THINKING LIKE A LAWYER

New Perspectives on Law, Culture, and Society
ROBERT W. GORDON AND MARGARET JANE RADIN, SERIES EDITORS

THINKING LIKE A LAWYER

An Introduction to Legal Reasoning

KENNETH J. VANDEVELDE
Thomas Jefferson School of Law

Westview Press
A Subsidiary of Perseus Books, L.L.C.

Copyright © 1998 by Westview Press, A Subsidiary of Perseus Books, L.L.C.

Published in 1996 in the United States of America by Westview Press, Inc., 5500 Central Avenue, Boulder, Colorado 80301-2877, and in the United Kingdom by Westview Press, 12 Hid's Copse Road, Cumnor Hill, Oxford OX2 9JJ

Library of Congress Cataloging-in-Publication Data
Vandevelde, Kenneth J.
  Thinking like a lawyer : an introduction to legal reasoning /
Kenneth J. Vandevelde.
      p.   cm. — (New perspectives on law, culture, and society)
  Includes bibliographical references and index.
  ISBN 0-8133-2203-0 (HC). — ISBN 0-8133-2204-9 (pbk.)
  1. Law—Methodology.   2. Law—Interpretation and construction.
I. Title.   II. Series.
K212.V36   1996
340'.11—dc20   95-48965
                                                                        CIP

The paper used in this publication meets the requirements of the American National Standard for Permanence of Paper for Printed Library Materials Z39.48-1984.

10   9   8   7   6

For Lidia, Jenny, and Shelly

Contents

Acknowledgments

I can recall the exact moment when the idea for this book was born. It was in Professor Mort Horwitz's torts class at Harvard Law School in the fall 1976 semester. The reader will see from the copyright date that twenty years elapsed before the book finally appeared.

The idea lay dormant until 1989, when I joined the faculty of Whittier Law School as an assistant professor of law. A two and one-half hour commute each way from San Diego gave me time to organize my thoughts, and I began to write snippets intermittently. Work continued after I moved to Thomas Jefferson School of Law in San Diego in 1991, and in spite of appointments as associate dean in 1992 and dean in 1994, I eventually brought the project to completion.

It is impossible to recall all those people whose ideas have shaped my thinking during the two decades that have intervened between the idea for, and the realization of, the project. I have listed in the bibliography the works that I found particularly interesting or helpful—either because they taught me something about legal reasoning or because their authors seemed to concur in conclusions I had reached independently. So much of this book builds on what others have written before me that I must acknowledge my enormous debt to the community of scholars working in this field.

Certainly, my deepest debt of gratitude is to Professor Horwitz, whose brilliant teaching stimulated my nascent interest in historical and structural analyses of legal doctrine, and to Professor Duncan Kennedy, who nourished those same interests with hours of provocative lectures and conversations. I am not sure that either of them would wish to be associated with this project, but their influence on my thinking was profound, and I owe them more than they will ever know.

Several of my former students at Whittier Law School were kind enough to read the manuscript and offer suggestions on making the material accessible to the undergraduate or entering law student. They are Jamie Batterman, Samantha Burris, Jan Buzanis, Debbie Deutsch, Kim Kirby, and Tom Zimmerman. I thank each of them.

I owe thanks as well to my colleagues, Professor Marybeth Herald, who read and commented on a draft of the entire manuscript, and Professors Lydia Clougherty, Stephen Root, and Ellen Waldman, who read and commented on various portions of the manuscript. Their suggestions were excellent and they are, of course, blameless for the many errors that I will find or have shown to me in the coming years.

At Westview Press, I have been most fortunate to have the constant encouragement and support of Spencer Carr. Professors Robert Gordon and Margaret Jane Radin, the editors of the series in which this book appears, made an invaluable contribution to the final product through their suggestions. I hope they know how much I appreciate their help and do not think the effort was in vain.

Kenneth J. Vandevelde

Introduction

People who have learned to think like lawyers usually also talk like lawyers, often to the considerable annoyance of their families and friends. Yet, many lawyers talk that way because they find legal reasoning so powerful that they cannot resist thinking about nearly everything in the same way they think about the law. The paradox, however, is that very few lawyers are consciously aware of what it means to think like a lawyer.

Although lawyers, law professors, and law students frequently refer in conversation to the process of "thinking like a lawyer," attempts to analyze in any systematic way what is meant by that phrase are rare. Law students may be told that they must learn to think like a lawyer but are not told precisely what that means. This book is an attempt to define this elusive phrase and, more specifically, to identify the techniques involved in thinking like a lawyer.

I. HOW LAWYERS THINK

The phrase "to think like a lawyer" encapsulates a way of thinking that is characterized by both the goal pursued and the method used. The method will be discussed momentarily. The goal of legal thought, which is addressed first, is generally to identify the rights and duties that exist between particular individuals or entities under a given set of circumstances.

As an illustration of the difference between lay thought and legal thought, imagine that two friends—a lawyer and a nonlawyer—are discussing a newspaper reporter who promised an informant anonymity and then published the informant's name.[1] The nonlawyer, astonished by the reporter's conduct, may say to the lawyer, "He can't do that, can he?" The nonlawyer's conception is that the law tells you what you "can" or "cannot" do.

Lawyers rarely think that way, although they may occasionally speak in those terms as a kind of shorthand for a more elaborate thought process. A lawyer would ask instead, "Has the reporter breached any legal duties to the informant, and if so, what rights to relief from the reporter does the

---

[1] This illustration is based on Cohen v. Cowles Media Company, 501 U.S. 663 (1991).

informant have?" That is, a lawyer's goal is to identify the rights and duties that exist between the reporter and the informant in the situation described.

As the illustration suggests, thinking like a lawyer essentially requires beginning with a factual situation and, through some process, arriving at a conclusion about the rights and duties of the persons or entities involved in the situation. Let us turn now to the method used by lawyers—a method known as legal reasoning.

Identifying a specific person's rights and duties requires a process of legal reasoning that includes five separate steps. They can be summarized briefly as follows: The lawyer must

1. identify the applicable sources of law, usually statutes and judicial decisions;
2. analyze these sources of law to determine the applicable rules of law and the policies underlying those rules;
3. synthesize the applicable rules of law into a coherent structure in which the more specific rules are grouped under the more general ones;
4. research the available facts; and
5. apply the structure of rules to the facts to ascertain the rights or duties created by the facts, using the policies underlying the rules to resolve difficult cases.

A lawyer may perform these steps in any of several different settings. A litigator may gather facts concerning events that have already occurred to determine whether the client has certain rights or duties with respect to the client's adversary. A business lawyer may be shown a contract and asked for advice concerning the rights and duties that the contract creates. In these two examples, the facts are fixed, and the lawyer's task is to identify the legal consequences of those facts.

In other cases, the process is reversed: The desired legal consequence is already known, and the lawyer's task is to identify the facts that would result in the desired consequence. A businessman may tell his lawyer, for example, that he wishes to obtain the right to purchase a thousand widgets for $1 each. The lawyer's task now is to create a set of events, such as the negotiation of a contract, that will give rise to a purchase right.

The rights and duties that lawyers identify through the legal reasoning process are those they believe would be enforced by a court of law. Regardless of how convinced a lawyer may be that a particular right or duty *should* exist, if a court would not enforce the right or duty, then it does not exist insofar as the legal system is concerned. Legal reasoning, then, is essentially a process of attempting to predict the decision of a court.

For reasons that will be made clear in Chapter 5, lawyers often cannot predict with certainty how a court will decide a dispute. In those cases, legal reasoning can do no more than identify some of the possible results, suggest the arguments that may lead a court to reach each of these possible results, and perhaps provide some indication of the relative probability that each possible result will occur.

II. THE PLAN OF THIS BOOK

This book is an introduction to the process of using legal reasoning to determine the rights and duties of specific persons in a given situation, that is, it exposes the process of thinking like a lawyer. It is divided into three parts.

Part One, Basic Legal Reasoning, provides an introduction to the five steps in the legal reasoning process, with each step treated in a separate chapter. It is written from the perspective of a self-aware practitioner and describes the orthodox version of mainstream legal reasoning as practiced by American lawyers at the end of the twentieth century, although not every lawyer would be equally conscious of using all the techniques described therein.

The reader may notice two conclusions in particular that emerge from the discussion of basic legal reasoning. First, although the legal reasoning process in form is structured as if it were based on mechanical logic, in reality legal reasoning is impossible without reference to the policies underlying the law. Second, these policies are in conflict, and thus legal reasoning requires a lawyer to make judgments about which policies are to prevail in particular circumstances.

Part Two, Advanced Legal Reasoning, consists of two chapters intended to guide the reader toward a deeper understanding of how the legal reasoning process operates. In the first of these chapters, the origins of the contemporary model of the legal reasoning process are traced. The purpose of the discussion is to explain how legal reasoning became a distinctive mixture of logic and judgment and to introduce the reader to some of the theoretical problems generated by this method of resolving legal disputes. In the second of these chapters, the focus shifts to the critical dimension of legal reasoning, the making of policy judgments. The purpose here is to develop a systematic approach to the analysis, synthesis, and application of policies through which the lawyer can construct legal arguments and predict judicial decisions.

Part Three, Applications, illustrates some of the ways in which the approach discussed in Parts One and Two might be applied to four distinct bodies of law: contracts, torts, constitutional law, and civil procedure, each of which is treated in a separate chapter. These chapters are not intended to constitute a complete summary of the law in any one area but are offered merely to illustrate a way to approach or think about each subject, thereby demonstrating that the same basic techniques of legal reasoning apply to all areas of the law.

PART ONE

Basic Legal Reasoning

1

Identifying Applicable Law

The first step in legal reasoning is to identify the law that is potentially applicable to a particular situation. Law is generally of two types.

One type is case law or, as it is sometimes referred to in American courts, "common law." This is law created by a court for the purpose of deciding a specific dispute as well as future, similar cases. Case law is announced by a court in the written opinion in which it decides the dispute.

The other type is enacted law. This consists of laws adopted, usually by a legislature or other elected body, not to decide a single dispute, but to stand as general rules of conduct. Enacted law governs all persons subject to the power of the government in all future situations in which the rule by its terms applies. Enacted law includes constitutions, statutes, treaties, executive orders, and administrative regulations. For the sake of brevity, the different forms of enacted law are often referred to collectively here as statutes.

Two differences between case law and enacted law are of particular importance in this study. First, because of the doctrine of legislative supremacy, discussed later in the chapter, enacted law binds the courts. Case law, however, may be changed by a court with sufficient justification. Second, enacted law is cast in authoritative language; that is, the precise words of an enacted law rule are clear and fixed until such time as the enacting body modifies them. Case law, by contrast, often cannot be captured by a single, authoritative and uncontroversial formulation. Rather, lawyers are likely to disagree among themselves concerning the law that was established by a particular case. The result of these differences is that the application of case law is considerably more flexible than the application of enacted law. The court can manipulate the language of the case or even overrule the case entirely, whereas the language of enacted law is subject to judicial interpretation but cannot itself be manipulated or changed by the court. This means that the application of enacted law tends to involve principally the interpretation of the text of the statute, whereas the application of case law may involve subtle refinements of prior articulations of the law, the introduction of new qualifications or exceptions, or the outright rejection of a well-established body of law.

As will be seen in this and later chapters, the method by which the lawyer identifies, analyzes, synthesizes, and applies both case law and enacted law depends upon which governmental entity creates the law. This chapter thus begins with a very brief introduction to the sources of American law, focusing on the role of each governmental entity in producing a particular type of law, with special emphasis on the judicial branch. Following that introduction, the discussion turns to its principal concern—the process of identifying potentially applicable rules of law.

I. THE SOURCES OF AMERICAN LAW

A. *Enacted Law*

The supreme law in the American legal system is the United States Constitution, which sets down principles of law binding on all branches of the federal and state governments. The Constitution was drafted in 1787 by a convention in Philadelphia and was ratified by each of the states. The Constitution begins with the words "We, the People of the United States" and purports to have been adopted directly by the people, who are regarded as the ultimate source of law in the United States.

The Constitution establishes three branches of the federal government: legislative, executive, and judicial. The legislative and executive branches produce enacted law and are discussed in this subsection. The judicial branch produces case law and will be discussed in the next subsection.[1]

The federal legislative branch is Congress, whose members are elected by the people and which is empowered by the Constitution to enact statutes governing various subjects of federal concern, such as interstate commerce and the national defense. As long as a congressional statute is consistent with the Constitution, that statute binds all persons subject to the laws of the United States. Further, under the doctrine of legislative supremacy,[2] the executive and judicial branches are obligated to apply and enforce the statutes enacted by Congress.

---

[1] Each of the fifty states has a constitution that establishes a similar tripartite government. Each state has a legislature; an executive branch headed by a governor; and a judicial branch, headed by an appellate court, usually called a supreme court. States also have various independent administrative agencies. These state entities function similarly to their federal counterparts but are bound by the state constitution as well as by federal law.

[2] The term "legislative supremacy" is misleading to the extent that it suggests that the legislature is supreme in all respects to the other branches. The term means simply that the legislature is the supreme lawmaking body.

The executive branch is headed by an elected president and is composed of various agencies responsible to the president, such as the Department of State, the Department of Justice, and the Department of Defense. The Constitution empowers the executive branch to administer and enforce the statutes enacted by Congress.

As the world has become more complex and the function of government more expansive, Congress has increasingly enacted statutes that establish only very general principles of law and has delegated to various agencies the authority to adopt more specific regulations consistent with the statutes. These administrative regulations define the terms of the statutes and explain how they apply to particular types of situations. The rationale is that Congress does not have the resources or the expertise to write detailed legislation.

The federal government includes a number of so-called independent agencies, which are created by statute and whose members are appointed by the president. Examples include the Federal Communications Commission, the Securities and Exchange Commission, and the Federal Trade Commission. These agencies are considered independent because their members are generally appointed for a fixed term and, unlike the heads of the executive branch agencies, cannot be removed at the discretion of the president. Independent agencies often have the authority not only to issue administrative regulations but also to resolve certain disputes involving those regulations through procedures that resemble the judicial process and, like judicial proceedings, result in case law.[3]

B. Case Law

The federal judicial branch consists of the federal courts. The judges of the federal courts are appointed by the president, subject to the advice and consent of the Senate. To ensure their independence from the other branches, federal judges are appointed for life.

The courts resolve disputes concerning the application of law to particular factual situations. In many instances, the law to be applied is enacted law. Courts, however, also have authority to create law, known as common law, to decide disputes.

Under the English legal system, on which the American system is based, courts were empowered to create rules of law in order to decide the disputes

---

[3] For example, the Federal Trade Commission has the authority to conduct an adversarial hearing to determine whether a business is engaged in an unfair or deceptive trade practice in violation of federal statute. If this agency proceeding determines that the business is in violation of the law, the commission is empowered to issue an order that the business cease the unlawful practice. Administrative agency decisions are subject to review by the federal courts under the Administrative Procedure Act, 5 U.S.C. §§ 551–559 (1988 and Supp. 1993). For the sake of brevity, administrative case law will not be discussed further.

brought before them. For example, originally, the law governing contracts and torts was not enacted by statute but was created by the courts. The law was called common law because it was common to the entire realm and was distinguished from local law.

Following the American Revolution, the individual states incorporated the English common law into state law, either by a provision in the state constitution, by a statute known as a reception statute, or by judicial declaration. State courts deciding disputes thus apply the common law as well as statutory law. Under the doctrine of legislative supremacy, mentioned previously, a state legislature has the power to modify the common law of that state at any time. State courts may also modify the common law of their state. Thus, the common law continues to evolve, and its substance varies from state to state.

Congress did not enact the equivalent of a federal reception statute. It did, however, pass the Rules Decision Act,[4] which provides that federal courts shall apply *state* law, except where the Constitution, treaties, or federal statutes otherwise require. Moreover, the Supreme Court held in 1938 in the famous case of *Erie R.R. Co. v. Tompkins*[5] that the federal courts do not have the constitutional authority to create a general federal common law.

As a result of the Rules Decision Act and the *Erie* decision, with a few exceptions, there is no federal common law.[6] In any case arising in which common law rules apply, a federal court generally applies state common law. The common law, in other words, with the exceptions just mentioned, is state law. Although the federal courts apply state common law, they usually do not modify it. Generally speaking, only the state legislatures and state courts have the power to modify the common law.[7]

Because so much of the legal reasoning process entails a careful analysis of judicial decisions, it is necessary to describe the operation of the judicial branch in some detail. To avoid needless complexity, the focus here is on the federal court system.

---

[4] 28 U.S.C. § 1652 (1988).

[5] 304 U.S. 64 (1938).

[6] There is federally created common law in two situations. First, federal courts create common law on a few subjects, such as foreign affairs, that are of special interest to the federal government. Second, federal courts create what is sometimes called interstitial common law, which is a body of judicial decisions interpreting and applying federal statutes.

[7] Because of the Supremacy Clause in the U.S. Constitution, discussed later in this chapter, Congress has the authority to enact statutes that become the supreme law of the land and thus override contrary state common law as well as contrary state statutory law. In addition, under the doctrine of judicial review, also discussed farther on, the federal courts have the power to declare state common law rules unconstitutional.

1. District Court

Disputes are initially brought before the trial courts, which in the federal system are known as district courts. In general, the court decides a dispute by applying law to fact. More specifically, resolving a dispute requires the court to decide three things.

The trial court must first decide precisely what the facts were that gave rise to the dispute; second, what laws govern those facts; and third, how the law applies to the facts. By applying the law to the facts, the court determines the rights and duties that exist between the parties under the law and thereby resolves the dispute.

The parties to a dispute usually have a considerable number of areas of agreement. They almost always agree on many of the facts underlying the dispute and often agree on much or all of the law. Frequently, the core of the dispute concerns how the law applies to the facts.

Anything on which the parties do not agree, assuming it is relevant to resolving the dispute, is put at issue. Thus, in legal reasoning, an issue is simply a question to be decided. The court resolves a dispute by identifying the issues and then deciding them.

a. Identifying Issues

Because there are only three things to be decided in a dispute, there are only three types of issues that can arise in legal reasoning. These are issues of fact, issues of law, and issues requiring application of law to fact.

Issues of fact all pose essentially the same basic question: What is the situation to which the law must be applied? In other words, what events have occurred to create the dispute?

Issues of law also pose essentially one basic question: What are the rules of law governing this situation?

Issues requiring the application of law to fact similarly pose one general question: What rights or duties exist between the parties under the governing law in this situation? These issues are sometimes called mixed questions of law and fact.

A single dispute may present all three types of issues or any combination of them. For example, assume that a man sues a female physician claiming that she was negligent in failing to administer a particular diagnostic test to him and that, as a result, he sustained injuries three years later that would have been preventable had his disease been diagnosed earlier.

The physician may put at issue some of the plaintiff's factual allegations. She may raise as issues of fact two questions: Would the diagnostic test actually have revealed that the patient was suffering from the disease? Would the disease have been less injurious had it been discovered earlier?

The parties may also disagree on the applicable law. For example, the physician may raise this question as an issue of law: Does the statute of limitations for negligence claims against a medical practitioner require the claims to be filed within two years of the time the negligence *occurred* or within two years of the time the negligence was *discovered?* If the law requires the claim to be filed within two years of the time the negligence occurred, then the patient would have no right to compensation from the physician.

In addition, the parties may disagree about the application of the law to the facts. For example, the parties may present another question to the court as a mixed issue of law and fact: In this situation, did the physician's failure to administer the test constitute negligence? This is a mixed question of law and fact because it requires the court to apply the legal definition of negligence to the facts to determine whether the physician's conduct constitutes negligence. If the physician was not negligent, then the patient has no right to compensation.

b. Deciding Issues

Determining which category an issue falls into is critical because it determines who decides the issue at trial and the extent to which the issue can be reviewed on appeal. This subsection presents a discussion of how each type of issue is decided by the district court. The next subsection sets forth how each type of issue is reviewed on appeal.

In determining how issues will be resolved by the district court, the threshold question is whether there are any relevant issues of fact. Issues of fact can be resolved only by a trial. Thus, if there are relevant issues of fact, the dispute will lead to a trial in the district court.

Trials are of two types: bench trials and jury trials. Either party may demand a jury trial if the Constitution or a federal statute creates a right to a jury trial in the type of dispute that is in litigation. If there is no right to a jury trial, then the dispute will be decided in a bench trial.

In a bench trial, the judge decides all issues; that is, the judge determines what law applies to the dispute, resolves any factual questions necessary to decide the dispute, and applies the law to the facts. The court then records its decision by entering judgment, which generally entails signing a formal document. The judgment is accompanied by a written statement of the court's findings of facts and conclusions of law.

In a jury trial, the judge decides any issues of law and presides over the trial. After the parties have presented all the evidence, the judge instructs the jury on the law applicable to the dispute. The jury then decides all issues of fact and applies the law to the facts. At the conclusion of its deliberations, the jury announces its decision, known as a verdict.

Occasionally it appears during a trial that the evidence presented is so one-sided that a reasonable jury could reach only one result. In such a case, upon a motion of a party,[8] the judge may simply rule in favor of that party without sending the dispute to the jury to decide, a process known as entering judgment as a matter of law.

Assuming that the judge does decide to send the case to the jury for resolution and the jury reaches a verdict, the judge must then determine whether to enter judgment in accordance with the verdict. Normally, the judge does enter judgment in accordance with the verdict. In some cases, however, if the judge believes the verdict is contrary to the clear weight of the evidence, the judge can order a new trial, which requires impaneling a second jury and retrying the case. Alternatively, if the judge believes that in light of the evidence no reasonable jury could reach the verdict that it did, then the judge can enter judgment as a matter of law in favor of one party.

If there are no relevant issues of fact, then there is no need for a trial, and the case will be decided by the judge upon the motion of a party. A number of different motions may result in a resolution of the litigation without a trial. For example, a defendant may dispute some of the plaintiff's factual allegations but may take the position that the factual disputes need not be resolved because, even assuming that the plaintiff's allegations are true, the plaintiff must still lose. In that situation, the defendant files a motion to dismiss the complaint for failure to state a claim upon which relief can be granted.

Alternatively, if either party believes that the evidence allows the factual issue to be decided only one way, that party may argue to the court that there are no genuine issues of fact and that the court should decide the legal issues and render a judgment, a process known as entering summary judgment. A genuine issue of fact exists if a reasonable jury could decide the issue in favor of either party. Whether there are issues of fact, of course, may be a matter on which the parties do not agree. If both parties agree that no genuine issue of fact exists, both may move for summary judgment.[9]

c. Distinguishing Issues of Law and Fact

The prior discussion implies that the distinction between the three types of issues is relatively sharp. In fact, however, at least two situations exist in which the theoretical distinction among the types of issues seems to collapse.

---

[8] A motion is a request for the court to issue a judgment or an order. Although the court's ruling on a motion may be oral, if the ruling is important the court is likely to prepare a written opinion explaining its decision.

[9] The discussion in this section assumes that the dispute is a civil case. If it is a criminal case, the Constitution places additional restrictions on the power of the judge to decide the case against the defendant. This difference is of enormous practical significance to the parties in a criminal case, but it will be ignored here in order to avoid complexities that are peripheral to this discussion.

The explanation for the collapse begins with the fact that the prototypical trial in the American legal system is the jury trial. In a jury trial, the judge decides questions of law, and the jury decides questions of fact and questions requiring the application of law to fact. Because the judge's function in a jury trial was traditionally to decide issues of law, lawyers have become accustomed to regarding any issue decided by a judge as an issue of law.

In any jury trial, however, at least two situations may arise in which a judge decides questions that, strictly speaking, are not questions of law. In both of these situations, the theoretical distinctions among the various types of issues seem to dissolve.

The first situation arises where a reasonable jury could decide an issue in only one way. As noted above, in such a situation, the judge may grant a motion for summary judgment or for judgment as a matter of law. In other words, if the facts cannot reasonably be disputed, the judge may take the factual issues away from the jury and decide them personally.

Where the judge takes an issue away from the jury and decides it, lawyers often say that the judge decided the issue "as a matter of law." For example, in the illustration above, if the evidence that the diagnostic test would have revealed the disease (a question of fact) or the evidence that the physician was negligent (a mixed question of law and fact) was so overwhelming that a reasonable jury could decide either of these issues in only one way, the judge may decide the issues, for example, by granting a motion for summary judgment.

The usage may be confusing because what the judge actually decided, in substance, was either a factual question or a mixed question of law and fact. Saying that the issue was decided as a matter of law is merely another way of saying that a judge, rather than a jury, decided the issue. In effect, questions of fact or mixed questions of law and fact can be converted nominally to questions of law if the evidence is sufficiently one-sided.

The second situation in which a question that might otherwise seem to be a question of fact or mixed question of law and fact is treated as a question of law occurs where the law states that the question shall be decided by a judge rather than a jury. For example, the determination of whether a term in a contract is ambiguous is sometimes said to be a question of law. Although as a theoretical matter one could argue that this determination falls within the definition of a question of fact or a mixed question of law and fact, some courts believe that judges are more suited than jurors to determining whether a contractual term is ambiguous and thus have declared that to be a question of law. Again, what that really means is simply that the question is decided by the judge rather than the jury.

The root of the confusion is that courts have often been ambivalent about giving juries too much discretion. In situations where the evidence on an issue is one-sided or where the issue seems especially appropriate for determination by a judge, courts have taken the issue away from the jury. Yet, because of the tradition that judges decide questions of law and juries decide the remaining questions, the only way to accomplish the task of taking an issue away from a jury while seeming to remain consistent with the tradition was to declare certain issues to be questions of law.

2. Court of Appeals

After a district court has entered judgment (based either on a motion or a trial), a party that has lost on one or more issues may appeal the decision of the district court to an appellate court. In the federal system, the district courts are organized into regional groups called circuits. Each circuit has a court of appeals that decides appeals from the decisions of the district courts in that circuit.

The court of appeals must determine as an initial matter which standard of review to use in deciding the appeal. The standard of review establishes the extent to which the court of appeals will defer to the decision of the trial court. At one extreme, the court of appeals could review the decision on the appealed issue de novo. A de novo review is one in which the court of appeals gives no deference at all to the trial court's decision and decides the issue entirely in accordance with its own interpretation of the law or the facts. At the other extreme, the court of appeals could defer completely to the trial court, holding that the trial court's decision on the issue was not reviewable on appeal.

The standard of review depends upon the nature of the issue and whether the issue was decided by the judge or jury. The court of appeals generally reviews de novo the district judge's determination of which law applies and its application of law to facts. If the court of appeals disagrees with the trial court's decision, it will usually reverse the judgment of the trial court.

The court of appeals' review of the district judge's factual findings, on the other hand, is not de novo. Rather, the court of appeals defers to the district judge on factual matters and thus overturns the judge's findings of fact only if they are clearly erroneous. Jury verdicts are given even greater deference and are overturned on appeal only if they are not supported by substantial evidence.[10]

---

[10] The appellate court defers to the factual findings made in the trial court in order to avoid what, in effect, would be a retrial of the entire case. The theory here is this: Because the trial judge or members of the jury actually saw and heard the witnesses testifying, they are in the best situation to assess the credibility of the evidence and to decide the facts. Trial judges, however, are in no better position to decide the law than the appellate court. Moreover, an incorrect decision on the law would be binding in future cases, whereas an incorrect finding of fact affects only one case, and thus it is particularly important that legal issues be correctly decided. It is for these reasons that appellate courts do not defer to trial courts on issues of law.

Other standards of review are applied in certain circumstances. For example, some decisions by a trial judge in the course of a trial are overturned by the appellate court only if considered an abuse of discretion.

3. Supreme Court

A party that loses on one or more issues in the court of appeals may seek a review of the decision of the court of appeals in the United States Supreme Court by filing a petition for a writ of certiorari. The Supreme Court has the discretion to grant or deny the petition.[11]

If the Supreme Court denies the petition, the decision of the court of appeals becomes final. If the Supreme Court grants the petition, it will then review the court of appeals' decisions on questions of law and the application of law to fact de novo but will give the district court's factual findings or the jury's verdict the same deference that the court of appeals did.

II. IDENTIFYING APPLICABLE LAW

In this section, the process of identifying the law that potentially applies to a particular set of facts is examined. As the first section suggests, the lawyer confronts an array of case law and enacted law that could potentially apply to a given situation. The process of determining which law applies is really a process of winnowing out the law that could not plausibly apply.

A law may not apply to a given situation for any of three reasons: (1) the governmental entity that adopted the law does not have power to prescribe law applicable to the specific persons or transactions involved in the situation; (2) the law by its terms does not apply to the situation; or (3) although the governmental entity that adopted the law may have power as a general matter, another entity of greater power has enacted a contrary law that prevails in this situation. By applying these three criteria, the lawyer can eliminate the inapplicable law.

The next three subsections examine each of these three criteria in turn.

A. Identifying the Government with Power: An Introduction to Choice of Law Theory

The first reason that a law may not apply to a situation is that the government that adopted the law does not have power over the persons or transaction involved in the situation. All governments are governments of limited powers; that is, no government has the power to govern all persons or

---

[11] In a very small number of cases, a losing party has a right to appeal to the Supreme Court and thus does not need to petition for certiorari. Rather, the party simply files a notice of appeal and the Supreme Court is then required to hear the case.

transactions anywhere in the world. Thus, for example, the United States generally has no power to regulate activity in the Netherlands that does not affect persons or property in the United States.

This means that some laws may appear by their terms to be applicable to a particular situation, but, in fact, do not apply. They do not apply because the government that adopted the laws does not have the power to regulate the persons or the transaction involved in the situation.

Accordingly, the lawyer's first inquiry in identifying the applicable law must be to determine which government's law applies. This determination is made based on a body of legal rules known as the conflicts of law or choice of law rules.

Choice of law is a complex area of law that cannot possibly be reduced to a few sentences here. Choice of law analysis, however, is absolutely critical to finding the applicable law, and thus a brief overview is necessary.

Assuming that U.S. law applies,[12] the choice of law analysis has two dimensions: vertical and horizontal. Vertical choice of law rules determine whether federal law, state law, or both, applies. Assuming that at least some state law applies, horizontal choice of law rules determine *which* state's law applies. If only federal law applies, then horizontal choice of law analysis is unnecessary.

1. *Vertical Choice of Law Analysis*

The key to understanding the significance of vertical choice of law analysis is recognizing that federal law and state law are generally not mutually exclusive. In most cases, if federal and state law both address a situation, then both apply. An exception exists where federal and state law conflict, in which case federal law prevails.[13]

As it happens, the great majority of events in daily life are governed by state law. For example, family relations, the transfer of property, the formation of contracts, and the redress of personal injuries are all governed by state law. In some instances, federal law also applies. For example, certain business conduct constitutes fraud under state common law and also violates federal antiracketeering statutes. Occasionally, some aspect of a transaction may be governed solely by federal law.

Vertical choice of law analysis thus ultimately results in one of three determinations: (1) federal law applies; (2) state law applies; or (3) both federal

---

[12] There is also the possibility that the law of another country or international law applies. These possibilities raise problems too complex for inclusion in this introductory survey. Thus, the assumption used here is that the applicable choice of law rules have identified U.S. law as the governing law.

[13] This situation is discussed further at the end of this chapter under the preemption doctrine.

and state law apply. In other words, vertical choice of law analysis *may* winnow out all federal law, or all state law, but very often it eliminates neither.

2. Horizontal Choice of Law Analysis

Horizontal choice of law analysis generally results in a substantial winnowing out of applicable law. This occurs because, to the extent that state law applies, it is usually the law of only one state that does so.[14] The laws of different states, generally, *are* mutually exclusive, and they are not applied simultaneously to the same transaction.

Fortunately, many transactions occur in a single state and involve residents of that state. Thus, the lawyer knows instinctively that, to the extent that state law applies, it is the law of that state that applies. Therefore, as a practical matter, legal reasoning often requires very little conscious horizontal choice of law analysis.

However, whenever a situation involves transactions affecting more than one state or involves residents of more than one state, the possibility always exists that the law of more than one state may be potentially applicable. Which state's law is applied is ultimately determined in either of two ways: by agreement of the parties or by filing a lawsuit.

An agreement in advance between the parties is the simplest way to determine the law applicable to a situation. Two parties preparing to engage in a transaction will often insert a provision in their contract specifying which state's law applies to the contract. These provisions, generally known as "choice of law clauses," will usually be enforced by the courts.

The other way to determine which state's law applies is to wait until a dispute arises and then file suit to resolve the dispute. Every jurisdiction has its own choice of law rules that tell the court which state's law to apply. Such rules differ from state to state, however, and thus which law applies may depend entirely on where the suit is filed.[15]

---

[14] An exception exists where a state court applies its own procedural law but uses the substantive law of another state. The difference between substantive and procedural law is discussed in the introduction to Part Three.

[15] An example may help clarify all this. Suppose that Slade, who is standing in state A, shoots Tenderfoot, who is standing in state B. Tenderfoot now wishes to sue Slade for battery. In a case involving physical injury, some courts apply the law of the state where the wrongful act occurred—in this case state A. Other courts apply the law of the state where the injury occurred—in this case state B. Thus, whether the law of state A or B applies depends on which court Tenderfoot files suit in. Tenderfoot would probably choose the court that would apply the most favorable law. It could even happen that state A would apply the law of state B, whereas state B would apply the law of state A. In some cases, Tenderfoot may choose to file suit in state C, even though it has nothing to do with the dispute, because state C would apply the most favorable law.

In short, the lawyer may not know with any certainty which state's law will apply until the situation leads to a lawsuit. Indeed, the lawyer deciding to file suit may choose to do so in the courts of a particular state solely because those courts will apply the law most advantageous to his client. Choosing a court for tactical reasons is a common practice known as "forum shopping."

When more than one state's law is potentially applicable, the lawyer's only recourse is to research all potentially applicable law. In the end, the lawyer could determine that, depending upon where suit is filed, the client may be subject to any of several different states' laws on a subject. If the client wants to be certain of acting in accordance with the law, the client may have to adhere to all of these varying statutes and cases, knowing that any dispute will ultimately be governed by only one state's law but that the identity of the state will remain unknown until the dispute reaches litigation. It is in part to eliminate this kind of uncertainty that parties agree to choice of law clauses in their contracts.

Choice of law analysis thus plays a major role in the winnowing process. It ideally results in the elimination from further consideration of all law except that of a single state and, perhaps, that of the federal government.

B. Identifying Law by Subject Matter: An Introduction to Rule Analysis

Having narrowed the potentially applicable law to that of one or two sovereigns—one state, the federal government, or both—the lawyer must next winnow out those statutes or cases that, by their terms, do not apply to the subject matter of the situation under review. Lawyers do so by using the process of rule analysis. Let us discuss precisely what that entails.

Each statute or case contains one or more rules of law. In the next chapter, the techniques to be used to identify the rules of law in a statute or case are discussed in some detail. For now, the reader should simply assume that the lawyer, upon reading each statute or case, is able to identify at least one rule of law in that statute or case. It is these rules of law that the lawyer must analyze to determine if the statute or case, by its terms, is potentially applicable to the situation.

1. The Nature of Rules: Form

In general, rules of law have the form "if x, then y," meaning that if these facts occur, then this legal right or duty arises.

Rules of law thus have a factual predicate and a legal consequence. For example, a case may announce the rule that a physician performing medical services for a patient has a duty to exercise reasonable care to prevent injury to the patient.[16] In other words, if these facts (a physician-patient relationship and the rendering of a medical service) occur, then this consequence (duty to exercise reasonable care) will result. The physician's performance of a medical service for a patient is the factual predicate, and the duty to exercise reasonable care is the legal consequence.

Usually the factual predicate requires some combination of facts. Each of these facts is referred to as an element. In the example above, the factual predicate has two elements: (1) the existence of a physician-patient relationship, and (2) the rendering of a medical service. When facts constituting all of the elements occur, then the legal consequence takes effect. The legal consequence is generally the creation of some right or duty between certain persons.

Identifying rules of law applicable to a particular situation means identifying those rules of law with factual predicates that accurately describe the situation.[17] If one or more elements of the rule is not present in the situation under review, then the rule will not apply. For example, the rule above would not apply to a physician assisting his patient with the latter's income tax return because the second element, the rendering of a medical service, is absent.

As this suggests, the only way to determine whether a rule is applicable to a situation is actually to endeavor to apply it. Applying a rule to a situation is a potentially complex process that is described in some detail in Chapter 5. Suffice it to say here that during the initial stage of identifying potentially applicable law, the lawyer looks for all laws that could plausibly apply. To put this another way, the lawyer searches for rules with factual predicates that could arguably be said to apply to the situation.

2. The Nature of Rules: Substance

Rules are presumed by the American legal system not to be mere arbitrary pronouncements but to be based on some underlying policy. That is, rules create a right or duty not for its own sake but in order to further a public policy.

When the rule is a statute, the underlying policy is generally that which the legislature intended to further when it enacted the statute. When the rule is a case law rule, the underlying policy is generally that which the court ar-

---

[16] *See, e.g.,* Keene v. Wiggins, 69 Cal. App. 3d 308 (1977).

[17] This does not require that the lawyer study every case decided or statute enacted in the jurisdiction. Rather, lawyers over the years have developed a series of research techniques intended to identify relatively quickly the statutes and cases within a given jurisdiction that could plausibly apply to various types of situations. The assumption is that if these techniques do not identify a statute or case then it is probably not applicable. Legal research techniques are far too complex to summarize here. *See, e.g.,* CHRISTOPHER G. AND JILL ROBINSON WREN, THE LEGAL RESEARCH MANUAL (2d ed. 1986).

ticulated as the justification for the rule at the time the rule was announced. Case law rules may also be based on the policies underlying legislative enactments, even in cases that do not involve a statute. For example, the court may adopt a rule favorable to consumers. In support, the court may cite recent legislation that may not be applicable to the case under consideration but nevertheless reflects a public policy of protecting the consumer against the superior bargaining power of merchants and manufacturers.

Rules, moreover, are usually not based on a single policy but represent compromises among sets of opposing policies. Typically, one set of policies favors creation of a broad right or duty, whereas an opposing set of policies favors restricting or eliminating the same right or duty.

If the policies favoring the right or duty were to prevail all of the time, the right or duty would become absolute—with no exceptions or limitations. If the policies opposing the right or duty were to prevail all of the time, the right or duty would disappear.

In fact, however, both sets of policies are important, so neither can be permitted to prevail in every situation. Rather, the policies supporting the right or duty will prevail in some situations, whereas the opposing policies will prevail in others.

The elements of the rule define exactly the situation in which the policies favoring the right or duty prevail. When the elements are satisfied, the right or duty exists; when they are not satisfied, the right or duty does not exist.

The policies underlying the rule are of great importance to the process of legal reasoning. If it would not further the underlying policies, then applying the rule to a particular situation would be undesirable and the court often will not apply it, especially if the rule is based on case law rather than enacted law. Further, at least where case law rules are concerned, even though the factual predicate of the rule may seem clearly not to apply, if the policy behind the rules would be furthered by finding the rule to be applicable, the court may nevertheless apply the case law rule by analogy, may synthesize a new case law rule to govern the situation, or may modify the rule so that it becomes applicable. Thus, as will be discussed in greater detail in subsequent chapters, the underlying policies provide much assistance in identifying those situations in which the rule will be applied.

3. *The Problem of Generality*

The elements of a rule are typically phrased in very general terms. This is especially true with respect to statutes and other forms of enacted law. Thus, for example, a rule does not usually refer to something as specific as a red Buick, or even an automobile, but refers more broadly to a motor vehicle. The elements, in other words, describe the facts in broad, generic terms.

The elements are phrased in general terms for reasons of both fairness and efficiency. If rules were written narrowly, legislatures and courts would

need to adopt far more rules, which would be inefficient and would carry
the risk that similar situations might not be treated the same way, which
would be unfair.

Imagine, for example, that instead of enacting a single rule for the speed
limit, the state enacted a different rule for every type of automobile. Such
detail would be enormously time-consuming for the legislature to write and
for the lawyer to research. Further, such a detailed code would create the
possibility that some cars might be overlooked or that certain cars might be
given preferential treatment. Our intuitive notions of fairness tell us that
there should be equal justice under the law and that like cases should be
treated in a like manner. A few rules of great generality are more efficient to
write and research and are usually thought to reduce the prospect of unequal treatment, since all persons are subject to the same rule.

Yet, this generality also impedes the legal reasoning process. The general
language is often so vague that it simply leaves unclear whether a particular
set of events satisfies the elements of the rule. In the case of the rule
described above, for example, it may be unclear whether someone who
casually asks a physician for advice at a cocktail party has established a
physician-patient relationship.

Thus, in reviewing rules of law, the lawyer must be alert to any rule with
a factual predicate that might *plausibly* be said to describe the specific facts
under review. Further, as will be seen in Chapter 5, case law rules can often
be phrased at different levels of generality, and thus, in examining those
rules, the lawyer must be alert to whether they can plausibly be said to
apply if rephrased in more general terms.

C. Identifying Void Rules:
An Introduction to Constitutionalism

Once legal research has identified all the statutes and cases that are plausibly applicable to the situation under review, the winnowing process is usually complete. It occasionally happens, however, that a statute enacted or a
case decided by one governmental entity is contradicted in some way by a
law created by another entity of superior authority, with the result that the
statute or case must be disregarded.

A few basic principles of constitutional law determine the hierarchy of
authority among the different sources of law. In this last section, some of
the most important of these principles are summarized.

First, as a fundamental principle of the American legal system, the Constitution prevails over all other law, federal or state. The Supremacy Clause
of the Constitution, set forth in Article VI, explicitly states that the Constitution and federal laws made pursuant to the Constitution are the supreme
law of the land. Thus, if one of the applicable rules is a constitutional pro-

vision, then it voids any contrary statute or case, whether federal or state, at least to the extent of the conflict. A state constitution prevails over all other state law.

Second, as just noted, the Supremacy Clause also provides that federal law made pursuant to the Constitution is the supreme law of the land. Thus, under a doctrine of constitutional law known as the preemption doctrine, federal law invalidates *all* state law on a subject where Congress has either explicitly or implicitly prohibited state regulation of the subject. Even where Congress has not explicitly or implicitly prohibited all state regulation of a particular subject, a specific state law is void if it directly conflicts with a federal law. Of course, there are countless situations in which federal and state law on the same subject are not in conflict and thus both may be applied.

Third, under the doctrine of legislative supremacy, the courts are required to apply the law enacted by the legislature. Thus, a statute prevails over contrary case law.[18] Nevertheless, the power of courts to interpret statutes allows them to apply the statutes in ways not intended by the legislature. As a result, a legislature occasionally enacts a statute specifically intended to overturn a prior judicial decision that it believes applied another statute incorrectly.

Fourth, under the doctrine of judicial review, the courts have the power to determine the constitutionality of all laws, including statutes. Thus, a judicial decision holding a statute unconstitutional renders the statute void. In practice, this amounts to a kind of exception to the doctrine of legislative supremacy because it permits a court to refuse to apply a statute.

Fifth, because administrative agencies are created by statute, their regulations are subordinate to statutes enacted by the same or a superior sovereign.[19] Thus, statutes generally prevail over contrary administrative regulations.

These various principles, all of which are rooted in the American system of constitutional government, require that certain statutes or case law rules be considered void in a particular situation and thus be disregarded simply because another entity with greater authority has adopted a contrary law also applicable to that situation. In the absence of the contrary law, the first rule might have been valid and applicable. Further, a rule that is void in one situation may be treated as valid in a second situation because the contrary

---

[18] This statement assumes that both the statute and the case law were issued by the same sovereign. Further, because of the Supremacy Clause, federal statutes prevail over contrary state case law, but state statutes cannot generally prevail over federal case law.

[19] Here I use the word "statute" in its technical sense to refer to legislative enactments and not to other forms of enacted law.

law of greater authority does not apply to that second situation.[20] Although the vast majority of statutes and case law rules are constitutional, occasionally these principles eliminate from consideration one or more otherwise applicable laws.

---

[20] An example may help to clarify this point. A state may enact a statute providing that all automobile sales shall be taxed at a rate of 8 percent. Under the Supremacy Clause of the Constitution, a state may not tax the federal government. Because the Constitution prevails over state law, the state tax law is void as applied to a sale of an automobile to a federal agency. The tax law is valid, however, as applied to the sale of an automobile to a law professor.

2

Analyzing Statutes and Cases

The second step in legal reasoning is to analyze the plausibly applicable statutes and cases to identify both the rules of law and the underlying policies contained therein. In this chapter, the techniques for analyzing the law are discussed. Enacted law, described generically here as statutory law, is discussed separately from case law.

I. Analyzing Statutes

The analysis of a statute for purposes of identifying the rule of law is simple because the statute itself is the rule of law. Thus, the process of identifying an applicable statute and extracting the rule of law are the same.

Identifying the policies underlying the statute can be quite difficult, however. The policies underlying a statute are those that the legislature sought to promote when it enacted the law.

Lawyers use a variety of approaches to identify the policy underlying a statute. One is to examine the statute itself. Occasionally, a legislature enacting a law, especially a comprehensive reform measure, includes a section that states explicitly at least some of the policies underlying the legislation. Another approach is to find prior case law applying the statute, which may contain a discussion of the policy behind the statute.

Often, neither of these approaches is helpful and the lawyer must then attempt to identify the underlying policies by researching the legislative history of the statute. This history may include the record of the committee hearings, the reports issued by the committees when they sent the bill to the full body, the debate on the floor of the legislature prior to passage, and statements made by the president or governor at the time the bill was signed or vetoed. This research, however, may also be inconclusive because, for reasons discussed in Chapter 7, legislative history is often incomplete or misleading or allows more than one interpretation.

Researching the history of a statute may involve inquiry into events beyond the formal process by which the statute was enacted, such as investigating the social conditions that prompted its passage. The lawyer then examines the circumstances prior to enactment of the statute and tries to determine the nature of the mischief that led to its enactment.

Identification of the mischief, however, does not necessarily reveal with sufficient clarity the policy underlying the statute. As explained in Chapter 1, lawyers prefer to draft rules using general language, and thus the legislature very likely used language in the factual predicate that covered more than the exact situation that prompted the legislative enactment. An anti-corruption law enacted after revelations that a senator had accepted very large honoraria from special interest groups might not simply prohibit honoraria but is likely to be much broader, prohibiting, for example, the giving of "any thing of value." Because the language is broader than the precise situation that the legislature had in mind, the lawyer must still decide what the legislature supposedly "intended" with respect to all of the situations that were arguably covered by the language but that did not constitute the precise mischief consciously addressed. Does the statute, for example, prohibit giving the senator information that has no commercial value but that the senator may nevertheless find useful and thus valuable?

The indeterminacy of the investigation into the history of a statute provides the lawyer with the opportunity for advocacy on behalf of a client. The lawyer may argue successfully that a particular policy underlies a statute, even though there is no external evidence that that policy was consciously in the minds of those involved in the enactment of the statute.

Because of the problems associated with ascertaining legislative intent, many courts have said that the best indication of legislative policy is the language of the statute itself and, therefore, if the meaning of the language is clear on its face, a court should not delve into its history. In this view, only when there is some doubt about the meaning of the statute should a court look beyond the statutory language.[1]

Some lawyers question, however, whether this rule accurately describes the process by which courts actually interpret statutes. In their view, the court virtually always examines the historical evidence to determine

---

[1] This is the so-called Golden Rule of statutory interpretation, which has been stated as follows: "The general rule is perfectly well settled that, where a statute is of doubtful meaning and susceptible upon its face of two constructions, the court may look into prior and contemporaneous acts, the reasons which induced the act in question, the mischiefs intended to be remedied, the extraneous circumstances, and the purpose intended to be accomplished by it, to determine its proper construction. But where the act is clear upon its face, and when standing alone it is fairly susceptible of but one construction, that construction must be given to it. . . . The whole doctrine applicable to the subject may be summed up in the single observation that prior acts may be referred to solve but not to create an ambiguity" Hamilton v. Rathbone, 175 U.S. 414, 420–421 (1899).

whether that evidence would support the interpretation it wishes to give to the statute. If so, the court can declare the statute unclear and then rely openly on the history. If not, the court can declare the statute clear on its face and then decline to discuss the history. Suffice it to say, in any event, that rarely would a competent lawyer deliberately omit an argument based on legislative history that was favorable to his client.

The lawyer's examination of the policies underlying a statute may also extend beyond the historical events that originally prompted its enactment to include an inquiry into contemporary notions of good public policy. Interpreting a statute according to current public policy, as opposed to the policy of the legislature that originally enacted the law, is controversial and is disfavored by most courts. Nearly all courts would agree, however, that no statute should be interpreted in a way that would lead to an "absurd" result. This position can be reconciled with the view that the intent of the drafters should prevail by assuming that the legislature would never have intended an absurd result.

As long as the result is not absurd, however, most courts would insist that the apparent intent or purpose of the legislature be followed. Thus, the lawyer's examination of current notions of public policy is usually very limited.

The choice between interpreting a statute by reference to its language alone and interpreting it by reference to extrinsic sources, such as the legislative history or current notions of public policy, is a fundamental tension that pervades the legal reasoning process. This tension will be further discussed in Chapters 5 and 7.

II. ANALYZING CASES

A. *The Components of a Case*

Analyzing case law is a much more complex undertaking than analyzing a statute. Discussion in this section covers the various components that may be found in a well-written judicial opinion, the significance of each, and how each should be analyzed. Because the overwhelming majority of published judicial opinions are appellate decisions, this discussion assumes that the case under analysis is an appellate decision.

1. *Facts*

A judicial opinion usually begins with a description of the facts. This is a narrative of the events that gave rise to the dispute submitted to the court for decision.

Many of the facts in the opinion are of meager significance but are there merely to provide a context for the facts that do matter. Without them, the rest would not make sense. On a first reading, however, the lawyer generally does not know which of the facts are significant. As will be seen, determining which facts are significant requires first identifying the rules of law and the underlying policies that govern the case.

2. *Procedural History*

Next, the procedural history is summarized. This portion of the opinion sets forth a description of the events that occurred in the trial or lower appellate court during the course of the litigation, beginning with the filing of a complaint.

Like the factual recitation, much of the procedural history is of minimal importance in itself but provides context. The procedural history generally indicates one detail that is of fundamental importance: the precise nature of the decision in the lower court from which one or both parties are appealing.

The nature of the decision from which the appeal is taken is critical because, as noted in Chapter 1, it determines the standard of review that the court of appeals applies to a trial court's decision. The standard of review, in turn, determines what the appellate court must decide and the effect that the appellate court's decision will have on future cases.

For example, if a physician is appealing a jury verdict that he was negligent in providing medical care, the appellate court reviews the verdict only to determine whether it was supported by substantial evidence. To affirm the judgment against the physician, the appellate court need not decide that the physician was negligent but only that there was substantial evidence to that effect, which is a much different determination. The appellate judges may believe that the physician in fact was not negligent. As long as there is substantial evidence that supports the verdict, however, the verdict will stand.

Moreover, because the appellate court is not deciding whether the physician was negligent but only whether there was substantial evidence that he was, the appellate court's opinion upholding the jury's verdict against the physician cannot be cited by lawyers in future cases as deciding that such conduct by the physician *was* negligent. Rather, the appellate court's opinion can be cited only as establishing that such conduct *could be* negligent. This point concerning the use of a prior decision will be returned to in Chapter 5.

3. *Questions Presented*

At the end of the procedural history, the opinion states the questions presented. These are simply the questions that the appellant has asked the court to decide. In other words, they are the issues on appeal.

Each question asks, in effect, whether some decision made in the trial or lower appellate court was erroneous, requiring reversal of the judgment. The entire rest of the opinion is devoted to deciding the questions presented.

4. Rules of Law

To decide the questions presented, the opinion begins by announcing rules of law. These are general principles of law that state that, under a particular set of circumstances, a certain right or duty exists.

The court announces these rules because it believes they govern the questions that it must decide. In effect, the rules establish the parties' rights and duties in this case as well as in all similar cases. Usually, most or all of the rules have been announced in prior cases, and the court cites the earlier cases from which each rule is taken.

The rules of law are of great importance. Much of the factual and procedural history is significant because it provides the context for some other part of the opinion, but the rules of law are important simply in themselves. Because they are thought to govern the reported case as well as similar cases, these rules may ultimately determine the results of the situation that the lawyer has been asked to review. The lawyer must carefully read and extract from the opinion each of the rules of law announced.

Identifying the rules of law can be difficult because they may not be stated in a clear, concise fashion. The elements may be scattered throughout a lengthy discussion, requiring the lawyer to construct the rules from a series of statements. The same rule may be stated more than once, in slightly different form, requiring the lawyer to choose the version that best explains the result reached.

As this suggests, extraction of the rule from a judicial opinion is not a mechanical process. Two lawyers reading the same opinion may well disagree on the rule of the case. And, because of the need at times to construct rules, the rule extracted by the lawyer may be phrased in the lawyer's own words rather than in the words of the court.

A case law rule thus differs from an enacted rule. Less importance is attached to the literal language of a case law rule simply because often there is not a single, authoritative version of the case law rule. The indeterminacy of the language of a case law rule, of course, provides the lawyer with the opportunity to articulate the rule in the form most favorable to the client's position.

5. Application of Law to Fact

The next portion of the opinion applies the law to the facts. This is a discussion of how the court has decided whether each element of each rule was satisfied by the facts before it.

Recall from Chapter 1 that the elements of a rule are typically phrased in very general terms. When writing an opinion, the court must decide whether the specific facts of the dispute before it fall within the meaning of the broad, generic facts set forth in the rule. In some cases, the court finds the language of the rule of law so clear that it believes only one result is possible. For example, a court would certainly hold that a red Buick is a motor vehicle.

In other cases, the court may decide that the language of the rule is too general to dictate a single result and that the policy behind the rule must be examined. The court would then be attempting to decide which result would best further the policies underlying the particular rule.

For example, if the rule to be applied prohibits the use of a "motor vehicle" in a park,[2] the court may have to decide whether a remote-controlled toy operated by a child falls within the definition of a motor vehicle. The court may decide that the purposes underlying the rule are to promote the recreational use of the park and to ensure the safety of pedestrians. Because a remote-controlled toy presents relatively little danger to pedestrians, ensuring pedestrian safety probably does not require that the toy be considered a motor vehicle. Moreover, promoting the recreational use of the park would require that the toy *not* be considered a motor vehicle. Thus, the court would further the policies underlying the rule by deciding that the toy does not fall within the meaning of the term "motor vehicle."

These discussions of policy are of considerable importance. They reveal the policies behind the rules and, as will be shown in Chapter 5, they provide a basis for deciding whether the elements of the rules are satisfied in future cases or even whether the rules should be changed.

Paradoxically, despite its importance, the policy discussion may be the portion of the opinion that is the least structured or methodical. The court may simply announce that public policy favors a particular result, without attempting to explain how the court knew there was such a policy.

It is almost always the case, moreover, that a judicial decision, rather than being based on a single policy, reflects a balance between at least two competing policies, one of which supported creation of the right or duty and the other of which opposed it. In the example above, the motor vehicle rule was based on policies of promoting the recreational use of a park and protecting pedestrians. On the one hand, the policy of ensuring pedestrian safety, taken to extremes, would have required banning the toy, since a pedestrian could trip over it or be startled by it. On the other hand, promoting the recreational use of the park, as noted, required that the toy be allowed.

The court has to decide, under the circumstances of the case before it, how to resolve the conflict. Explanations of how such conflicts are resolved

---

[2] This example was inspired by a well-known hypothetical case suggested by H.L.A. Hart.

are very often brief and conclusory. The court may note that there are conflicting policies and that one policy outweighs the other, without any real discussion of how the court determined the relative weights of the policies. The court may decide that the result is necessary to further a particular policy, ignoring competing policies altogether.

Courts are sometimes not explicit about the policies that underlie their decisions, and thus it is left to lawyers and judges in later cases to infer those policies—in effect to explain the basis for the decision after the fact. A creative lawyer litigating subsequent cases can attribute policy judgments to the court that plausibly explain the earlier decision and simultaneously support the client's position in the later case.

In any event, it is the completion of this analysis that permits the lawyer to ascertain which were the dispositive facts in the opinion. The dispositive facts were those on which the court relied in deciding whether the elements of the rule were satisfied. Perhaps the court decided that the toy was a motor vehicle because it was motorized, even though minuscule. The lawyer would infer from this that the existence of a motor is a dispositive fact.

Or, perhaps the court decided that the toy was not a motor vehicle because, even though it had a motor, it could not carry a driver or passengers. The lawyer would infer that the inability to carry people was a dispositive fact. Although other details, such as the shape, color, or price of the toy may have been mentioned in the opinion, the court did not rely upon them in deciding whether the element of a motor vehicle was met, and thus they were not dispositive facts.

In identifying the dispositive facts, the lawyer must distinguish between necessary and sufficient facts. Necessary facts are those that *must* be present for the element to be satisfied. If a necessary fact is not present, the element cannot be satisfied and the rule cannot apply. The absence of a necessary fact thus means that the element is not met. The presence of a necessary fact, on the other hand, does not mean that the element *is* met. The fact may be necessary, but not sufficient, to establish the element.

For example, if a device is deemed a motor vehicle only if it has a motor and is capable of carrying passengers, then the presence of a motor is a necessary fact, but it is not sufficient. The device must also be capable of carrying passengers.

Sufficient facts are those whose presence establishes the element but which need not be present for it to be satisfied. If a sufficient fact is present, then the element is satisfied. At the same time, its absence does not mean that the element is not satisfied, because some other sufficient fact may be present. The fact is sufficient to establish the element but not necessary.

The discussion that follows draws a distinction between the holding in a case and dictum. The holding essentially is the decision in the case, whereas dictum consists of statements made by the court that were not strictly necessary to the decision and will not be binding in future cases. In a technical sense, no court can ever hold that a particular fact was necessary to the result. To hold that the fact was necessary would be to hold, in effect, that in any situation where the fact is not present the result would be different. Such a situation, however, is not before the court and thus the court's statement concerning the result that would occur in the absence of the fact is dictum. For this reason, a court, strictly speaking, can hold only that a fact is sufficient for the result, not that it is necessary. This point is of limited importance, however, given that dictum, very often, *is* followed in subsequent cases and thus the fact will be treated in future cases as if it were necessary.

6. Holding

The decision of the court with respect to a question presented is called the holding. This is the most important part of the decision. In some cases, the court announces the holding with an expression such as "we hold." In other cases, it leaves to the lawyer the task of identifying the holding.

All of the problems attendant on identifying rules may exist in equal or greater measure in identifying the holding. When the court does not clearly state the holding, the lawyer may have to construct it from scattered statements. This process can be an indeterminate one, which may leave lawyers in disagreement about what the case actually held and which may present a lawyer with the opportunity to articulate the holding in the terms most favorable to the client.

7. Disposition

Finally, the opinion contains the disposition. A disposition is essentially a procedural directive of some kind that gives effect to the court's decision. Typically, the disposition is either that the trial court's judgment be affirmed or that it be reversed. In some cases, in addition to reversing the judgment of the trial court, the appellate court remands the case to the trial court for additional proceedings, such as a new trial. Although the disposition is critical to the parties to the case, it is of relatively little interest to a lawyer analyzing the case for purposes of identifying applicable law for future situations.

B. An Introduction to Stare Decisis

Whereas statutes are binding on the courts because of the doctrine of legislative supremacy, case law is binding because of the doctrine of stare decisis. This term is a shortened form of the Latin phrase *stare decisis et non quieta movere,* meaning "to stand by decisions and not to disturb that which is settled." Under this doctrine, a court is expected to decide "like" cases in the same way. That is, a decision in one case is binding in all future like cases.

The principle of stare decisis is not a rigid rule. When there is sufficient justification, a court may overrule a prior case, in effect, deciding a similar case differently than it did the last time such a case arose. Yet, stare decisis imposes a heavy presumption that prior cases will be followed.[3]

Stare decisis is thus a source of both certainty and flexibility in the law. New cases are generally to be decided in a way that is consistent with prior cases, thus promoting certainty. At the same time, because it is not an inflexible rule, stare decisis permits change when the underlying policies seem to require it.[4] Stare decisis also promotes both justice and efficiency. It promotes justice by requiring that like cases be decided in the same way, thus leading to equal justice under the law. It promotes efficiency by avoiding the need to relitigate the same issue anew each time it arises.

The doctrine of stare decisis is qualified by a distinction between the holding of a case and dictum. Dictum is any statement by the court that is not strictly necessary to the decision of the case before it. The word "dictum" is an abbreviation for the Latin phrase *obiter dictum,* which can be loosely translated as "a word said incidentally."

Under the doctrine of stare decisis, only the holding is considered binding; dictum is not. Dictum indicates the policy of the court, and it offers clues as to how the court would decide future cases. And, barring changes in circumstances or the membership of the court, dictum will likely be followed in

---

[3] Cases are generally binding only in the same jurisdiction, unless a court in a second jurisdiction is applying the law of the first jurisdiction. Thus, for example, decisions of the Massachusetts state courts do not bind the California state courts, unless California has decided to apply Massachusetts law. (The situation in which one state may apply the law of another state is discussed in Chapter 1.)

Cases, moreover, bind a court only if decided by that court or a higher court. Thus, the federal court of appeals must follow its own decisions and those of the U.S. Supreme Court but is not bound by federal district court decisions.

A court may overrule its own decisions with sufficient justification. It may not overrule decisions of higher courts under any circumstances, however. If a lower court believes that the decision of a higher court would no longer be followed by the higher court, it occasionally decides not to follow the prior case, which leaves the higher court with the choice of overruling the prior case or reversing the trial court's decision.

A case that is not binding may still be considered persuasive authority; that is, a court may look to such a case for guidance, but it is free to reach a different conclusion than was reached in the nonbinding case.

[4] The circumstances in which a court is likely to change case law are discussed in Chapter 5.

future cases. Dictum, however, need not be followed, whereas the holding must be, unless there is sufficient justification to depart from the doctrine of stare decisis.

For this reason, the holding is the most important part of a judicial opinion. It is the only part that, strictly speaking, will be binding in future cases. Above all else, case analysis must result in identification of the holding. Everything else is secondary.

The claim that the holding is of primary importance seems oddly inconsistent with the emphasis in prior pages on identifying rules of law. There really is no inconsistency, however, because a holding is in essence a rule of law stated at a lower level of generality; a holding is merely a rule of law restated in terms of the facts of a particular case.

For example, a particular case may state the rule of law that an individual who fails to exercise reasonable care for his or her own physical safety is contributorily negligent.[5] The case may go on to hold that a person who fails to look both ways before crossing a railroad track is contributorily negligent. The factual predicate in the rule is the failure to exercise reasonable care, whereas the factual predicate in the holding is the failure to look both ways. Failure to look both ways is merely a specific instance of failure to exercise reasonable care. The holding is just a specific instance of the more general rule of law.

Indeed, courts in later cases may not even distinguish between a rule of law and a holding taken from a prior case. For instance, a statement of a rule of law that constituted dictum in an earlier case may be characterized in later cases as a holding, in order to give it greater weight.

The distinction between the holding and dictum, like the doctrine of stare decisis that it qualifies, promotes both certainty and flexibility in the law. By stating general rules in dictum, the court indicates how it intends to decide future cases that are in some way analogous to the present case, thus promoting certainty. At the same time, however, because dictum is not binding, the court may at any time refuse to follow dictum without having to overrule the prior case, a circumstance that promotes flexibility.

The distinction between the holding and dictum also enhances the quality of judicial decisionmaking. Matters not strictly necessary to the decision of the case may not have been fully researched or argued by the parties to the litigation and thus may not have been carefully considered by the court. A

---

[5] Contributory negligence is negligence by the injured party. The traditional rule, now changed in nearly all jurisdictions, was that a party whose injury was partly attributable to that person's own negligence could not recover compensation from another party whose negligence also was a partial cause of the injury; that is, the injured party's contributory negligence barred recovery.

broad rule that appears to promote public policy in the situation before the court may be counterproductive in other situations not contemplated by the court when it articulated the rule. Because the rule is only dictum, courts may disregard it in subsequent cases without seeming to have abandoned the principle of stare decisis. In this way, the potentially adverse consequences of an ill-considered rule are avoided.

The arguments that may lead a court not to follow dictum are discussed in Chapter 5. In general, the arguments used to avoid the application of dictum are similar to those used to overrule a prior case. There is a difference, however; because dictum is not binding, a court can be more easily persuaded to disregard dictum than to overrule a holding.

The doctrine of stare decisis rests on a paradox. On the one hand, a court has the power to decide only the dispute before it, and the rules that it announces are binding only in like cases. On the other hand, it is left to the courts deciding future cases to determine whether those cases are like the prior case and, therefore, whether the prior case must be followed. The paradox is thus that a prior case binds a court, but only if the court decides that the prior case is binding.

Most lawyers, noting this paradox, eventually come to the understanding that the common law is not a set of fixed rules, but rather a process. It is a process whereby later cases are decided in a way that seems consistent with prior cases, although it is only when the later cases have been decided that the true meaning of the prior cases becomes known. By continually deciding which cases are similar or dissimilar to prior cases, courts in effect are shaping the content of the previously announced rules. The rules are defined as they are applied, and the law is in a constant state of evolution, explication, and elaboration.

III. ANALYZING RIGHTS AND DUTIES

In identifying rules of law, whether those rules are drawn from case law or from enacted law, the lawyer must be careful to characterize correctly the precise right or duty created. In this last section, some of the important characteristics of a right or duty are explained.

A. *The Meaning of Right and Duty*

As an initial matter, rights and duties should be understood as types of legal relationships among persons or entities. The law sometimes uses terms other than right or duty to identify a legal relationship. Other such terms include power, liability, privilege, and immunity.

Some scholars have attempted to give each of these terms a specific meaning that would distinguish it from the others.[6] An immunity, for example, may be thought of as a legal relationship that exempts a person or entity from some power, liability, or duty. Thus, sovereign immunity exempts the state from the power of a court. Such efforts at refining the terminology, however, have not met with widespread or lasting acceptance.

Most lawyers in practice tend to use the two terms "right" and "duty" in a sense broad enough to encompass nearly all legal relationships. The term "duty" generally refers to a legal relationship that requires a person to take some action, as in the case of the duty to exercise reasonable care in performing a surgical operation. The term "right" is often used in two different ways. First, it refers to a legal relationship that entitles a person or entity to take some action, as in the right to vote in an election. Second, it also refers to a legal relationship that entitles a person or entity to action from another, as in the right to receive payment of compensation.

The discussion in this book follows the common practice of using right and duty in a broad sense to refer to legal relationships generally. Occasionally, when common usage has settled on one of the other terms, as in the case of the attorney-client privilege, the other term will be used.

The terms "right" and "duty" can often be used to describe exactly the same legal relationship, although from the perspective of a different person in the relationship. For example, a lawyer may say that a negligent physician has a duty to pay compensation to an injured patient and that the patient has a right to receive compensation from the physician. The two have a single relationship that can be described from the patient's perspective as a right and from the physician's perspective as a duty.

The terms "right" and "duty" can also be used to refer collectively to several more specific rights or duties. Thus, for example, the landowner's right of property refers collectively to a number of rights, such as the right to exclude others from the land and the right to convey the land to another.

B. *Three Characteristics of Rights and Duties*

Describing a right or duty requires the lawyer to identify three characteristics of the legal relationship. Each of these is discussed in turn.

First, the lawyer must identify the persons between whom the relationship exists. Assume, for example, that the patient has a right to compensation from the physician. That right would create a legal relationship

---

[6] *See, e.g.,* Hohfeld, *Some Fundamental Legal Conceptions as Applied in Judicial Reasoning,* 23 YALE L.J. 16 (1913); Hohfeld, *Fundamental Legal Conceptions as Applied in Judicial Reasoning,* 26 YALE L.J. 710 (1917).

between only those two persons. It would create no relationship between the patient and the physician's uncle in Louisville.

Legal relationships may exist among more than two persons. Indeed, some rights create a legal relationship between one person and the entire world. The owner of real property, for example, is generally said to have a right to exclude everyone in the world from that property. Rights that exist against all people generally are referred to as rights in rem. Rights that exist only against specified individuals are often referred to as rights in personam.

The second characteristic of a legal relationship that the lawyer must identify is its subject matter, that is, the type of conduct that the right or duty governs. For example, the duty to pay compensation requires one person to pay money to another. The right to exclude others from land may entitle the owner to build a fence but not to place land mines around the perimeter. Each of these rights or duties requires or permits only specified types of conduct.

The third characteristic that the lawyer must identify is the nature of the relationship, assessing whether the legal relationship is mandatory or permissive. Thus, the lawyer must be alert to whether a legal relationship *requires* or merely *permits* certain conduct.[7] For example, the right to exclude others from one's land permits the owner to build a fence but does not require that the landowner do so.

C. *The Significance of the Three Characteristics*

As has been demonstrated, legal reasoning is the process of using rules to draw conclusions about the existence of particular rights or duties in a given situation. More specifically, the lawyer must reach some conclusion about whether the right or duty described in the legal consequence of a rule also applies to the situation under review. In applying a rule to facts, the lawyer must be careful to ensure that the right or duty found to exist in the situation has the same characteristics as the right or duty described in the governing rule.

For example, returning to the illustration from the Introduction, the lawyer may conclude that the reporter has a contractual duty not to publish the informant's name. In analyzing the rules describing the legal consequences of a breach of contract, the lawyer must be precise about whether

---

[7] Arguably, there is a third possibility—that the relationship is *prohibitory*; that is, the relationship may prohibit certain conduct by certain persons. Prohibitions and requirements, however, may be regarded as merely two different ways of articulating the same relationship. One can say, for example, that Michelle is required to attend school or that she is prohibited from missing school. To simplify matters, the text treats requirements and prohibitions as conceptually indistinct and refers to them collectively as requirements.

the promisee's right as described in the rules is to obtain performance of the promise or compensation for the breach. That, in turn, will determine whether the informant's right is to obtain a court order prohibiting publication of the name or merely to obtain compensation after the name is published. Failure to be precise could result in reaching the wrong conclusion, such as a conclusion that the reporter's promise conferred on the informant the right to stop publication when it conferred only the right to obtain compensation in the event of publication.

One source of difficulty is that references to a right—such as the right of property, the right of privacy, or the right of free speech—can mean different things in different contexts. In each context, the term may have slightly different characteristics. It may be that in announcing the existence of a right or duty the court itself was not precise about the characteristics of the right or duty.

Another source of difficulty is that lawyers can manipulate the level of generality at which a case law rule is stated. In so doing, the lawyer changes the characteristics of the right or duty described in the legal consequence of the rule. The right or duty found to exist in the situation under review thus has different characteristics than the right or duty described in the governing rule.

As this suggests, in some cases, the lawyer in the course of applying a rule to a situation may deliberately change one or more of the characteristics of the right or duty described in the governing rule in order to change the result that the rule seems to require. For example, the lawyer may find a rule stating that a landowner has a right to build a fence around his land to exclude others but may restate the right more generally as a right to exclude others from the land. The lawyer now argues that the client has a right to plant land mines around the perimeter of the land. By manipulating levels of generality, the lawyer attempts to transform the right to build a fence into a right to plant mines.

3

Synthesizing the Law

The third step in legal reasoning is to synthesize the rules of law into a single, coherent framework that can be applied to the facts. This requires that the lawyer determine the relationship that each rule bears to the others.

In addition, legal reasoning at times requires that the lawyer construct a second, somewhat different type of synthesis: the synthesis of a single rule from a number of holdings to govern a situation not within the confines of any prior rule or holding. Thus, in this second type of synthesis, the result is not a framework of rules but a single rule. This rule, of course, once constructed, is integrated into the larger framework of rules.

This chapter discusses both types of synthesis. In Section I, the techniques for organizing rules into a framework are described. In Section II, the ways in which a lawyer may synthesize a new rule to be placed within the framework are discussed.

I. Synthesizing Rules: General to Specific

Synthesizing the rules into a coherent framework means, in effect, that the lawyer creates an outline of the applicable rules, with more specific rules categorized under more general rules. To the extent that the lawyer's analysis of statutes and cases has identified the policies underlying the rules, the lawyer should include those in the synthesis as well.[1]

As will be discussed in Chapter 5, not all rules are applied the same way. Thus, in synthesizing the rules, the lawyer must make note of the source of the rule and, if the rule was derived from case law, observe whether it was a holding.

A. The Basic Organizing Principle

The key organizing principle in legal reasoning is to move from the general to the specific. For this reason, the lawyer usually begins with general rules

---

[1] The analysis, synthesis and application of policies is discussed in detail in Chapter 7.

of law, which directs the search to more specific rules, which then can be applied to specific facts to produce a conclusion.

Thus, in constructing a synthesis, the lawyer similarly moves from the general to the specific, endeavoring to identify the general rules, under which the more specific rules can be categorized, essentially in an outline form. These more specific rules may be thought of as "subrules" to the more general rules.

The categorization process is carried out by determining the type of relationship each rule bears to the others. The relationship between the rules determines the placement of each rule in the synthesis or outline.

B. Relationships Among Rules

For the most part, any two rules have only one of a few possible relationships to each other. In this subsection several possible relationships are described.[2]

1. Rules Defining a More General Rule

First, one rule may define an element of another rule. For example, a rule found in a first case may state that one who intentionally touches another in an offensive way is liable for a battery. A rule found in a second case may state that a touching is offensive if a reasonable person under the circumstances would find it so. In this example, the second rule defines an element—the element of offensiveness—of the first rule. The second rule is more specific than the first and should be categorized as a subrule of the first. Other cases may have produced rules defining the other elements of a battery, and they too would be categorized under the more general rule creating liability for the commission of a battery.

When the general rule is a statutory rule, the more specific rules defining its elements are likely to include both statutory and case law rules. In enacting a statute, a legislature very commonly enacts specific sections that have the sole function of defining the elements of a statutory rule. Many statutes include a section that is explicitly labeled as a "definitions" section. If the legislature fails to define an element of the statute, the courts may need to create case law rules defining the element in order to apply the statute to particular disputes. It also may happen that the legislature does enact a definition, but the definition itself may be unclear. In that case the courts must

---

[2] The terminology used in describing the relationships is my own. Very little has been written on how to perform the task of organizing rules according to their relationship to each other, and thus there is no widely accepted terminology for these relationships.

accordingly create case law rules defining the elements of the definition. In any event, the elements of statutory rules are usually defined by a mixture of statutory and case law rules.

Where the general rule is a case law rule, the lawyer often finds that the more specific rules defining elements of the general rule are based only on case law. It is unusual to find a statute that was enacted for the purpose of defining an element of a case law rule. Statutory definitions are enacted almost exclusively for the purpose of defining the elements of statutory rules.

2. Rules Applying a More General Rule

Second, one rule may serve as an application of another rule. In other words, one rule may state the manner in which a more general rule applies to a specific situation.

For example, a case may announce the rule that a physician who performs surgery on another person without consent is liable for a battery. This rule is really nothing more than a specific application of the rule just described, creating liability for the commission of a battery. The rule imposing liability on a physician is more specific than the first rule, imposing liability on any person for the commission of a battery, and should be categorized as a subrule of the first.

A specific rule applying a more general rule to a particular sets of facts may technically be a holding of a case. As has been seen, holdings are very often merely particularized applications of rules. For reasons that will be explained in Chapter 5, the fact that a particular rule is the holding of a case, as opposed to dictum, should be noted by the attorney, but that will not affect the placement of the rule in the synthesis.

A specific rule applying a more general rule may also have the effect of illustrating the definitions of the elements. For example, the rule imposing liability on the physician for a battery in effect designates a surgical operation as an illustration of what is meant by an offensive touching.

Regardless of whether the general rule is a statutory rule or a case law rule, the more specific rule applying it is usually created by case law. Indeed, the principal function of the courts is to apply statutes and case law rules to specific situations.

It is unusual for a statutory rule to serve as the specific application of a more general statutory or case law rule. As has been explained in Chapter 1, legislatures generally attempt to enact statutes that operate at a high level of generality and usually do not enact statutes that are merely more specific applications of another statute already in force.

Recalling, however, that the word "statute" is being used here in a broad sense to refer to all enacted law, the reader should note that there are instances where one enacted rule is actually the application of another enacted rule. This is perhaps most likely in situations where an administrative agency has issued regulations implementing a statute. Certain of the administrative regulations may be nothing more than statements applying the statute to specific factual situations.

3. Rules Limiting a More General Rule

Third, one rule may serve as a limitation on the scope of another rule, which means that one rule may specify situations in which another rule does not apply.

For example, a case may state the rule that one who uses reasonable force against another person necessary for self-defense against imminent bodily injury is not liable to that other person for a battery. At first glance, this rule concerning self-defense seems to contradict the general rule imposing liability for a battery. And, in a sense, there is a contradiction here. But the contradiction exists only in a specified set of circumstances—those circumstances where force is necessary for self-defense. Because the self-defense rule describes the circumstances under which it prevails over the general rule, the contradiction can be resolved by treating the self-defense rule as simply a limitation on, or an exception to, the general rule.

A rule that creates an exception to, or limits the scope of, another rule, is obviously more specific than that other rule. Thus, the narrower, limiting rule should be categorized as a subrule of the more general rule.

When two rules contradict each other, the question sometimes arises as to which is the general rule and which is the exception. The general rule, of course, is simply the rule that applies to the broader set of circumstances.

Often, the rule that constitutes the exception will be obvious on the face of the rules. For example, a rule may state explicitly that it is an exception to a more general rule. Even if a rule does not state explicitly that it is an exception, its exceptionality may be implicit because it defines a relatively narrow set of circumstances in which it prevails over another rule, leaving it clear that the other rule prevails in all other circumstances.

At times, the question of which is the general rule and which the exception will be open to some doubt. Moreover, the answer may change over time. It is not uncommon in the law that an exception is applied to an increasingly broader range of circumstances until the supposed exception becomes more broadly applicable than what previously had been considered the general rule. Lawyers speak of this situation as one in which "the exception swallows the rule." Eventually, the "exception" is openly acknowledged to be the new general rule.

Statutory rules, of course, are likely to state explicitly which is the general rule and which the exception. Further, because the language of statutes is fixed, statutory rules are less likely to produce the phenomenon in which an exception grows until it swallows the rule.

Where the general rule is a case law rule, most of the exceptions are also case law rules. Occasionally, a legislature enacts a statute intended to modify the common law in some respect and that statute in effect may create a limitation on a case law rule.

Where the general rule is a statute, the exceptions are nearly always statutory rules. The doctrine of legislative supremacy, described in Chapter 1, precludes the courts from modifying statutes through case law. Occasionally, however, a court may create what amounts to a case law limitation on a statute, provided it can reconcile the limitation with the doctrine of legislative supremacy.

One way for a court to remain consistent with legislative supremacy in limiting a statute with case law is to find that the limitation is implicit in the language of the statute or is consistent with the underlying legislative intent. The theory is that the court is not overriding the legislature but is achieving the result that the legislature would have intended, had it anticipated the particular situation before the court.

Another way for a court to remain consistent with legislative supremacy while limiting a statute with case law is to find that the statute would be unconstitutional without the limitation. As noted in Chapter 1, the doctrine of judicial review, in which courts have the power to determine the constitutionality of legislation, amounts in practice to an exception to legislative supremacy.

4. Rules Cumulative to Another Rule

Fourth, one rule may be cumulative to another. In other words, one rule may describe a different right or duty than another rule. Or, it may describe a different set of facts that will give rise to the same right or duty.

In either case, the two rules are not mutually exclusive alternatives because both may apply simultaneously. Because the rights or duties are cumulative, there is no contradiction between the two rules; that is, neither rule limits the other.

For example, a case may state a rule that one who intentionally causes another the apprehension of an imminent offensive touching is liable in tort for an assault. This rule defines a liability—the liability for an assault—that is cumulative to the liability for a battery. One may commit an assault, without also committing a battery, by putting a victim in fear of bodily harm that ultimately is not inflicted. Or, one may commit a battery, without also committing an assault, by offensively touching a sleeping victim. Further, one may commit both torts by causing the fear of bodily harm, accompanied by the actual infliction of the harm. These rules are cumulative in the sense that either or both may apply to the facts without affecting the applicability of the other.

Where two rules create cumulative rights or duties, they occupy parallel places in the synthesis. Neither is more general than the other. Thus, neither is categorized as a subrule of the other. Rather, they exist at the same level of generality.

Cumulative rules can be case law rules or statutory rules, or they can be a combination of the two. It is not unusual, for example, for common law rules imposing liability for certain conduct to exist side by side with statutory rules imposing liability for similar conduct. One instance of this occurs where statutory rules imposing liability for unfair and deceptive trade practices exist cumulatively with common law rules imposing liability for fraud.

5. Rules Contradicting Another Rule

Fifth, one rule may contradict another. That is, one rule may provide that a particular right or duty exists under a specific set of circumstances, whereas the other rule provides that no such right or duty exists under those same circumstances.

This state of affairs, in theory, is not supposed to occur. The law is assumed to be an internally consistent framework of rules that can be harmonized so that they lead to only one result in a given situation.

Traditional legal reasoning thus requires that the contradiction between the two rules be resolved. There are at least three ways to resolve a contradiction between rules.

One resolution is found by treating one rule as simply superseding the other rule. If the rules emanate from different sources, then constitutional principles may provide a basis for subordinating one rule to another. For example, a federal rule generally prevails over a contrary state law rule.[3]

If the rules emanate from the same source, then the rule that was developed later in time is often treated as displacing the earlier rule. Where both rules are statutory, this resolution is virtually unavoidable because of the principle of statutory interpretation that directs that a later statute prevail over a prior, inconsistent statute. Where both rules are case law rules, it may be far less clear whether the later case supersedes the earlier case. In some instances, the court in the later case states explicitly that the earlier decision is overruled and thus no contradiction exists. In other instances, the later case so thoroughly repudiates the reasoning of the earlier case as to suggest implicitly that the earlier case no longer states the law, a situation in which the earlier case is said to have been overruled *sub silentio,* that is, by silence. In still other instances, however, the effect of the later case on the earlier case may be unclear.

---

[3] *See* Chapter 1.

Because of the doctrine of legislative supremacy, statutory rules can supersede case law rules, but rarely can a case law rule supersede a statutory rule. The principal situation in which a case law rule supersedes a statutory rule occurs where the court declares a statute unconstitutional. In addition, a case law rule may effectively supersede a statutory rule by interpreting or applying it in a way that is seemingly inconsistent with its language.

A second way to achieve resolution is by treating one rule as a limitation on, or an exception to, another rule. As discussed earlier, this explanation of the relationship between the rules is especially plausible if one rule, by its terms, applies only to a limited set of circumstances. In those exceptional circumstances, the narrower rule prevails, but in all other circumstances the general rule applies. This form of resolution thus requires that the situations to which the two rules apply be somehow distinguished, preferably on grounds related to furthering the underlying policies.

A third method of resolution treats neither rule as the general rule but regards them as applicable to mutually exclusive sets of circumstances. Here, in effect, there is no general rule that applies in all situations. Rather, there are two complementary rules, each of which applies to certain situations. As in the case of cumulative rules, these mutually exclusive rules are parallel to each other. Neither is more general and neither is categorized as a subrule of the other.

For example, tort law establishes certain duties that owners and occupiers of land owe to persons who come onto their land. In some states, the extent of the duty depends upon whether the person coming onto the land is classified as a trespasser, a licensee, or an invitee. A different rule defines the duty owed by the landowner to each of these types of persons. In short, there is no general rule that defines the duties owed by landowners to persons on their land. Rather, there are three complementary rules, each of which applies to a particular set of situations.

This resolution also requires that the lawyer articulate a distinction between the types of situations to which the two rules apply. Again, the distinction should be one related to the underlying policies. The lesser protection afforded trespassers, for example, may be related to the policy of protecting property rights by discouraging trespassing.

In some cases, the exact boundary between the situations governed by two contrasting rules is left unclear. Two rules that are plainly inconsistent are acknowledged to exist and each has been applied to specified circumstances. Which rule would be applied to some novel situation, however, is left undetermined until the situation arises.

For example, one rule of constitutional law states that the government may not condition the receipt of a benefit on the surrender of a right. Thus, the government cannot require that all clerical employees refrain under all circumstances from criticizing the president because that would condition the receipt of a benefit (a government job) on the surrender of a right (the right of free speech).[4] At the same time, the courts have also recognized the rule that the government may refuse to subsidize speech with which it disagrees. Thus, the government may refuse to allow public funding for medical clinics to be used to promote abortion as a method of family planning.[5]

The two rules are clearly inconsistent. Thus, if the first rule were applied to the second situation, it would lead to precisely the opposite result. That is, the court would hold that the government may not condition the receipt of a benefit (funding for a clinic) on the surrender of a right (the right to endorse abortion). Despite their inconsistency, both rules are part of constitutional law, although it remains unclear in which circumstances a court would apply the first rule and in which it would apply the second.

C. *Outlining the Synthesis*

The rule synthesis just described can be sketched as an outline in the form that follows. By determining each rule's relationship to the other rules, the lawyer establishes its place in the outline. Rules defining, applying, or limiting a more general rule are organized together under that more general rule. Cumulative rules, on the other hand, occupy the same relative position in the outline.

OUTLINE

I. Battery: Rule imposing liability for a battery

   A. Definition of elements

      1. Definition of intent
      2. Definition of a touching
      3. Definition of offensiveness
      4. *Etc.*

   B. Rule applications

      1. Case of surgeon operating without consent
      2. *Etc.*

   C. Exceptions

      1. Self-defense
      2. *Etc.*

---

[4] *See, e.g.,* Rankin v. McPherson, 483 U.S. 378 (1987).
[5] *See, e.g.,* Rust v. Sullivan, 500 U.S. 173, 111 S.Ct. 1759 (1991).

II. Assault: Rule imposing liability for an assault

   A. Definition of elements

      1. Cases defining individual elements
      2. *Etc.*

   B. Rule applications

      1. Cases applying the rule
      2. *Etc.*

   C. Exceptions

      1. Cases creating exceptions to the rule
      2. *Etc.*

III. Owners and occupiers of land

   A. Rule defining the liability to invitees

      1. Definition of elements
         a. Cases defining the elements of the rule
         b. *Etc.*
      2. Rule applications
         a. Cases applying the rule
         b. *Etc.*
      3. Exceptions
         a. Cases creating exceptions to the rule
         b. *Etc.*

   B. Rule defining the liability to licensees

      1. Definition of elements
         a. Cases defining the elements of the rule
         b. *Etc.*
      2. Rule applications
         a. Cases applying the rule
         b. *Etc.*
      3. Exceptions
         a. Cases creating exceptions to the rule
         b. *Etc.*

   C. Rule defining the liability to trespassers

      1. Definition of elements
         a. Cases defining the elements of the rule
         b. *Etc.*

    2. Rule Applications
      a. Cases applying the rule
      b. *Etc.*
    3. Exceptions
      a. Cases creating exceptions to the rule
      b. *Etc.*

II. Synthesizing a Rule: Specific to General

Situations arise in which the lawyer wishes to establish the existence of a rule not previously recognized in explicit terms. The lawyer's client, for example, may be in a situation that is essentially unprecedented. Or the situation may be one that is not unprecedented but one in which courts in times past have declined to impose rights or duties.

The lawyer can address these situations by synthesizing a new rule based on the holdings of prior cases.[6] Indeed, some of the most influential examples of legal scholarship consist of analyses of a number of cases followed by a conclusion that these cases have established a general rule not previously recognized.[7]

In this section, the way a lawyer can fill a gap in the law by synthesizing a new rule is described. Once the new rule is synthesized, the lawyer places it in the larger framework discussed in the preceding section.

The lawyer in this situation would probably not admit that he or she is synthesizing a new rule, arguing instead that, in fact, there already *is* an applicable rule, although it has not yet been explicitly recognized as such. The rule would be described as newly discovered rather than newly invented because, if the rule already exists, then under the doctrine of stare decisis the court must apply it. An existing rule, in other words, is binding.

A second reason that the lawyer would prefer to argue that the rule has been discovered rather than invented is that some courts question whether the creation of new rules of law by a court is consistent with democratic principles. The court thus may be reluctant to adopt a new rule but may be quite willing merely to apply a rule that supposedly already exists. This matter is discussed further in Chapter 6.

---

[6] Another important way to resolve a dispute for which no obviously applicable rule exists is to create an analogy between the novel situation and another situation for which rules do exist. The use of analogies to decide cases is discussed in Chapter 5.

[7] *See, e.g.,* Warren and Brandeis, *The Right of Privacy,* 4 Harv. L. Rev. 193 (1890); Fuller and Perdue, *The Reliance Interest in Contract Damages,* 46 Yale L.J. 52, 373 (1936, 1937).

A. *The Basic Model*

The lawyer synthesizes the new rule by a method similar to the logical process of induction.[8] Induction is a method of reasoning that, in essence, proceeds from the particular to the general.

For example, after tasting several raisins and finding that each of them is sweet, one may reason by induction that all raisins taste sweet. Induction produces a conclusion that is probable, though not certain. No matter how many raisins one eats, the possibility always exists that the next one may taste different from the others.

Nevertheless, courts formulate rules of law by a process that is inductive in form. If a number of cases have been decided in which a particular right or duty was found to exist, then the court may conclude that the same right or duty exists in all similar cases. By studying several particular instances, the court formulates a general rule.

For example, assume that various courts decide a number of cases imposing a duty on landowners to warn guests about various conditions on the land, such as a concealed pit, quicksand, or an unstable slope. As the number of cases grows, it becomes possible to think of these cases as collectively establishing a rule that requires the landowner to warn guests about hazards. In this situation, a rule is formulated by a process of induction. The rule, however, is broader than any of the specific cases on which it was based. The whole thus becomes greater than the sum of the parts.

By creating a rule broader than any one prior case, the court creates a rule broad enough to apply to the novel case. The novel case, accordingly, can be decided by application of the newly synthesized rule.

As noted above, induction does not compel a particular conclusion but can only suggest that the conclusion is probable. In the same way, the court is not compelled to accept the new, broader rule. Just as tasting a few raisins does not force one to conclude that all raisins taste the same, the prior decisions in cases involving certain specific hazards do not require the court to decide that other hazards are subject to the same rule. The court may

---

[8] In this book, I discuss three different logical processes: induction, deduction, and analogy. The latter two are discussed extensively in Chapter 5.

In broad terms, I am defining induction as the process of reasoning from specific cases to a general rule. I define deduction as reasoning from a general rule to a specific case. I define analogy as the process of reasoning from one specific case to another specific case.

I acknowledge that some logicians would regard these definitions as technically inaccurate. The definitions do, however, serve my purpose, which is to demonstrate that lawyers reason in three different ways—sometimes using specific cases to create a general rule, sometimes using a general rule to decide specific cases, and sometimes using a specific case to decide another specific case.

correctly note that the holdings in the prior cases did not reach beyond quicksand, a concealed pit, and an unstable slope and may decide not to extend the holdings beyond those situations.

The more such cases the lawyer finds, however, the more likely the court is to accept the existence of the new rule. The techniques that the lawyer uses to propose or oppose recognition of the new rule are discussed later in this chapter.

B. *The Problem of Indeterminacy*

The premise for using inductive reasoning is that several similar items have been identified about which a generalization can safely be made. Yet, the lawyer will find that the process of formulating a generalization is not a mechanical one. Rather, it is a process that requires the exercise of judgment and that can lead to more than one result.

The lawyer must make at least two decisions in synthesizing the rule. First, the lawyer must decide which facts to include in the factual predicate, thus determining how to characterize the prior cases. Each of the prior cases may be subject to multiple characterizations, depending upon which facts of those cases the lawyer chooses to emphasize. In deciding how to characterize the cases included in the rule, the lawyer in effect is choosing the elements of the rule.

For example, the lawyer may characterize the cases involving the quicksand, the concealed pit, and the unstable slope as cases involving abnormal conditions, provided that each condition was abnormal for that area. Or, the lawyer may characterize them as cases involving hazards, because each condition was dangerous. Alternatively, the lawyer may characterize them as cases involving concealed hazards, on the theory that none of the hazards was obvious to the casual observer. Or, the cases may be characterized as involving natural hazards, if they were not the result of human activity. Finally, the lawyer may choose to emphasize the especially dangerous nature of the hazards and characterize the cases as involving life-threatening hazards.

All of these characterizations may be equally accurate. No one characterization is the "correct" one that must be chosen to the exclusion of the others. The process of characterizing the facts is indeterminate. The lawyer can reach a particular characterization only by the exercise of judgment.

A second decision the lawyer must make is to set the level of generality at which the new rule should be formulated. This means deciding whether the prior cases are to be described in broad, general terms or in narrow, specific terms.

In the case of the concealed pit, the unstable slope, and the quicksand, for example, the lawyer must decide at what level of generality to characterize the conditions on the land that give rise to a duty to warn. At one extreme, they could be characterized as hazards. In that case, the lawyer could conclude that the various cases identified by research establish a general rule that the landowner has a duty to warn guests about all hazards on the land.

At the other extreme, the lawyer could characterize the conditions as falling within the three narrow categories of quicksand, concealed pits, and unstable slopes. Each of these categories might be characterized even more narrowly so that, under the lawyer's characterization of the rule, a landowner has a duty to warn only of concealed pits of a certain depth, unstable slopes of a specified angle, and quicksand pools of a particular size.

Between these extremes is a range of possible rules of differing levels of generality. The term "life-threatening hazards," for example, is more specific than the term "hazards."

Each of these levels of generality may yield a rule that is equally accurate. No particular level of generality is correct to the exclusion of the others. The choice of the level of generality at which to state the rule is indeterminate. The lawyer's selection of a particular level of generality must therefore be based on the exercise of judgment. Different lawyers generalizing about the same group of cases will produce rules at different levels of generality.

The judgments concerning which facts to include in the factual predicate and the level of generality at which to state a rule are interrelated. The more general the rule, the fewer the facts that need to be specified. For example, if the rule is formulated as applying to all hazards, then whether the hazards are natural or life-threatening is irrelevant and would not be specified in the rule. Put another way, stating the rule at a high level of generality allows the lawyer to be agnostic about which of various specifics to include in the factual predicate. The corollary, of course, is that if the lawyer decides to include numerous detailed facts in the factual predicate, then, necessarily, the rule cannot be stated at a high level of generality.

C. Addressing Indeterminacy Through Policy Judgments

The lawyer may attempt to solve the indeterminacy involved in synthesizing a rule by referring to the policies underlying the cases. In this situation, the lawyer uses the underlying policies as a guide in selecting the facts to include in the factual predicate of the rule and in choosing the level of generality at which to state the rule. As will be seen, however, use of the underlying policies does not entirely solve the problem of indeterminacy.

The first decision the lawyer must make is to select the facts to include in the factual predicate of the rule. As an initial matter, some of the prior cases may have specified that certain facts were dispositive. For example, the case involving the pit may have specified that a duty to warn was imposed because the pit was a concealed hazard; that is, the case made clear that the holding imposing a duty was based on the presence of two facts—the fact that the condition was hazardous and the fact that it was concealed.

To the extent that the prior cases leave unclear which facts were dispositive, the lawyer selects for inclusion in the newly synthesized rule those facts in the prior cases that were relevant to accomplishing the underlying policies. For instance, if the policy was solely the protection of personal safety, then the fact that the conditions were natural probably should not matter, since a condition may be hazardous whether it is natural or not. Nor perhaps should it matter that the conditions were concealed, since even an obvious hazard can threaten safety. If the policy, however, was to encourage people to be responsible for their own safety, then the fact that the condition was concealed becomes more relevant. In such situations, the court may wish to deny recovery to guests who put themselves at risk by encountering an obvious hazard.

A second decision the lawyer must make is to select the level of generality at which to state the elements in the newly synthesized rule. As a practical matter, the lawyer must state the elements in terms general enough to include the facts of any prior case from which the rule is being synthesized. Thus, if the lawyer wishes to include the quicksand, the slope, and the pit cases, then a term at least as general as "hazard" may have to be used. Any narrower term could arguably exclude some of the cases.

The lawyer must also state the elements in terms at least general enough to include the novel case to which the rule will be applied. For example, assume that the lawyer concluded that, in the prior cases, the quicksand, the pit, and the slope were all in some way concealed, and thus the term "concealed hazard" would include all prior cases. The lawyer's client, however, was injured by a hazard that was not really concealed, although the client unfortunately did not notice it. If the lawyer characterizes the facts of the prior cases as involving concealed hazards, the very case for which a rule is being formulated will be excluded. Accordingly, the lawyer characterizes the facts of the prior cases in still more general terms—perhaps as "hazards"—in order to include the case under consideration.

The lawyer, however, also has the choice of synthesizing a rule in terms broader than is absolutely necessary in order to include the prior cases and the current case. Assume for a moment that the term "concealed hazard," in fact, would embrace all of the cases the lawyer wishes to include. If "concealed hazards" would include all of the cases, then so would the more general term "hazards" and the even more general term "potentially dangerous conditions." The lawyer must decide whether to use one of these more general characterizations or to be only as general as is absolutely necessary to include the current case.

In choosing the level of generality, the lawyer must avoid overreaching. In other words, the lawyer cannot formulate the rule in terms so broad that it includes new cases that make the policy judgments underlying the prior cases inapplicable. If the rule is too broad, application of the rule can yield undesirable results.

For example, assume that in the quicksand, pit, and slope cases the courts were attempting to strike a balance between, on the one hand, compensating injury and, on the other hand, encouraging safety by refusing to compensate the careless. In each case, the court held that because the hazard was concealed, the victim could not have avoided injury by exercising care. Thus, the policy of encouraging safety did not preclude imposing liability on the landowner.

The lawyer who characterizes these cases as imposing liability for all "hazards" may well be overreaching, because the policy judgments in the prior cases would not apply to any case in which the hazard was obvious. In the case of an obvious hazard, the victim might well have avoided injury by exercising care, and thus the policy judgment made in the prior cases does not apply. In cases in which the hazard is obvious, the policy of encouraging safety could require leaving the careless plaintiff uncompensated by not imposing liability on the landowner.

Thus, the lawyer must state the newly synthesized rule at a level of generality sufficient to include the prior cases and the client's case. At the same time, the rule must not be stated at a level of generality high enough to encompass new cases in which the policies underlying the prior cases would require a different result.

Between these extremes, however, the lawyer may well have some degree of choice. Thus, reference to the underlying policies may not eliminate all of the indeterminacy in synthesizing a new rule.

D. Using Rule Synthesis as an Advocate

The discussion in the previous section implicitly assumed to some extent that the lawyer, in synthesizing a new rule, was acting as a dispassionate observer, looking for the "true" nature of the rule that would explain the prior cases as well as govern the new case.

Yet, the lawyer engaged in the synthesis of a new rule is very often acting as an advocate, with the purpose of either constructing a new rule that will compel the result the client seeks or opposing the creation of the new rule. Let us consider the tactical moves that a lawyer in either situation may make in support of a client's position.

1. Supporting the New Rule

First, the lawyer attempting to create the rule probably wants to generalize from as many cases as possible. Recall that the lawyer would probably argue that the rule being advocated is not a new rule at all but rather a well-established rule perhaps not previously articulated in explicit terms. The more cases that have recognized the rule, the more the rule looks like a well-established rule of law that the court must apply and the less the court feels that it has ventured onto new terrain.

Second, the lawyer obviously wants to include in the factual predicate of the rule only those facts that clearly have counterparts in the current case. At times, that may be difficult because the court in a prior case may have stated explicitly that a particular fact—say, the fact that the hazard was concealed—was dispositive. If the fact was dispositive in the prior case from which the new rule is to be synthesized, then the fact generally has to be included in the new rule as well.

There is at least one argument the lawyer can make for excluding the dispositive fact from the new rule, and this is to contend that the dispositive fact was a sufficient, but not a necessary, condition for the result reached in the prior case. Thus, the fact need not be an element of the rule. This argument is bolstered considerably if the dispositive fact was absent from some prior cases. Even if it was present in all of them, the lawyer can argue that it was only a sufficient fact. This is done by demonstrating that the policies underlying the rule do not dictate that it be present. The lawyer might argue, for example, that the only policy mentioned by the court in the prior case was protecting persons against avoidable injury and that policy would have required imposition of a duty to warn whether the hazard was concealed or not. The lawyer is arguing, in effect, that the fact of concealment was not truly necessary to the result and any statements about the necessity of the fact should be considered dictum. Further, because the policy underlying the rule does not require that the hazard be concealed, the prior court's dictum to the effect that a concealed condition was a necessary fact should not be followed.[9]

Third, the lawyer probably wants to formulate the rule in the most general terms possible, without overreaching. A more general rule embraces more prior cases because the broad language used obscures the minor differences among the cases, thus allowing more cases to fall within the rule. As explained above, the more cases that seem to have embraced the rule, the more willing the court will be to apply it in the novel case. At the same time, the broader the rule, the more likely it is to encompass the lawyer's case.

2. Opposing the New Rule

A lawyer opposing recognition of the new rule may also employ a set of standard tactical moves. First, the lawyer attempts to restrict the number of cases on which the generalized rule may be based. This is done by confining the prior cases to their facts. That is, the lawyer points out that the

---

[9] As noted in Chapter 2, any statement by a court that a fact is necessary to its holding can technically be regarded as dictum. The policy discussion here, however, provides a basis for arguing not merely that the prior statement *need* not be followed, but that it *should* not be followed.

quicksand case addressed only quicksand; the concealed pit case, only concealed pits; the unstable slope case, only unstable slopes. Therefore, anything beyond quicksand, concealed pits, and unstable slopes is mere dictum that need not be followed. Ultimately, the argument is that no general rule exists; there are only several specific rules, none of which applies here. This argument, in essence, is an appeal to the reluctance of courts to make new law.

Second, the lawyer tries to identify dispositive facts in the prior cases that are not present in the novel situation, searching through the prior cases for as many details as can be found and arguing that all of these details were necessary to (not merely sufficient for) the decisions and thus belong in the factual predicate of any newly synthesized rule. Thus, for example, the lawyer may argue that the quicksand, pit, and slope are all concealed, life-threatening natural hazards and thus the rule should be limited to concealed, life-threatening natural hazards. Obviously, the strategy is to formulate a rule that excludes the current case.

Third, the lawyer tries to formulate the rule as narrowly as possible, again with the hope that it will exclude the current case. One way to do this is to characterize the facts narrowly—a concealed pit would be called a concealed pit, not a hazard or an abnormal condition. For this argument to be effective, the lawyer must be prepared to explain why the policy judgments that underlie the rule do not apply in the same way when the rule is formulated in more general terms; that is, the lawyer must explain why a rule formulated in more general terms would overreach.

4

Researching the Facts

The fourth step in legal reasoning is to research the facts to which the law must be applied. In a real sense, it is misleading to suggest that factual research follows the process of analysis and synthesis described in the prior chapters. As should have been clear from the Introduction, the lawyer cannot even begin the legal reasoning process without a general idea of the circumstances to which the law is to be applied. Thus, a limited factual inquiry is, in fact, the first step of the legal reasoning process.

I. THE ROLE OF FACTUAL RESEARCH

There is a constant interplay between factual research and the other steps of legal reasoning. The lawyer uses the basic facts known at the beginning of the inquiry to identify the likely sources of applicable law. As potentially applicable general rules are identified, the lawyer may realize that additional facts are needed to determine the applicability of the more specific rules defining, applying, or limiting the general rule. Thus, the lawyer continues to alternate between legal and factual research until all of the plausibly applicable rules have been identified.

At some point, the lawyer believes that the governing rules have been identified and synthesized into a framework. It is at this point that the lawyer must complete the factual research to make certain that all the relevant facts have been discovered. Thus, the fourth step really marks not so much the beginning as the end of the lawyer's factual investigation.

The rules of law identified by the lawyer shape the factual research. At the very beginning of the research, the lawyer conceives of the process as an attempt to determine simply what happened. As the legal research progresses, however, the lawyer comes to understand the potential legal consequences of the facts being researched. Very quickly, the lawyer begins to ask not simply what happened but whether the elements of the rules have been met.

Assume, for example, that the lawyer's client was injured while on the land of another person. The lawyer is attempting to determine whether the landowner had a duty to warn the client about the particular hazard that caused the injury. Legal research identifies a rule providing that the landowner would have had a duty if the client was an invitee but not if the client was a trespasser. The lawyer's factual research now shifts to determining whether the client was an invitee. If a factual detail does not make it more or less likely that the client was an invitee, then the lawyer regards that fact as irrelevant to the inquiry. The rules of law thus guide the attorney's selection of facts.

The rules also shape the lawyer's characterization of the facts. The lawyer cannot usefully characterize the facts in any way that seems intuitively appealing. Rather, the facts must be characterized as demonstrating that the elements were or were not met. Thus, in the example, the lawyer would characterize the facts as establishing that the client either was or was not an invitee.

II. The Rules of Factual Investigation

The law has its own unique rules for factual investigation. To a scientist, a fact is that which can be empirically observed. To a lawyer in a dispute, a fact is that which can be proven to a jury or to a judge sitting as the finder of fact. Although a scientist may find it highly probable as an empirical matter that the accused was present at the scene of the crime, if a jury finds otherwise, then it is a "fact" for purposes of the trial that the accused was not present.

One way to keep this point in mind is to draw a distinction between evidence and facts. In a trial, evidence is the empirical information that the lawyer presents to the jury.[1] A fact is that which the jury finds to be true, which may or may not be consistent with most of the evidence.

The facts found by the jury may differ from the evidence adduced by the lawyer for at least two reasons. First, the law of evidence may exclude from the trial some of the information in the lawyer's possession, and thus the

---

[1] Although, as explained in Chapter 1, in many trials no jury is impaneled and the judge decides all factual issues, for the sake of simplicity the discussion in the remainder of this chapter refers only to the process of presenting evidence to the jury. Unless otherwise noted, however, the discussion applies equally to the presentation of evidence to a judge sitting as the finder of fact.

jury may know less about the client's situation than the lawyer does.[2] Second, even assuming that all available evidence is admitted at trial, the evidence is very often incomplete or contradictory, and thus fact-finding will require some degree of inference and judgment, about which reasonable people can differ. The balance of this section discusses each of these two problems in turn.

A. The Problem of Evidence Law

The law of evidence prescribes rules that govern factual investigation in a court of law.[3] A lawyer engaged in legal reasoning can assume that a fact is true only if that fact can be proven in court using admissible evidence. Like any rule, the rules of evidence may lead to injustices in a particular case, but they exist because they are thought on balance to result in more accurate fact-finding in most cases and, thus, to produce more justice in the trial courts.[4] A description of a few of the main principles of evidence law illustrates the kinds of restrictions on the use of information at trial that the law imposes.

1. Types of Evidence Admissible

In general, the jury is permitted to consider two types of evidence: sworn oral testimony given in court; and physical objects, such as a document, a

---

[2] It is, of course, the judge who decides whether evidence will be admitted at trial or not. Where the judge is sitting as the finder of fact and rules that certain evidence is inadmissible, that judge quite obviously must hear the evidence to rule on its admissibility but, at least in theory, the judge will disregard any evidence that he or she has determined to be inadmissible.

[3] There is at least one other commonly encountered body of law, apart from evidence, that regulates factual investigation. The procedural rules that govern civil and criminal litigation typically contain rules of discovery. Under these discovery rules, either party may be able to compel the other party to provide certain types of information upon request. These rules, of course, are of assistance in factual research only where the client has already commenced litigation.

Moreover, the fact that the lawyer has obtained the information through discovery does not mean that it is admissible. Each item of information obtained will be admitted at trial only if it is admissible under the rules of evidence.

Although in theory the lawyer, prior to litigation, has investigated the facts to determine the client's rights and duties, the discovery process yields so much otherwise unavailable information that by the end of discovery the facts may look very different than they did prior to the commencement of litigation. Furthermore, the lawyer may learn still more facts once trial begins. Because the information available changes, the lawyer engaged in litigation must often continually reapply the law to the latest version of the facts to determine whether his or her prior conclusion is still sound.

[4] For further discussion of the problem that rules often lead to injustice in particular cases, see Chapter 7.

photograph, or a knife. All evidence must be authenticated. If the evidence is in the form of testimony, the witness testifying authenticates his or her testimony by swearing to tell the truth and then identifying himself or herself. If the evidence is in the form of a physical object, then a sworn witness must usually identify the object. In this way, the jury knows that all evidence is what it purports to be—the observations of Mr. Clark, the contract between Smith and Jones, the knife found at the scene of the killing.

Further, the witness testifying or authenticating an object must lay a foundation for the testimony; that is, the witness must explain how he or she knows the information about which he or she is testifying. For example, if the witness is going to testify that Frank shot Ned, that witness must first testify to being present at the time of the shooting and being able to see it occur or must give some other acceptable explanation for having obtained the information. The witness can testify only to facts gained through direct observation and is usually not permitted to inject opinion or speculation.

A witness's opinion *is* admissible when the witness is testifying as an expert. For example, the court would admit testimony by an expert in the field of surgery to the effect that a surgeon's failure to utilize a particular procedure caused the patient's injury. Expert opinion testimony is admissible because it is thought that lay jurors can decide certain kinds of issues only with the assistance of those with specialized knowledge or training.

2. The Requirement of Relevance

Evidence is admissible only if it is relevant; that is, the evidence must tend to prove or disprove a fact of consequence to the action. For example, if the plaintiff is claiming that the defendant committed a battery by punching him in the nose, the color of the defendant's shoes is probably not relevant because it does not tend to prove that the defendant's conduct did or did not meet the elements of a battery.

3. Reasons to Exclude Relevant Evidence

Even though evidence is authenticated and relevant, it may nevertheless be excluded because of concerns about its reliability or its potential to prejudice the jury, or for other reasons. It may be useful to consider an example of evidence that is excluded based on each of these concerns.

a. Unreliability: The Example of Hearsay

Hearsay is the classic example of evidence excluded because of its unreliability. Hearsay is an out-of-court statement offered into evidence for the truth of the matter asserted in the statement. Because the statement was made out of court, the jury cannot assess its reliability, and thus it is excluded.

For example, assume that an issue at trial is whether the gun belonged to the defendant. Assume, moreover, that the defendant's ex-girlfriend Marsha had told a police detective that the gun *did* belong to the defendant. The detective nevertheless could not testify about Marsha's statement because her statement is hearsay. That is, her statement was made out of court and is being offered into evidence to demonstrate the truth of the matter asserted in her statement, which is that the gun belongs to the defendant.

Like most hearsay, Marsha's statement is of questionable reliability. Perhaps Marsha was intoxicated at the time she asserted this, or perhaps she was angry with the defendant, or mistaken. If the prosecutor wishes the jury to know that Marsha believes that the gun belongs to the defendant, he would probably have to call Marsha as a witness and have her make the statement under oath, allowing defense counsel the chance through cross-examination to test the reliability of the testimony.

The statement would not be hearsay if it were offered to prove something other than the matter asserted in the statement. For example, assume that the prosecution wished to prove that Marsha feared the defendant because she thought he was a gun-toting gangster and thus was testifying reluctantly.[5] Her statement that the gun belonged to the defendant might be admissible to show not that the gun actually did belong to him but only that she *believed* that it belonged to him and thus feared him. In that situation, the fact that her statement is unreliable is unimportant because it is being admitted only to show her belief, not the actual fact of ownership. Since the unreliability of the statement does not undercut its usefulness, the court is likely to admit it into evidence for the purpose of showing Marsha's state of mind. The statement would continue to be inadmissible for the purpose of proving ownership of the gun.

If the judge did admit Marsha's statement, he would probably instruct the jury that her statement is to be considered only as evidence of her belief and not as evidence of the defendant's ownership. Yet, some jurors might not be able to compartmentalize the information in that way and, despite the judge's instruction, would consider it as evidence of the defendant's ownership.

In the end, the hearsay rule can often be circumvented by thinking of a reason to admit the testimony other than to prove the truth of the matter

---

[5] The prosecution may want to prove that Marsha is a reluctant witness for a variety of reasons. First, to the extent that she does incriminate the defendant, the jury may give her testimony special weight on the assumption that one who testifies at personal risk must be telling the truth. Second, to the extent that she tends to exonerate the defendant, the jury may disbelieve her because of the assumption that she is too frightened to testify accurately. Third, if she is a reluctant witness, the court may permit the prosecutor to ask leading questions, thus allowing the prosecution to control her testimony more tightly.

asserted. Lawyers speak of this as offering the evidence for a "nonhearsay purpose," and it is an effective way of putting before the jury testimony that may be helpful to one's case but which would otherwise be inadmissible as hearsay.

It also is possible to get out-of-court statements admitted into evidence by persuading the court that the statement fits within one of the exceptions to the rule excluding hearsay. These exceptions are generally based on the idea that certain hearsay, because of the circumstances in which the statement was made, is sufficiently reliable to be admitted into evidence. For example, statements made by someone against his or her own interest can often be introduced into evidence even though they are technically hearsay, on the assumption that anyone who admits something against his or her own interest is probably telling the truth.

b. Prejudice: The Example of Prior Bad Acts

Evidence of prior bad acts by a criminal defendant provides an example of evidence that may be excluded because of the possibility of prejudice. Such evidence is often excluded because even though the evidence may be relevant to establishing guilt, courts are concerned that a jury may give too much weight to such evidence. In other words, the jury may convict the defendant solely because he had committed prior crimes. However, when the evidence establishes a certain pattern to a crime, as when a con artist has used a similar scam in the past, such evidence is more probative of a later crime involving the same pattern than is evidence of bad acts generally. Such evidence is often allowed.

c. Other Policies: The Example of Privilege

A statement made by a client to his attorney for the purpose of obtaining legal advice provides an example of evidence excluded for other policy reasons. Such a statement is a privileged attorney-client communication and is generally not disclosed to the jury unless the client waives the privilege. The statement, of course, may be of enormous relevance and reliability, but the policy of encouraging people to seek legal advice by permitting them to speak freely to their lawyer is thought to outweigh the value of admitting the privileged communication into evidence.

B. *The Problem of Credibility*

Even assuming that all available evidence can be brought before the jury, lawyers must anticipate that the evidence on which they have based their reasoning may be disbelieved. For example, the lawyer may have advised the client that the client has a binding contract based on the client's description of certain conversations with another party. If the jury disbelieves that testimony, however, then insofar as the law is concerned, there is no contract and the lawyer's reasoning was based on a false factual premise.

If a client is trying to create the facts necessary to give rise to a right or duty, as in the case of a client who is trying to create some kind of contractual right, the lawyer must keep in mind that only those facts that can be proven to a jury will give rise to the enforceable right or duty that the client seeks. Thus, lawyers often emphasize the need to enhance the credibility of the client's version of the facts by keeping written records or having witnesses to transactions. At the same time, when the events already have occurred and the client wants simply to know the legal consequences of those events, the lawyer should be alert to the fact that legal reasoning should be based only on those facts that can be established in a court of law.

5

Applying the Law

The final step in the legal reasoning process is to apply the law to the facts to determine the rights and duties of the people involved in the situation. The law, as we have seen, consists of rules and the underlying policies.

The lawyer may attempt to use the rules to determine the rights or duties that exist in a particular situation. This requires the application of one of two methods: deduction or analogy. When using deduction, the lawyer determines whether the facts of the situation are or are not described by the factual predicate of a rule and thus whether the legal consequence imposed by the rule does or does not apply to the situation. When using analogy, the lawyer determines whether the facts of the situation are or are not like those described by the factual predicate of the rule and thus whether the legal consequence imposed by the rule does or does not apply to the situation. In applying either of these methods, the lawyer uses rules to determine the rights and duties that exist in the situation and thereby completes the legal reasoning process.

As will be seen, however, deduction and analogy often produce indeterminate results; that is, the lawyer cannot determine with sufficient certainty whether the facts of the situation are described by, or are like, the situation described in the factual predicate of the rule. In that case, the lawyer must refer to the underlying policies to ascertain the rights and duties that exist in the situation.

The application of policies to a situation involves the use of methods quite different from those used to apply rules. Rather than comparing the situation of the case to that described in the factual predicate, the lawyer determines whether imposing the legal consequence described in the rule would further the underlying policies to a greater extent than not imposing the legal consequence. The application of policies is thus neither deductive nor analogical. It involves a process of weighing policies and assessing the relationship between ends and means.

The relative extent to which the lawyer relies on the rules and the policies is to some degree a matter of choice. For example, the lawyer may take the position that disputes should be settled by the application of rules and that policies will be consulted, if at all, only when there is extreme uncertainty concerning the applicability of the rule. Alternatively, the lawyer may take the position that it is always preferable to seek the result that would further the underlying policies, unless (or perhaps, even if) that result would be contrary to very clear language of the rules.

The choice between rules and policies is profound. In applying rules, the lawyer seeks consistency with past decisions, regardless of whether the result seems desirable. In applying policies, the lawyer seeks the most desirable result. Rules refer the lawyer to prior decisions, whereas policies refer the lawyer to future consequences. Rules require the use of the logical methods of deduction and analogy, whereas policies require the use of an empirical method for assessing ends-means relationships and a normative method for weighing values.

The relative role of rules and policies is perhaps the most debated issue in modern American jurisprudence. The debate proceeds on both descriptive and normative grounds.

The descriptive question that lawyers debate is whether in fact courts resolve issues primarily by the application of rules or by the application of policies. The orthodox theory is that judges apply rules through the logical processes of deduction and analogy, turning to policies only in the occasional hard case. The competing theory is that judges in reality intuit the best result, that is, the result that is most satisfactory to them as a matter of policy, and only then do they turn to the rules to explain and justify the result they have reached on other grounds. In this view, the judge may even have the sensation of following the rules, but the interpretation of those rules as the judge applies them is guided by prior intuition about the most desirable resolution. In this way, the rules can seem to produce the correct result.

The normative question that lawyers debate is whether rules or policies should be given primacy in deciding disputes. For reasons of political theory described in Chapter 6, the orthodox position again is that courts should give primacy to rules, referring to the underlying policies only to resolve indeterminacies or to decide whether the rules should be changed. Policy application is thus treated as a supplement to rule application.

The account of contemporary mainstream legal reasoning continues in this chapter, where the application of law to fact is treated as involving either of two methods: deduction or analogy.[1] In the next two sections, these

---

[1] As I have explained in Chapter 3, some logicians would consider my use of the terms induction, deduction, and analogy technically inaccurate. I have used these terms, however, to demonstrate that legal reasoning has three different modes: moving from specific cases to a general rule (induction), moving from a general rule to a specific case (deduction), and moving from a specific case to another specific case (analogy).

two methods are described, and then how that method is supplemented by the application of policies is briefly discussed. The principal concern here is thus the application of rules. A fuller discussion of the application of policies is reserved for Chapter 7.

I. DEDUCTION

A. *The Basic Model*

Reasoning in the deductive form using a syllogism is the dominant style of legal reasoning. A syllogism of the type used in legal reasoning has an established structure, consisting of a major premise, a minor premise, and a conclusion. The major premise posits a statement that is true of a class of objects, the minor premise characterizes a particular object as belonging to the class, and the conclusion asserts that the statement is therefore true of the particular object.

For example, one might be told that all Kentucky colonels wear string ties (major premise). Upon hearing that Mr. Sanders is a Kentucky colonel (minor premise), one could deduce that Mr. Sanders wears a string tie (conclusion). The major premise, which posits a statement true of a class of objects, states that all Kentucky colonels wear string ties. The minor premise, which describes a particular object, states that Mr. Sanders is a Kentucky colonel. The conclusion asserts that the statement about Kentucky colonels generally is true of Mr. Sanders specifically.

In legal reasoning, the major premise states a rule of law applicable to a class of situations described in the factual predicate, the minor premise characterizes a particular situation as either satisfying or not satisfying the elements of the factual predicate, and the conclusion states whether the general rule has therefore been shown to apply to the particular situation. That is, the major premise announces a rule of law, the minor premise describes the facts of the client's situation, and the conclusion states whether or not the right or duty described in the rule of law has been demonstrated to exist under the facts of the client's situation.

For example, assume that the lawyer must decide whether the client, a man who punched a neighbor in the nose, is liable for a battery. A legal rule may state that a person is liable for a battery if through some voluntary act that person causes an offensive touching of another with the intent to cause the touching. This rule states the major premise.

Having formulated the major premise, the lawyer must next formulate a minor premise that characterizes the facts of the client's situation. The minor premise characterizes the facts as either satisfying or not satisfying each of the elements of the factual predicate of the rule.

One may think of the lawyer's treatment of the facts as a process of categorization. The rule creates a category of facts that gives rise to a legal consequence. The lawyer must decide whether the client's situation is included in the category or excluded from it.

In the case of the rule stated above, the factual predicate has four elements: (1) voluntary act (2) causing (3) an offensive touching (4) with intent. The lawyer with some degree of confidence can state a minor premise that the client (1) did perform a voluntary act (2) that caused (3) an offensive touching (4) with the intent to cause the touching. Combining the major premise with the minor premise, the lawyer concludes that the client is liable for a battery. In other words, the lawyer has categorized the facts of the client's situation as falling within the factual predicate of the rule. The conclusion is that the legal consequence stated in the rule of law exists in the client's situation.

This basic model of syllogistic reasoning assumes that the lawyer can apply the law to facts by reference solely to the language of the legal rule, an approach that is sometimes called textualism (because of the exclusive focus on the text of the rule), or formalism. In effect, the lawyer examines the words of the rule and attempts to decide whether the general facts set forth in the rule embrace the specific facts of the client's situation.

B. The Problem of Indeterminacy

Legal reasoning in the deductive form, however, is often indeterminate. When it is, the lawyer cannot reach a firm conclusion merely by applying the plain language of the rule to the facts.

Legal reasoning is indeterminate because the elements of the factual predicate are stated in such general terms that the lawyer cannot determine with certainty whether they include the facts of the client's situation.[2] Thus, it is often possible to characterize the facts of the client's situation in more than one way and thereby derive two or more alternative minor premises. The conclusion of the legal reasoning process depends entirely upon which minor premise the lawyer selects.

Consider the example of the client who punched his neighbor in the nose. Few would doubt that a punch in the nose satisfies the elements of a battery, including the element of a touching. Thus, the only plausible minor premise would include an assertion that the client did cause a touching.

Assume now, however, that the client, rather than punching the neighbor in the nose, had tugged on the neighbor's necktie, pulled on his shirtsleeve, pushed his hat off his head, or knocked a box of pizza out of his hand. Or consider less tangible contacts, such as blowing air on the neighbor's face,

---

[2] The reasons for writing rules in such general terms are discussed in Chapter 1. They also are discussed in Chapters 6 and 7 under the topic of formalism.

causing sound waves to reverberate in his ear, or sending electromagnetic radiation through his body.

The problem is that the term "touching" is so general that lawyers may differ over which, if any, of these examples constitutes a touching. Whether the client has satisfied the elements of a battery in each case depends upon how the lawyer characterizes the client's conduct.

The problem of indeterminacy is especially difficult if the factual predicate incorporates a legal standard, such as "reasonable" or "good faith." Rather than stating the facts that must be present, standards merely characterize the facts at a high level of generality. Whether the characterization applies may depend upon innumerable circumstances that cannot be, and are not, specified in the factual predicate. Thus, standards are so general that their language is particularly unlikely to decide a case.

For example, one tort law rule states that a person is negligent if he or she fails to exercise reasonable care. Driving a car at sixty miles per hour is unreasonable if the road passes through a school zone and children are present but may be entirely reasonable if the road is a deserted four-lane highway and the driver is rushing an expectant mother to the hospital. In short, standards do not create a sharply defined category of facts that gives rise to the legal consequence, and thus they can intensify the indeterminacy of a legal rule.[3]

C. *Addressing Indeterminacy Through Specificity*

The problem of indeterminacy, as noted above, stems from the fact that the language of rules is so general that the lawyer cannot be certain whether the language embraces the facts of a particular situation. In other words, it is unclear whether the facts should be characterized as constituting the elements of the rule.

Because the problem of how to characterize facts arises from the generality of the language of the rule, the difficulty can sometimes be addressed by finding a more specific rule that defines the elements with greater precision. Recall that, in step three, the lawyer has organized the rules into a framework in which specific rules are categorized as subrules of more general rules.

One type of subrule is that which defines an element of a more general rule. Thus, for example, the lawyer may identify a rule defining the element of a touching. Such a rule may state that a touching occurs when the defendant causes physical contact with the plaintiff's person or with something

---

[3] Legal standards are discussed in more detail in Chapter 7, under the heading Formalism and Instrumentalism.

closely identified with the plaintiff's person. This rule adds a degree of specificity to the word "touching."

Once a more specific rule is identified, the lawyer again performs syllogistic reasoning, now using the specific rule as the major premise. The new major premise in this syllogism is that one who causes physical contact with the plaintiff's person or something closely identified with the plaintiff's person commits a touching. The minor premise might be that a necktie is closely identified with the plaintiff's person. The conclusion then would be that pulling on the necktie constitutes a touching.

A similar syllogism might be used in an effort to decide whether pushing the hat off the plaintiff's head is a touching. In this case, however, even the more specific rule may be too general. It simply may not be self–evident to the lawyer whether the hat is "closely identified" with the person. The lawyer may look for an even more specific rule defining the specific rule and if there were such a rule, the lawyer would again use it syllogistically to decide about the hat. If no more specific rule exists, the lawyer will be in a quandary over how to determine whether the hat is closely identified with the plaintiff's person and, thus, whether pushing the hat is a touching.

In short, identifying more specific rules at times may seem to solve the problem of indeterminacy. Lawyers often find, however, that even the most specific rule is sufficiently general to leave room for doubt. Something other than formal reasoning is necessary to reach a conclusion.

D. Addressing Indeterminacy Through Rules of Statutory Interpretation

Before turning to nonformal techniques for addressing the problem of indeterminacy, a few words should be said about special rules for the textual analysis of enacted law. The law especially favors textualism in applying statutes and other forms of enacted law. Indeed, as noted in Chapter 2, courts are openly suspicious of attempts to ascertain the meaning of statutes through extrinsic sources, such as legislative history or contemporary ideas of public policy. In any event, these extrinsic sources may be inconclusive and therefore of limited assistance, even assuming the court is prepared to rely upon them. Thus, the lawyer applying a statute to a set of facts often has little more than the plain language to guide interpretation.

The relatively greater emphasis on textual or formal analysis with respect to enacted law is defensible. If a rule has been created by enacted law, the exact wording of the rule was adopted by the sovereign entity upon whose authority the rule rests. If a rule has been created by case law, however, as explained in Chapter 2, there may not be a single authoritative version of the text of the rule. The rule may have been constructed by the lawyer from several passages in a prior case or synthesized from the holdings of several cases in the manner described in Chapter 3. Without an authoritative version of the text, arguments that interpretation of a rule should rest on analysis of the precise terms of the text are difficult to maintain.

1. The Special Rules of Statutory Interpretation

In part because of the strong preference for textual analysis when statutes are being applied, courts have adopted a number of special rules for interpreting statutes. These rules are intended to assist the lawyer in resolving questions concerning the meaning of the language. In general, they permit the lawyer to make inferences about the meaning of a statutory rule by looking at the text alone.

For example, one rule of statutory interpretation is that every word or phrase in a statute is to be given effect. Thus, if an interpretation can be reconciled with the language of a statute only by assuming that a certain word is redundant or without effect, the court will generally reject that interpretation.

Another rule, sometimes expressed in the Latin maxim *expresio unius est exclusio alterius* (meaning "The expression of one thing is the exclusion of another"), is that lists are presumed to be exhaustive. Thus, if a statute lists certain instances to which it applies, the court will presume that the legislature meant to exclude any instance not listed.

A third rule, known as the doctrine of *ejusdem generis* (a Latin phrase meaning "of the same kind"), states that when a statute contains a list of instances to which it applies followed by general language indicating other instances, the statute will be presumed to apply to other instances only if they are of the same type as those listed. For example, a statute that authorized an investigator to inspect "books, papers, and other data" would authorize inspection only of other data that were like books and papers.

A fourth rule, which is also frequently summarized by a Latin maxim—*generalia specialibus non derogant* (meaning "The general does not derogate from the particular")—provides that a specific statute prevails over a more general one. For example, if one statute provides that claims of negligence must be brought within three years and a second statute provides that malpractice claims against physicians must be brought within one year, the latter statute would probably govern a negligence suit brought by a patient against a surgeon. Because malpractice actions against doctors are a narrower category of lawsuits than negligence actions generally, the malpractice statute is likely to be considered more specific and thus the governing statute.

Still another rule provides that statutes in derogation of the common law shall be construed narrowly. This means that the legislature is presumed to intend as little change to the common law as necessary. Thus, a statute that alters common law rules will be interpreted, in doubtful cases, so as not to apply.

Not all of the rules of statutory interpretation, however, limit the lawyer to the text of the statute. One well-established rule, for example, is that a statute will not be interpreted in a way that leads to an absurd result. A court may thus apply this rule to avoid a result that otherwise seems plainly required by the text of the statute.

2. *The Indeterminacy of These Special Rules*

Even with numerous other rules of statutory interpretation like those just described, textual analysis of a statute is often indeterminate for two reasons.

First, the rules of interpretation themselves are often too general to lead to but one conclusion. For example, in the case of the doctrine of *ejusdem generis,* lawyers may disagree concerning the features that the listed items have in common.[4] Thus, in the illustration just given, one lawyer may conclude that the kinds of materials that the investigator may inspect include only those that are in printed form on paper, which would exclude microfilm and computer discs, whereas another lawyer may conclude that they include any material that is in printed form whether on paper or not, which would include microfilm but not computer discs. A third lawyer may conclude that the investigator is authorized to inspect any existing record regardless of the medium but is not authorized to order the creation of new records. All three of these characterizations accurately describe books and papers, but each has a somewhat different scope and, if used, would give a different meaning to the term "other data." Thus, the rules of interpretation are very often victims of the same problem of generality that they are intended to address. For that reason, the rules of statutory interpretation can be indeterminate.

Second, rules of statutory interpretation may be indeterminate because they are sometimes contradictory on their face. Indeed, Professor Karl Llewellyn, who taught at Columbia Law School in the mid-twentieth century, wrote a well-known article in 1950 in which he attempted to show that, for each of numerous rules of statutory interpretation, one could state another rule that seemed to contradict it, at least in part.[5] For example, Llewellyn noted that one commonly stated rule to the effect that "[i]f lan-

---

[4] Deciding which features that several items on a list have in common for purposes of applying the doctrine of *ejusdem generis* is a process similar to deciding which features several cases have in common for purposes of creating a new rule through legal reasoning in the inductive form. This latter process and the problems of judgment involved are discussed in Chapter 3.

[5] Llewellyn, *Remarks on the Theory of Appellate Decision and the Rules or Canons About How Statutes Are to Be Construed,* 3 VAND. L. REV. 395, 401–405 (1950).

guage is plain and unambiguous it must be given effect" was contradicted by another rule stating that a literal interpretation will not be adopted if it would "lead to absurd or mischievous consequences or thwart manifest purpose."

One explanation for this phenomenon is the underlying tension in statutory interpretation concerning the extent to which a lawyer should consult extrinsic sources in interpreting a statute. Put another way, conflicts between rules of statutory interpretation are rooted in a dispute about the relative primacy to be afforded the language of the rule and the underlying policies. As discussed in Chapter 2, a lawyer may attempt to interpret a statute by examining its language alone or by consulting extrinsic sources. If the lawyer decides to consult extrinsic sources, there are at least two types of extrinsic sources that might be consulted. One is the legislative history, which would be researched in an effort to interpret the statute in accordance with the intent of specific legislators. Another is the subsequent understanding of what is just or wise, which could lead to an interpretation of the statute in accordance with current notions of justice or good policy.

Each of these theories of statutory interpretation is reflected in a variety of rules of statutory interpretation. Thus, whereas some of the rules confine the lawyer to the language of the text, others authorize the lawyer to look outside the text—at either legislative history or current notions of justice or sound public policy. That is, some of the rules confine the lawyer to the language of the rule, whereas others broaden the inquiry to include the underlying policies.

Note how each of these theories is reflected, for example, in the two maxims taken from Llewellyn's article. The first theory—that interpretation is based on the language alone—is reflected in the maxim that plain and unambiguous language is to be given effect. The competing theory—that interpretation may be based on extrinsic sources—is reflected in the second maxim. Under the second maxim, the literal language is not to be followed if it would "thwart manifest purpose" (i.e., run contrary to legislative intent) or lead to "absurd and mischievous consequences" (i.e., contradict current notions of sound policy or justice). Thus, the first maxim tends to restrict the lawyer to the text alone, whereas the second encourages the lawyer to look outside the language of the statute at legislative history and common notions of justice and sound policy.

The rules of statutory interpretation, in other words, are based on competing theories of statutory interpretation, that is, on different conceptions of the relative importance of rules and policies. Because the theories point in opposite directions, the rules also point in opposite directions. Thus, the result reached depends upon which rules of statutory construction are applied.

E. *Addressing Indeterminacy Through Policy Judgments*

The principal nontextualist or nonformal technique for addressing the indeterminacy of rules is the use of policy judgments. The lawyer must decide whether the policies underlying the rule would be furthered by characterizing the facts as satisfying or as not satisfying the elements of the rule.

1. *The Two Types of Judgments Required*

The use of policies to address indeterminacy requires the lawyer to make two different kinds of judgments, discussed in this subsection.

The first type of judgment required is a judgment about the relationship between ends and means. In the battery example given earlier, one end is to preserve the peace. The lawyer must decide whether that end would be served by requiring the client to pay compensation for, say, pushing a hat off someone's head.

In theory, the extent to which a particular means will further a given end is an empirical question. Obviously, however, controlled experiments to determine the effects of a particular rule are rarely possible as a practical matter.[6] Thus, lawyers and courts generally use a combination of experience and intuition to make judgments about the relationship between ends and means. In making the judgments, lawyers may reach conclusions about which reasonable people can differ.

The second type of judgment required is a judgment about the relative importance of policies. This judgment is required because all rules represent a compromise among a number of opposing policies. For example, the rule defining a battery may be based on the policy of preserving the peace, but it is also based on the opposing policy of discouraging litigation over trivial offenses. The lawyer must decide which policy is to prevail in a given situation. Again, such judgments may yield conclusions about which reasonable people may differ.

The lawyer, in effect, makes two judgments: which policy to prefer, and which means are effective in furthering that policy. In the next subsection, the nature of policy judgments is described, and in the subsection thereafter, discussion centers in general terms on how these judgments are combined to decide a case. These topics are discussed in further detail in Chapter 7.

---

[6] Occasionally, a sociologist becomes interested in the effectiveness of a particular rule and attempts to study whether the rule actually furthers the ends for which it was enacted. For example, some have attempted to determine whether the death penalty furthers the end of deterring crime by comparing crime rates in societies with and without the death penalty. Drawing conclusions is difficult because of the inability to control for only a single variable. Thus, in the case of the death penalty example, the societies studied may be different in so many ways that differences in crime rates, if any exist, cannot necessarily be attributed to the use or nonuse of the death penalty.

2. *The Nature of Policy Judgments*

The lawyer begins the process of making policy judgments by identifying the policies articulated by the legislature or the courts in formulating the rule to be applied. In the battery example, for instance, the lawyer may have found language in the case law stating that the tort of battery is based on several policies. One may be a policy of preserving the peace, which is furthered by encouraging the victim to go to court rather than retaliating or instigating a feud. Another may be a policy of discouraging frivolous litigation, which is furthered by limiting tort liability to conduct causing significant injury. The lawyer must now decide whether these policies require compensation in the particular situation under review.

One may be tempted to state the application of the policies to the hat example in a syllogistic form. To simplify matters, assume momentarily that there is but one policy—preserving the peace. In this proposed syllogism, the major premise is that one commits a touching by causing a physical contact with something closely identified with the person of another such that the contact is likely to cause a breach of the peace. The minor premise is that pushing a hat off someone's head is likely to cause a breach of the peace. The conclusion would be that pushing the hat is a touching.

Using policies to decide cases, however, is not truly deductive. This is so because policies do not state a major premise from which one can reason deductively; policies are not general rules describing an entire category of cases that have a particular legal consequence. Rather, policies are the ends for which rules are the means. Thus, policies by their terms are stated as absolutes, as goals to be sought in all circumstances by any means, whereas legal rules by their terms create a specified legal consequence only in the limited circumstances set forth in the factual predicate.

In using policies to complete the legal reasoning process, the lawyer is not reasoning from a general rule to a specific case. Rather, the lawyer is reasoning from a specific case toward at least one, and probably several, policy goals. This form of reasoning requires the lawyer to make empirical judgments about the relationship between ends and means and value judgments about the relative weight of policies.

Policies, of course, can be stated at different levels of generality. The policy of protecting individual liberty, for example, can be stated more specifically as the policy of protecting free speech and more specifically still as the policy of protecting newspapers against libel actions. As policies are stated at lower levels of generality, they become limited in their scope of application and begin to take on the character of rules. Thus, as policies become more specific and rules become more general, the distinction between the two dissolves. This idea will be discussed in greater detail in Chapter 7. At the moment, suffice it to say that policies can be stated at different levels of generality and that, as will be shown further on, lawyers can manipulate the level of generality in order to create arguments for or against the application of a rule.

3. Combining the Judgments to Decide Cases

a. In General

Deciding a case requires that the lawyer combine the two judgments to determine the overall policy benefit yielded by each possible result. The preferred result is that which yields the greatest policy benefit.

The lawyer cannot simply decide that one policy is more important than the others and then propose any result that furthers that policy. The problem with such an approach is that a particular result may not further the preferred policy enough to justify the cost to the competing policy. In predicting the result that a court is most likely to reach, the lawyer chooses the result estimated to provide the most benefit, taking into account the relative weight of the competing policies and the extent to which each result will further or impede those policies.

For example, the rule creating liability for a battery, as already noted, is based on policies that include deterring violence and avoiding wasteful litigation. Assume that the court decides that the former policy is more important than the latter. Using that assumption, the court might well adopt a rule that all physical contacts result in liability for a battery, in order to discourage any physical contact that could even remotely lead to violence. The objection to such a rule is that it would encourage too much litigation—the morning commute on a crowded subway could spawn thousands of lawsuits. Thus, although the rule would further the policy of deterring violence, it would be too costly in terms of the policy of avoiding wasteful litigation. In combining the judgments, then, the lawyer considers both the importance of the policies and the degree to which they will be furthered or impeded by each result.

Although reasonable persons may differ about the relative weight of policies and the degree to which particular results will further or impede a given policy, policy judgments are not wholly indeterminate. As will be discussed in Chapter 7, policy judgments are made in a particular context that includes the historical setting, the individuals who are making the judgments, the facts to which the judgments will be applied, and prior judicial decisions. This context often constrains, even if it does not wholly determine, judgments about the weights of policies and the relationships between ends and means.

b. Line Drawing

Some lawyers describe the application of law to facts by using the metaphor of line drawing; that is, by adopting a rule, the lawyer draws a line between two categories of factual situations. In the category of situations on one side of the line, the right or duty created by the rule exists. In the category on the other side of the line, the right or duty does not exist. The location of the line is very much a matter of judgment because the lawyer must decide the relative importance of each policy and the extent to which applying the rule to any given situation will further or impede each policy.

Ideally, the situations on one side of the line should be qualitatively different from those on the other side. This qualitative difference justifies treating the situations differently. In practice, however, it is characteristic of line drawing that, no matter where the line is drawn, there will be situations on either side that appear *not* to differ qualitatively, that is, the difference will seem to be one of only very slight degree. Given that the situations on either side differ only slightly, the precise location of the line will seem arbitrary.

In extreme cases, the decision about which side of the line to place the case on will seem easy. To return to the example of the landowner's duty to warn about hazards, at one extreme it may seem obvious that a twenty-foot pit is so dangerous that the court should impose on the landowner the minimal burden of warning about the pit. At the other extreme, it may seem equally obvious that a one-inch deep depression in the ground poses so little danger that no discernible benefit would result from imposing a duty to warn. The twenty-foot-pit case and the one-inch-depression case seem clearly to belong on different sides of the line. The situations are qualitatively different, and this difference justifies their having different legal consequences.

As additional pit cases arise, however, the situations on opposite sides of the line will begin to resemble each other rather closely. At some point, the distinction between two cases on opposite sides of the line may seem arbitrary because there is no qualitative difference between them.

Nevertheless, the line must be drawn somewhere. The alternative would be to allow one policy to prevail all of the time. The landowner either would have no duty to warn of any hazard, no matter how dangerous, or would have a duty to warn of any potentially dangerous condition on the land, no matter how trivial. Because both of these rules are highly undesirable, people generally tolerate the drawing of a line that may seem arbitrary in close cases, as long as the location of the line seems to reflect a qualitative difference and to yield a desirable result in most situations.

c. Balancing

Some lawyers describe legal reasoning by using the metaphor of a set of scales, referring to "balancing" the policies in a particular situation. If the benefit to public policy associated with creating a right or duty in a particular situation outweighs the cost to public policy associated with creating the right or duty, the right or duty will be determined to exist. If the cost outweighs the benefit, then the right or duty will not be determined to exist.

The metaphor of balancing seems to suggest that deciding a case requires the lawyer to make only the first type of judgment—a judgment about the relative importance of policies. And, indeed, most lawyers, to the extent that they think about it all, probably do think of balancing tests as just that: a stark weighing of one policy against another.

In fact, however, balancing generally requires both types of judgments. The lawyer is not simply weighing, for example, free speech against the state's desire to suppress speech. If that were so, then one would outweigh the other, with the result that free expression would be either always protected or never protected.

Rather, the lawyer is really weighing the value of this particular act of suppression against the value of this particular instance of speech. The lawyer must make judgments about the extent to which this instance of speech truly furthers the policies underlying free expression as well as about the extent to which this instance of suppression truly furthers the policies underlying the state's desire to suppress, both of which are judgments about the relationship between ends and means.

For example, the lawyer may decide that the policy of free speech is more important than the policy of preserving a tranquil neighborhood. If that were the full extent of a balancing test, then the lawyer, if asked to decide whether the law permits a man to use a loudspeaker in a residential neighborhood at 3:00 A.M., would have to answer in the affirmative—because free speech outweighed tranquility.

In fact, however, the lawyer engages in a more sophisticated balancing test. More specifically, the lawyer also considers the relationship between the policy goals and the means adopted by the state to advance those goals. Thus, the lawyer considers the extent to which a ban on the loudspeaker at 3:00 A.M. would promote tranquility and impede free speech. If the speaker were permitted to use the loudspeaker during other times of the day to broadcast the same message, the lawyer may conclude that the ban's strong nexus with preserving tranquility justifies the minimal interference with free speech.

F. The Special Problem of Dictum

Thus far in this section it has been assumed that the rules identified and synthesized into a framework are binding if they apply and that the critical task for the lawyer is to determine whether the rules do indeed apply to the situation under review. Although this assumption is correct concerning enacted law, it is problematic in regard to case law.

The difficulty is that not all case law rules have the same force. As has been noted, it is traditional to distinguish between the holding of case, which is binding in future cases, and dictum, which is not.

The distinction, however, is not as clear in practice as it is in theory. Apart from the problem that two lawyers may not agree on which aspects of a case are the holding and which are dictum, courts in later cases may choose to treat a statement that rather plainly was dictum as if it were a binding rule of law.

That is, although a court need not follow dictum, it very often does so. Dictum represents, in effect, the court's prediction of how it would decide all future cases within the scope of the rule. The more cases that have cited a particular rule in dictum, the greater are the chances that a later court will follow it.

A court, however, will not apply dictum if the lawyer can persuade the court that the rule would lead to an undesirable result in the present case. As an illustration, assume that the lawyer in the battery example finds a prior case stating that clothing worn by someone is "closely identified" with that person's body and, thus, pulling on someone else's clothing is a touching. In the prior case, however, the clothing was a necktie worn by the plaintiff. Because it was necessary to decide only whether a necktie is closely identified with the plaintiff's body, to the extent that the rule refers to any clothing besides a necktie, the rule is dictum.

Now assume that the lawyer learns that his client pulled the shirtsleeve of the neighbor. A shirt quite obviously is an article of clothing. The rule is dictum, however, except concerning neckties, and thus the court need not characterize the shirtsleeve as an article closely identified with the body. But should it?

The court decides whether to follow dictum through the exercise of policy judgments. For example, the court will have to assess the extent to which imposing a duty of compensation on the client will further the end of deterring violence. That is, the court will have to decide whether pulling on a shirtsleeve is as likely to provoke violence as pulling a necktie. The lawyer may argue, for example, that a breach of peace is less likely to result from pulling a shirtsleeve than a necktie because tugging on a shirtsleeve does not pose a potential danger of strangulation and therefore the wearer may feel less threatened or invaded. Thus, imposing liability for tugging on the shirtsleeve is less closely related to the end of deterring violence than imposing liability for pulling on the necktie. At the same time, the argument will continue, pulling on shirtsleeves is such a common device for calling someone's attention that to impose liability for that act could lead to frivolous litigation. Accordingly, imposing liability for tugging on the shirtsleeve would hinder the policy of discouraging litigation more than imposing liability for the much less common act of pulling on the necktie. In short, the lawyer will conclude, the greatest policy benefit will be derived from disregarding the dictum and not imposing liability for the tugging on the shirtsleeve.

As is explained in the final section of this chapter, a court makes the same type of policy judgments in deciding whether to overrule a prior case entirely. Because dictum is not binding, however, the court in theory finds it easier to disregard dictum than to overrule the prior decision. Any attempt to overturn a prior decision must overcome the heavily weighted policy of stare decisis and thus requires very strong policy grounds for changing the law.

The distinction between holdings and dictum adds a further dimension of indeterminacy to the legal reasoning process. As has been illustrated, very often the lawyer cannot be certain what result a given rule requires in a particular case. That is, the terms of the rule are indeterminate. If the rule is dictum, however, then the lawyer cannot even be certain that the rule will be applied. In attempting to predict the decision of the court, the lawyer must include in the calculation the possibility that the dictum will not be followed.

G. Using Deduction as an Advocate

It has generally been assumed thus far in the discussion of legal reasoning in the deductive form that the lawyer is a disinterested observer attempting to determine how the law applies to the facts. In many instances, however, the lawyer applying law to fact is acting as an advocate and wants to reach a conclusion favorable to the client.

Although the legal counselor may be frustrated by the indeterminacy of the law, to the legal advocate this same indeterminacy provides opportunities to fashion arguments in support of the client's position. The indeterminacy of the law results from the generality of rules and from the fact that the underlying policies can be applied only through the exercise of judgment. Indeterminacy, in other words, is built into the very structure of the legal reasoning process.

The advocate seizes on these structural sources of indeterminacy and attempts to manipulate the levels of generality and the policies to produce a favorable result. Because the indeterminacy has its roots in certain constant features of the legal reasoning process, lawyers have developed standard techniques for manipulating the indeterminacy to their clients' advantage.

In this section some of these standard techniques are described. The case of the lawyer arguing that a rule does apply is examined first, followed by the case of the lawyer arguing that the rule does not apply.

1. Supporting Application of the Rule

The lawyer arguing for application of a case law rule typically seeks to broaden the factual predicate of the rule, stating the elements in relatively general terms. At a minimum, the factual predicate must obviously be stated in terms general enough to include the facts of the current case.

Often, this will require that the lawyer rely not on the narrow holding of a prior case but on the broader rules set forth in dictum. The prior case may have stated the rule that a hazardous condition on the land gives rise to a duty on the part of the landowner to warn of the hazard and may then have held that the landowner had a duty to warn of a concealed pit. The lawyer for the plaintiff in the current case, unless the client was injured by a concealed pit, would want to cite the broad rule stated in dictum rather than the narrower holding. Alternatively, the lawyer may synthesize a new rule from the holdings of several prior cases in the manner described in Chapter 3.

The lawyer may also choose to formulate the *legal consequence* of the prior cases at a high level of generality. Assume, for example, that in one prior case the landlord was held to have a duty to post a warning about an unstable slope. In the current situation, the client's host did post a sign warning his party guests about the hazard, but the client, distracted by the party, was inattentive and sustained injury. The lawyer may formulate the duty in the prior case as a duty to give adequate notice to guests about a hazard, a somewhat broader formulation, arguing that the posted warning was adequate notice under the circumstances of the prior case. The lawyer can now argue that the warning posted by the client's host was not adequate notice under the circumstances of a boisterous party, and thus the host is liable to the client.

Another way to broaden the legal consequence of a rule is to synthesize a new rule from several prior cases. For example, if in addition to the case imposing a duty to warn about an unstable slope, there is another prior case imposing a duty to put a fence around a concealed pit, the lawyer citing both cases may synthesize a broader rule imposing a duty to exercise reasonable care, arguing that the warning and the fence constitute the exercise of reasonable care under the circumstances of the prior cases but that the posted warning was not an exercise of reasonable care under the circumstances of the client's situation.

It may be necessary for the lawyer to find or synthesize rules that are applicable only at a very high level of generality. If no cases involving hazards on the land can be found, the lawyer may look for cases involving defective consumer products in which there is dictum stating, or from which the lawyer can synthesize a rule stating, that one has a duty to warn those who may be foreseeably injured by a danger of which one is aware. Although the prior cases dealt with defective consumer products, when the applicable rule is stated with sufficient generality, it seems to apply directly to the hazardous land.

At the same time, the lawyer must avoid overreaching, being careful not to state the rule at such a high level of generality that it seems to apply to cases in which it would produce a clearly undesirable result. For example, the rule from the consumer products cases stated above is probably too broad. Read literally, it suggests that a landowner would have a duty to warn others about hazards on someone else's land, merely by being aware of them, or that a manufacturer would have a duty to warn others about defects in another company's products.

In describing a rule or an argument that goes too far, lawyers sometimes say that it "proves too much." That is, although the rule or argument produces desirable results in some instances, it produces undesirable results in others. Thus, a rule that proves too much is often rejected by a court in favor of a narrower rule.

A second technique for arguing that a case law rule applies to a situation is to hold to a minimum the number of elements in the rule. The more numerous the elements in the rule, the greater the likelihood that one of them will be found not to apply to the client's situation. In quoting the rule or holding from a prior case, the lawyer attempts to eliminate from the factual predicate any fact that was not absolutely necessary to the decision. As just explained, any fact that the lawyer *does* include will probably be stated in general terms. Facts that have no counterparts in the current case will be characterized, if possible, as representing either special instances of the general, necessary facts or sufficient but not necessary grounds for applying the rule.

A third technique for arguing that a rule applies to a case is to demonstrate that the policies underlying the rule would also be furthered by applying the rule to the current case. The lawyer may argue, for example, that the policy that required imposition on the landlord of a duty to warn about a concealed pit equally requires imposition of a duty to warn about an unstable slope. Thus, although a slope, concededly, is not a pit, the difference between the two is irrelevant to the accomplishment of the underlying policies.

This technique may require the lawyer to manipulate the level of generality at which the policies underlying the rule are stated. Assume that the rule imposing a duty to warn about pits arose in cases involving commercially excavated pits and that the courts had stated that the policy underlying the rule was to ensure that those who profit from economic activity compensate those injured by that activity. Stated at this level of generality, the policy would seem inapplicable to a later case involving a naturally occurring slope. If the policy is restated more generally, however, as being one that requires those who own a property to compensate those injured by the property, then the policy seems to apply to the slope case. In other words, if the policy is stated at a sufficient level of generality, the distinction between economic and noneconomic activity disappears.

2. Opposing Application of the Rule

The lawyer opposing application of the rule employs techniques that are the mirror image of those employed by the adversary in the case. First, the lawyer opposing application of a case law rule tries to phrase the rule as narrowly as possible and may attempt to state both the factual predicate and the legal consequence in narrow terms.

Thus, the lawyer quotes the narrowest possible version of the holding, noting, for example, that the prior cases referred to pits—not hazards. The effort, obviously, is to state the factual predicate of the rule in such specific terms that it clearly cannot include the facts of the current case. The lawyer may note as well that the duty imposed in the prior cases was to warn those invited onto the land for business purposes. It was not a duty to warn persons generally, nor was it a duty to eliminate the hazard. Here, the attempt is to narrow the legal consequence.

As an adjunct to this argument, the lawyer opposing application of the rule may note that the adversary is citing mere dictum and that no case has ever adopted a rule as broad as that proposed by the adversary. He may suggest that the adversary, rather than applying existing law, is trying to persuade the court to make new law. Further, because the dictum would lead to an undesirable result in this case, it should not be followed. In other words, the dictum proves too much.

Second, the lawyer tries to include as many elements in the factual predicate as possible. In stating rules, courts often focus on those elements that are doubtful in the dispute before them, perhaps omitting elements that have clearly been met. The lawyer opposing application of the rule may look for several different formulations of the rule and combine elements from each formulation to produce a rule that contains every element ever included in any prior formulation. The goal, of course, is to include an element that is not satisfied in the current case.

Third, the lawyer may contend that the policy judgments underlying the rule do not apply to the current case. This argument may actually follow either of two different approaches.

One approach is to argue that the policies that underlie the rule would not be furthered by the result sought by the adversary. For example, assume that the adversary is arguing that a rule imposing liability on a landowner for failing to give adequate warning about a hazard should impose liability on a landowner who made only a single announcement at a party, because the single announcement was not an adequate warning for a boisterous and intoxicated crowd. The lawyer for the landowner may reply that the policy of protecting human life, on which the duty to warn was based in prior cases, would not be furthered by requiring repeated warnings because such a requirement could result in compensating those who failed to exercise care for their own safety.

Note that to make the argument it may be helpful to manipulate the level of generality at which the underlying policies are stated. The prior cases may have stated that the duty to warn was based on a policy of requiring landowners to maintain safe premises. At that level of generality, the policy would seem to require application of the rule. By stating the policy more generally as promoting safety, the lawyer makes the policy less determinate. Safety can be promoted by requiring the guests *or* the host, or both, to exercise reasonable care.

The other approach is to argue that this situation affects policies not contemplated by the legislature or court that formulated the rule. Because every rule is a compromise among conflicting policies, the lawyer is virtually always able to find a policy that would be impeded by application of the rule.

For example, assume that the adversary is arguing that the rule imposing liability for injuries caused by an unstable slope should apply to a construction site. More generally, the adversary is arguing that the rule imposes liability for hazardous conditions, which include construction sites, in furtherance of the policy of fairness to the injured individual. The policy of protecting individual rights is in tension with utilitarian theories of justice that promote the greatest happiness for the greatest number.[7] Utilitarianism thus provides a potential argument against application of the rule, particularly if the new situation seems to conflict with utilitarian values in ways that the prior cases did not. The lawyer may argue, for example, that imposing liability on a landowner for injury caused at a construction site penalizes beneficial economic activity that was not penalized by the rule imposing liability for injury caused by natural hazards. Thus, the rule should not apply to the construction site.

Fourth, the lawyer can argue that to apply the rule to this case would require that it be applied to other cases in which it would yield undesirable results. This argument is sometimes referred to as the "parade of horribles" or the "slippery slope" argument. The lawyer demonstrates that any definition of the elements of the rule broad enough to encompass this case would also encompass other hypothetical cases in which application of the rule would be undesirable. Application of the rule to this case would start the court down a slippery slope to an undesirable result; it would produce a parade of horrible results.

Note that what distinguishes this last argument from the others is that it does not require demonstrating that application of the rule would lead to a bad result in this case. It requires persuading a court only that application of the rule to this case would entail application of the rule to other cases in which it would produce an undesirable result. Note as well that in making this argument the lawyer attempts to state the elements of the factual predicate at as high a level of generality as possible in order to bring within them as many undesirable cases as possible.

---

[7] The distinction between these forms of justice is discussed in Chapter 7.

For example, the lawyer arguing that knocking a hat off someone's head should not be considered a touching could assert that to define contact with an article of clothing as an offensive touching would mean that one who brushed another's coat on a crowded bus, for example, or stepped on another's shoe could be liable for a battery. Thus, the concept of a touching should be defined narrowly enough to exclude this case as well as those cases in which a finding of the existence of a touching would lead to clearly undesirable results. The concept, therefore, should not be extended to contact with articles of clothing.

Again, however, in making this argument the lawyer must be careful not to overreach, to try to prove too much. If the lawyer's characterization of this case and the undesirable cases is too broad, the adversary may be able to suggest a narrower characterization that would exclude the undesirable cases and yet be coterminous with the cases to which the underlying policies suggest the rule should apply.

Assume, for example, that the lawyer argues that to define contact with a hat as a touching would mean that contact with any other personal belonging was a touching and thus could lead to liability for brushing against someone's car in a parking lot. The term "personal belonging" is arguably much too broad. The lawyer's adversary is likely to reply that a touching should be limited to contact with the victim's person or articles of clothing worn against the skin of the victim. Such a definition would apply the rule defining a touching to the hat case but not to the car case.

The adversary could assert that contact with articles of clothing worn against the skin is a relatively intimate invasion and is much more likely to prompt a breach of peace than contact with other belongings held at a greater distance. The adversary is likely to persuade a court to accept this definition and to apply the rule to the hat case by demonstrating that the policy judgments underlying the rule also apply to this case and to other cases that would be covered by this definition but that these policy judgments do not apply to the overbroad definition proposed by the lawyer.

H. *Addressing Indeterminacy Through Analogies*

Another approach to addressing the problem of indeterminacy is to examine the case law for analogies to the current situation. Recall that the lawyer's synthesis may include specific holdings that apply a general rule. The cases from which these applications are drawn provide a basis for reasoning by analogy.

Assume that the lawyer is attempting to determine whether a box of pizza held by someone is closely identified with the body and that the lawyer's synthesis contains a holding that a tray carried in one's hand is closely identified with the body. Note that the tray case does not define a touching but merely illustrates it. If a box of pizza were a tray, one could perform another syllogism: Striking a tray held in another's hand is a touching, a box of pizza is a tray, and therefore the client committed a touching.

Even if a box of pizza is not a tray, the lawyer may nevertheless use the tray case by way of analogy to form a conclusion about how to characterize or categorize the box of pizza. Specifically, the lawyer may decide that because a box of pizza is like, or analogous to, a tray in relevant respects, a box of pizza should also be considered closely identified with the body.

The use of analogy is discussed in greater detail in the next section. For now, it is sufficient to see that reasoning by analogy can be used to supplement reasoning in the deductive form. More specifically, the lawyer may use analogies to assist in attempts to decide how the facts should be characterized for purposes of reasoning in the deductive form.

II. ANALOGY

A. The Basic Model

The second form of reasoning through which lawyers apply law to facts is reasoning by analogy. An analogy is a form of logic by which one reasons that because two items are alike in at least one respect, they are alike in at least one other respect.

For example, if one had been told that the 9:03 A.M. train for London had left Cambridge station on time, by reasoning by analogy one might then conclude that the 11:15 A.M. train for London had also left Cambridge on time. That is, because the two phenonema were alike in that they were British morning trains headed for London from Cambridge, the observer reasoned by analogy that they would also be alike in being punctual.

Legal reasoning by analogy operates in the same manner, except that the objects being compared are judicial decisions. In the preceding example, the purpose of the analogy is to determine whether the second train would be punctual. In legal analysis, the purpose of the analogy is to determine whether, in the second case, a person has some legal right or duty that existed in the first case.

Under reasoning by analogy, the lawyer identifies at least one prior case—that is, one precedent—that seems to have facts in common with the client's situation. The lawyer analyzes the case to identify the legal consequence of those facts.

If the lawyer believes that the facts of the client's situation are analogous to those of the precedent—that is, if the lawyer believes that the facts of the client's case are like those of the precedent—then the lawyer concludes that the precedent should be followed. In other words, the client's situation should yield the same legal consequence as the facts in the precedent.

If the lawyer believes that the facts of the client's situation are different from those of the precedent, the conclusion is then that the precedent should be distinguished; that is, the precedent should be treated as if it were not a like case, and therefore it need not be followed.

Analogy, like deduction, involves three steps. First, the lawyer identifies a rule or holding announced in a prior case. The rule or holding serves the same function as the major premise in a syllogism: It is the statement of law potentially to be followed. Second, the lawyer determines whether the facts of the client's situation are like those of the prior case. Characterizing the facts as like or unlike those in the precedent is similar to the characterization of the facts in the minor premise of a syllogism. Finally, the characterization of the facts as like or unlike those of the precedent yields the conclusion that the client's situation should or should not have the same legal consequence as the facts in the precedent.

Analogy differs from deduction, however, in that a lawyer reasoning by analogy is using one specific case to decide another specific case. By contrast, a lawyer using legal reasoning in the deductive form is using a general rule to decide a specific case.

B. The Problem of Indeterminacy

The problem for the lawyer using legal reasoning by analogy is to determine whether the precedent and the client's situation are alike. If they are identical, the lawyer can refer to the precedent as like the client's situation and conclude that the two cases have the same legal consequence.

No two cases, however, are identical in every respect. If nothing else, the date of the events or the names of the parties are different. Thus, in theory every case is distinguishable from every other case and no precedent need ever be followed.

To permit every difference to be a basis for distinguishing prior cases would render analogy useless. Accordingly, for the doctrine of stare decisis to apply to a later case, it is not necessary that the facts of the later case be identical to those of the precedent in every respect but only that they be identical in most or all relevant respects. Thus, the lawyer must determine which were the dispositive facts in the prior case.

The dispositive facts are those upon which the court relied in deciding the prior case. The court in the prior case may have specified which were the facts giving rise to the right or duty that it found to exist. Alternatively, it may have left to future lawyers the task of inferring which facts were dispositive.[8] In the same way that an attorney can later attribute policy

---

[8] The method used to identify the dispositive facts in a case was discussed in Chapter 2.

considerations to a court that in fact were not explicitly part of the court's reasoning, an attorney can also attribute legal relevance to facts that the court may not actually have considered dispositive. In other words, in a practical sense, a judicial decision means whatever a lawyer can persuade another court that it means.

Having identified the dispositive facts, the lawyer must then decide whether the facts of the later case are like those of the precedent. The determination, however, is not mechanical. The lawyer can often manipulate the extent to which two cases seem alike by changing the level of generality at which the relevant facts are described.

For example, assume that the lawyer's client wishes to know whether he has a duty to warn guests about a concealed two-foot-deep pit on the land. Legal research identifies a case holding that a landowner has a duty to warn guests about a concealed ten-foot pit. If the two cases are described simply as cases involving pits, they are alike. If the two cases are described more specifically as involving a two-foot-deep pit and a ten-foot-deep pit, they are distinguishable. By stating the relevant facts at a very low level of generality (i.e., at a high level of specificity), the lawyer creates differences between the cases. Two cases can always be distinguished by stating the facts with sufficient specificity.

At the same time, cases can often be made to seem more alike by stating the facts with greater generality. Assume, for example, that the lawyer finds no precedents involving pits, but does find one holding that the landowner has a duty to warn about an unstable slope. A slope, of course, is not the same thing as a pit. The lawyer can eliminate the difference, however, by restating the relevant facts of the slope precedent in more general terms. The precedent can be characterized as holding, for instance, that the landowner has a duty to warn of hazards, a term that would include a pit. By restating the specific facts of the precedent in terms broad enough to encompass the facts of the later case, the lawyer can characterize the two cases as alike.

Note that legal reasoning in the analogical form presents the same problem as legal reasoning in the deductive form. The problem with deductive reasoning is that because of the generality of the rule, it is often possible to characterize facts in more than one way, and thus the lawyer must somehow choose from among more than one minor premise, thereby permitting a conclusion that the rule either does or does not apply. Similarly, the problem with analogical reasoning is that by manipulating the generality at which facts are described the lawyer can characterize facts in more than one way and thus conclude that the two cases either are or are not alike. This exercise permits the lawyer to choose whether to distinguish or to follow the precedent.

C. *Addressing Indeterminacy Through Policy Judgments*

The problem of indeterminacy in analogical reasoning is addressed in much the same way that it is in deductive reasoning: by recourse to the underlying policies. The lawyer must determine which characterization of the facts would further the policies that underlie the precedent. As in the case of legal reasoning in the deductive form, however, policy determinations require judgments about the relative importance of policies as well as about the relationship between ends and means.

In general terms, the lawyer must decide, based on these judgments, whether characterizing the facts of the current case as like those of the prior case would yield more policy benefit than characterizing them as unlike those of the prior case. If so, then the prior case will be followed. If not, then the prior case will be distinguished.

For example, a prior case may have held that a landowner has a duty to warn guests about a concealed pit on the land. The holding represented a compromise between competing policies of preventing injury and permitting landowners to use their land as desired.

The holding must be described as a compromise because either policy, taken alone, would have led to a different result. On the one hand, if the prevention of injury were the only relevant policy, the court would probably have required the landowner to eliminate the hazard, since that is the surest way of preventing injury. On the other hand, if permitting landowners to use their land as they wish were the only relevant policy, the court would probably have imposed no duty at all on the landowner.

The holding that the landowner has a right to maintain a concealed pit on the land, subject to a duty to warn guests, essentially represented the compromise between these two policies that the court believed would yield the greatest policy benefit. The posting of a sign would greatly further the policy of protecting life, while only slightly restricting the landowner's use of the land. The alternative result—not requiring a warning—would permit a potentially grave threat to life, while providing only minimal benefits for the policy of landowner control. Accordingly, the court imposed a duty to warn.

Now assume that the lawyer must decide, in a new case involving a landowner with an unstable slope on the land, whether the concealed pit case should be followed or distinguished. The lawyer can do so by applying the prior policy judgment to the facts of the current case.

In applying that same judgment to the slope case, the lawyer would note that the burden of warning a guest is the same, whether the hazard is a pit or a slope. If the slope is as dangerous as the pit, or more dangerous, then the policy judgment that underlay the pit case would require a duty to warn in the slope case as well.

Applying the prior judgment to the facts of the current case is not a mechanical process, however. In the example, the lawyer must evaluate the relative dangers of a slope and a concealed pit. This is essentially a judgment about the relationship between ends and means. The lawyer is making a judgment concerning whether the slope impedes safety less than, as much as, or more than the pit. Although there may be empirical evidence, usually the judgment is based largely on intuition and experience, matters about which reasonable persons can differ.

The indeterminacy of applying the prior policy judgments is even more apparent in the situation where the lawyer concludes that a slope is less dangerous than a concealed pit. The prior case decided that the danger of a concealed pit outweighed the burden of a warning. If a slope is less dangerous, then how does the lawyer know whether the danger still outweighs the burden? The lawyer again has to make judgments about the relative weight of policies and the extent to which a particular result would further or impede the various policies. These judgments have to be combined to determine whether the greatest policy benefit results from treating the slope case like the pit case or treating it differently.

As noted in the section on deduction, lawyers often conceive of making policy judgments as a process of line drawing or balancing. The lawyer must draw a line that separates those situations in which the danger justifies the requirement of a warning from those in which it does not. Or, to use the language of balancing, the lawyer must balance the danger against the burden of a warning in each particular situation.

Logic alone cannot dictate how policies are to be balanced or where the line is to be drawn. The decision requires judgments about the relative importance of the competing policies and about the extent to which a particular result will further or impede each policy.

As noted in the section on deduction, this does not mean that results are wholly indeterminate. Judgments are made in a particular context that includes factors such as a historical setting, the identity of the person making the judgments, the facts to which the judgments will be applied, and prior judicial decisions. As discussed in Chapter 7, the context constrains, even if it does not wholly determine, the nature of the judgments that can plausibly be made.

D. *The Special Problem of Dictum*

Reasoning in the analogical form is similar to reasoning in the deductive form in that it must take account of the problem of dictum. The court in the later case will generally follow dictum and may do so without even acknowledging that the statement is dictum.

Dictum, however, is not binding and may be disregarded by courts in later cases without departing from the principle of stare decisis. A lawyer typically persuades a court not to follow dictum by arguing that the case in which the dictum appears is distinguishable. The argument is stronger if the lawyer can demonstrate that the policy judgments underlying the dictum do not apply in the same way to the current case. Examples of this technique have been given earlier.

The concept of dictum thus brings indeterminacy to the process of analogy, just as it brought indeterminacy to the process of deduction. In applying the rules set forth in a precedent, the lawyer must be alert to the fact that some of the rules are dictum and can be disregarded on a much weaker showing than would be necessary to persuade the court to overrule the precedent entirely.

E. Using Analogy as an Advocate

The indeterminacy of analogy often frustrates a lawyer's attempts to predict the result in a given case. The legal advocate, however, knows that this same indeterminacy offers the opportunity to fashion arguments in support of the desired result.

Because indeterminacy is rooted in the generality of language and in the existence of opposing policies, the lawyer as advocate exploits both of these features to support the arguments. Indeed, these features give rise to a set of standard arguments for following and distinguishing a prior case. In this subsection, some of those arguments are described.

1. Arguments for Following the Precedent

As an initial matter, the lawyer arguing that a prior case should be followed in a later case emphasizes the numerous factual similarities between the two cases. Strictly speaking, the only relevant facts are those whose existence would further or impede one of the underlying policies. The advocate arguing that a prior case should be followed, however, rarely limits the argument to those facts. Rather, the advocate includes in the recitation of similarities virtually any fact that is not a trivial coincidence.

Second, the advocate argues that the inevitable dissimilarities are irrelevant, the basic contention being that none of the facts that make the cases different is relevant to furthering or impeding any of the underlying policies. Obviously, for example, the fact that the parties' names differ is irrelevant to any legitimate policy. To the extent possible, the advocate makes a parallel argument with respect to any dissimilarity between the cases.

This argument may be difficult to make where the court in the prior case has stated explicitly that a particular fact, not present in the current case, is dispositive. The best argument for following the case in that situation is to point out that in light of the policies underlying the prior case, the prior case would have been decided the same way even without the so-called dispositive fact. The lawyer is arguing, in effect, that the fact was not truly necessary to the result. Since it was not actually necessary to the result, any discussion of that fact should be considered dictum and need not be followed. It may be difficult to prevail in this argument because it requires the court to disregard how another court characterized its own decision.

A third technique for arguing that a precedent should be followed is to state the factual predicate of the precedent at a higher level of generality. For example, if the prior case held that the presence of a concealed pit on the land gives rise to a duty on the part of the landowner to warn a guest, but the current case involves a guest who fell down a slope, the lawyer for the injured guest may characterize the prior case as involving a "hazard" rather than a concealed pit. As the language becomes more general, it will tend to encompass the facts of the current situation.

The lawyer can also manipulate the level of generality of the legal consequence. For example, assume that a prior case held that married couples have a constitutionally protected privacy right to use contraceptives and thus a statutory ban on contraceptives was unconstitutional. A lawyer wishing to use that case to invalidate a statutory ban on sodomy among married persons would characterize the prior case as holding that married couples have a right of privacy with respect to their sexual relations. By restating the legal consequence of the prior case in sufficiently broad terms, the lawyer transforms the case into one that appears to involve the same right as the current case.

In restating the factual predicate or legal consequence of the prior case in more general terms, the lawyer must avoid overreaching. The more general the lawyer's statement, the more likely it is to include factual situations in which the rule, as restated by the lawyer, would lead to results that are undesirable as a matter of policy.

For example, if the lawyer restates the contraceptive case as creating a right to privacy in sexual relations for all persons, that statement would seem to apply equally to unmarried minors. Arguably, it suggests, for example, that statutory rape laws would be unconstitutional. A court would very likely be unwilling to characterize the contraceptive case as creating such a broad right of privacy. In that situation, the court would reject the lawyer's overly broad characterization of the legal consequences from the prior cases.

A fourth technique is to characterize the prior case, not in terms of its facts but in terms of the underlying policy judgments, which the lawyer argues should be followed. For example, the lawyer seeking to impose on a landowner a duty to warn customers about concealed hazards on the land may rely on cases holding that a manufacturer has a duty to warn consumers of product defects. The lawyer would then argue that the prior cases adopted a policy of protecting the unwary against physical injury and that such policy should prevail in the current case as well.

This technique may require manipulating the level of generality at which the policy underlying the precedent is stated. The product defect cases, for example, may have described the underlying policy as protecting the stream of commerce against unsafe instrumentalities. By restating the policy more generally as protecting the unwary, the lawyer makes the policy seem applicable to the subsequent case. That is, the impression is created that the result the lawyer seeks in the later case would further the policies articulated in the earlier case.

2. *Arguments for Distinguishing the Precedent*

The arguments for distinguishing a prior case mirror those for following it. First, the lawyer emphasizes every possible difference between the two cases, being especially alert to facts that the court in the prior case regarded as dispositive. Even if the facts were only sufficient for the holding and not necessary, the lawyer notes that the dispositive facts are not present in this case. If the later case differs concerning some such dispositive fact, then it is likely the court will distinguish the two cases. Assuming that the cases do not differ concerning any fact explicitly considered dispositive in the earlier case, the lawyer attempting to distinguish the precedent may nevertheless point to differences in other facts in an effort to make the cases appear as different as possible.

Second, the lawyer attempts to dismiss similarities between the cases as irrelevant. If possible, the lawyer argues that particular facts in the precedent that are similar to those in the later case were not explicitly found to be dispositive and are therefore irrelevant coincidences. If the facts were held to be dispositive, the lawyer can attempt to argue that the facts were not relevant to accomplishing the underlying policy, although this can obviously be a difficult argument to make.

Third, the lawyer attempting to distinguish the cases characterizes the precedent in the narrowest possible terms. The lawyer states the facts and the legal consequence with great specificity, noting that any broader reading would constitute dictum, which the court need not follow. By stating the facts at very specific levels, the lawyer produces new dissimilarities. Thus, a pit is not merely a pit, but a concealed, life-threatening, 20-foot-deep pit.

Fourth, the lawyer may contend that the policy judgments underlying the prior case do not apply to the current case. This argument may follow any of several different approaches.

One approach is to argue that the policies that prevailed in the prior case require a different result in this case than was reached in the prior case. For example, assume that the prior case held that the government has the power to prohibit the use of offensive language on a television broadcast because the danger that a youngster might be injured by hearing the language outweighed the broadcaster's right to use it. In a later case, a television station broadcasts a documentary that realistically portrays the lives of young drug users in an effort to persuade juveniles that drug use could ruin their lives. To make the documentary more realistic and thus more credible, the station broadcasts film of drug users engaged in conversation with the police, their families, and each other—conversation involving the use of the same offensive language. The lawyer might argue that, in this case, the policy of protecting children actually would be *furthered* by permitting the offensive language to be broadcast.[9] Thus, to further the policy that prevailed in the prior case the court should distinguish the prior case and void, rather than uphold, the ban on offensive language.

Note that this argument requires manipulating the level of generality at which the policies are stated. In the first case, the policy was to protect children against the moral corruption caused by offensive language. In the second case, the policy was to protect children against the quite different injury caused by illegal drugs. By restating the policy of the first case more generally as protecting children, the lawyer creates the appearance that the result being sought in the second case would further the policy underlying the first case.

Another approach is to argue that this situation affects policies that were not relevant to the prior case. Because every decision represents a compromise among conflicting policies, the lawyer can almost always find an opposing policy that provides grounds for distinguishing the prior case.

As an illustration, assume that the adversary has found a precedent holding that a contract between two large businesses must be enforced even if one business, through its failure to investigate adequately the value of what it was purchasing, was the victim of an unequal exchange. The adversary now argues that this precedent requires enforcing a one-sided agreement signed by an illiterate consumer. Enforcement of contracts to which parties agree is consistent with a policy of autonomy, which generally enforces the choices made by individuals. The policy of autonomy is in tension with the policy of paternalism, which calls upon the court to scrutinize choices to make sure that they were not the result of private domination.[10] Thus, the policy of paternalism may provide a basis for a contrary argument by the

---

[9] The first case in this example is based on F.C.C. v. Pacifica Foundation, 438 U.S. 726 (1978), in which the Supreme Court held that the Federal Communications Commission could, consistent with the First Amendment's guarantee of free speech, regulate a radio station's broadcast of George Carlin's comedy routine on the seven dirty words you cannot say on television because the regulation would further the policy of protecting children. The second case is based on a hypothetical question posed by Doc Anderson, one of my former constitutional law students.

[10] The distinction between the policies of autonomy and paternalism, as those terms are used here, is discussed in Chapter 7.

lawyer. For example, the lawyer may argue that the contract was in fact co-erced because the consumer did not have the mental or financial resources to make a free choice. The precedent did not implicate the policy of pater-nalism in the same way because the two businesses were of approximately equal power. Thus, the precedent should be distinguished.

Finally, the lawyer can argue that if the precedent is applied to this case, stare decisis would require that it also be applied to other cases in which it would produce a clearly undesirable result. This, again, is the parade of horribles or the slippery slope argument. The lawyer demonstrates that this case is indistinguishable from other hypothetical cases in which application of the precedent would lead to undesirable results. As with legal reasoning in the deductive form, this argument is distinguished by not requiring a demonstration that following the precedent would lead to a bad result in this case, only that it would entail application of the precedent to other cases in which it would produce an undesirable result.

To return to the example above, assume that the adversary is arguing that a case holding that a contract signed at gunpoint is void should apply so as to void a one-sided contract signed by an illiterate consumer to purchase a refrigerator needed for storing perishable medicine. The adversary asserts that the consumer is like the man threatened with violence because neither had any realistic choice but to sign. In both cases, signing the contract was a matter of life or death.

The lawyer attempting to distinguish the precedent must decide which facts to characterize as distinguishing this case from the precedent. The lawyer may argue, for instance, that this case involves coercive circumstances rather than coercion from the other party and that to treat them as equivalent would lead to absurd results in other cases. For example, all contracts for the purchase of food would arguably be void because people have no realistic choice but to buy the food. The same would be true of the contract to pur-chase an automobile needed to drive to the market to buy the food (and the medicine and the refrigerator). Ultimately, only contracts for luxury items would be enforceable. Thus, the lawyer would conclude, coercive circum-stances should not be confused with coercion from the other party.

Again, however, in making this argument the lawyer must be careful not to overreach, to try to prove too much. For example, by characterizing the refrigerator case as involving coercive circumstances, the lawyer has ar-guably overreached. The adversary can counter with a narrower character-ization of the refrigerator case that would exclude the undesirable cases and yet be coterminous with the cases to which the underlying policies suggest the rule should apply. Thus, the adversary may assert that the refrigerator case is like the gunpoint case because both involved serious, imminent threats to life or safety. Although food may be a necessity, any specific pur-chase of food may not be a matter of immediate survival. An automobile purchase is very likely even less urgent. Thus, the likelihood that a consumer did not freely exercise his or her will is much greater in the gun or refrigerator case than in the food or car case. The adversary, in other words, demonstrates that the policy judgments underlying the precedent also apply to this case, though not to the hypothetical cases suggested by the lawyer. The adversary may thus persuade the court that applying the precedent to the refrigerator case is consistent with the policies underlying the precedent but will not entail applying it to the food or automobile cases.

F. *The Problem of Competing Analogies*

The prior discussion has assumed that the lawyer was attempting to determine whether one precedent should be followed or distinguished in deciding a current dispute. The precedent must be followed if it is like the current case.

Often, however, the lawyer encounters a situation where there are two or more precedents, each of which is like the current case in some respects. The problem is that the two precedents reached opposite results and thus both cannot be followed. In other words, the lawyer must choose between competing analogies.

For example, assume that the lawyer has identified two precedents, one of which holds that a ban on films depicting nudity is unconstitutional because it limits the constitutional right of free speech and the other of which holds that a ban on live nude dancing in a bar is constitutional because it is directed at the conduct of nudity rather than speech. The current case on which the lawyer's advice is sought involves a prohibition on a bar in which live nude dancers perform in a secluded studio from which patrons are excluded, but the dancers are seen by the patrons on a giant closed-circuit television screen.[11] The lawyer must decide which of the competing analogies governs.

The choice between competing analogies is often characterized as a matter of line drawing. On one side of the line are cases suppressing speech (in the form of films), whereas on the other side are cases suppressing conduct (such as live dancing). The lawyer must decide on which side of the line televised live nude dancing falls. Competing analogies may present line drawing in its most difficult context because each of the two analogies may be quite similar to the current case. Placing the current case on either side of the line may require a particularly precise series of judgments.

The lawyer nevertheless chooses between the competing analogies using the same techniques that are used to decide whether to follow or distinguish

---

[11] This example is based on a problem developed by the California Young Lawyers' Association for use in the 1992 Roger Traynor Moot Court Competition.

a single precedent. The correct analogy is the one that seems most like the current case, taking into account all similarities and dissimilarities.

The lawyer arguing to uphold the ban can note that this case is like the nude dancing precedent because live nude dancing is occurring on the premises and is being observed contemporaneously by the patrons. Those same features distinguish it from the film precedent, in which the viewer is detached in time and space from the performance.

The lawyer arguing to void the ban can note that this case is like the film precedent because the viewer sees an image of the dancer rather than the dancer herself. It is distinguishable from the nude dancing precedent because the patrons are unable to communicate with or touch the dancers.

In addition to citing the similarities between this case and the precedent the lawyer wishes the court to follow and the dissimilarities between this case and the precedent the lawyer wishes to distinguish, the lawyer also attempts to characterize as irrelevant to any underlying policy the similarities between this case and the precedent that should be distinguished. For example, the lawyer arguing to void the ban can note that it is irrelevant that the dancing is being viewed contemporaneously. The bar could hypothetically videotape the dance and show it on a delayed basis, which would eliminate the contemporaneity but would have no impact from the standpoint of furthering or impeding the relevant policies. This thought experiment thus suggests that whether the viewing occurs contemporaneously with or subsequent to the dancing is irrelevant to furthering the underlying policies.

If the process of deciding whether one case is like another is often indeterminate, the process of tallying similarities and dissimilarities is even more so because some similarities or dissimilarities may be of greater importance than others and there are no fixed criteria for weighing them. The lawyer thus may turn to the underlying policies, seeking to ascertain the policy benefit that would result from following each of the competing analogies. The "correct" analogy is the one that, when applied, would yield the greater policy benefit.

For example, the lawyer arguing that the ban on the televised dancers should be upheld would note that the policy underlying the ban on live nude dancing, which is to reduce the crime associated with establishments featuring adult entertainment, requires that the televised dancers be treated the same as live dancers. The types of crime linked with nude bars, such as prostitution, substance abuse, and related violent crimes, would occur whether the dancers are observed directly during the dance or not. Not to treat the two types of dancing the same would impede the policy furthered by the rule upholding the ban on live dancing.

At the same time, the argument would continue, upholding the ban would impede the policy of free speech *less* than banning nudity in films.

Films communicate a far broader range of ideas to a much greater audience than nude dancing in a bar, and thus the regulation of nude dancing on closed-circuit television does not impede free speech to nearly the same extent as a ban on nudity in films would.

The lawyer arguing that the ban on televised dancers should be voided may argue that the policy underlying the right to display nudity in films—the protection of free expression—requires that the televised dancers be treated the same as the actors in film. The relationship in time and space between the dancers and the viewers makes no difference to the value of the speech. Not to treat the televised dancers like film actors would impede the policy furthered by the rule upholding the right to show nudity in films.

At the same time, the argument would continue, voiding the ban would impede the policy of preventing crime *less* than voiding a ban on live nude dancing would. Televised nude dancing does not contribute to crime in the same way that live nude dancing does because the inability of patrons to communicate with the dancers reduces the likelihood that prostitution and related crimes will occur.

Lawyers frequently argue cases involving competing analogies by demonstrating that to accept the analogy urged by the adversary would lead to undesirable results in other cases. To do this, they employ the slippery slope or parade of horribles argument described previously. In that way, the lawyer establishes not so much that the precedent being cited is the correct one as that the precedent being cited by the adversary is the incorrect one.

For example, assume that the lawyer is arguing that the bar with the televised dancers should be analogized to the precedent involving live nude dancing and thus the ban should be upheld. The lawyer may assert that to treat the dancers as if they were analogous to actors in a film merely because they are not directly observed would lead to absurd results. For example, it would permit a bar to feature live nude dancers in the same room as the patrons as long as they were seen in a mirror image, rather than directly. Thus, the fact that the patron sees an image rather than the dancer should be treated as irrelevant.

The lawyer arguing that the televised dancers should be analogized to actors in a film and thus the ban should be struck down may assert that to treat dancers who never appear in the same room with the patrons as if they were live dancers merely because their performance is viewed contemporaneously from the same premises would lead to absurd results. For instance, if the adversary's analogy is taken as correct, a film depicting nudity would be protected, but the state could criminalize the making of the film since it would involve contemporaneous viewing of nudity on the same premises. Thus, the fact that dancing occurs contemporaneously on the premises should be treated as irrelevant.

III. Comparing Deduction and Analogy

Despite underlying similarities, deductive and analogical reasoning perform somewhat different functions in the legal reasoning process. In deduction, one concludes that what is true of an entire class of objects is true of a single object in that class. In analogy, one compares two objects and concludes that because they are alike in at least one respect, they must be alike in another respect.

Legal reasoning in the deductive form, in other words, requires a general rule applicable to an entire class of situations. Statutes, of course, are general rules, and thus enacted law is applied through reasoning in the deductive form, often supplemented by analogies to particular cases to determine how to characterize certain facts.

Because analogy compares one object with another, analogy is generally the appropriate form of legal reasoning through which to decide one case by reference to another. The problem, however, with using analogy to compare precedents to a current situation is that because of the sheer volume of previously decided cases, to analogize a single factual situation to every prior case involving similar facts would be a practical impossibility. It is far easier to extract from the case law a general rule that governs an entire category of cases. For that reason, courts much prefer to base their decisions on general rules drawn from cases and applied in deductive form to the facts.

The general rules may have been stated in the cases as dictum, or the lawyer may have used the inductive process described in Chapter 3 to synthesize a general rule that seemed to encapsulate the holdings of a category of cases. In either event, once the rule is derived, the lawyer uses legal reasoning in the deductive form to apply it to the facts of the case.

As a technical matter, deduction may be the wrong form to use because the rule being applied very likely was dictum and thus does not actually bind the court in any later case. Deduction presupposes a rule governing all cases in a category, but dictum does not govern.

Strictly speaking, the lawyer is comparing the client's situation to a number of other cases. Thus, the correct form is really analogy. Yet, rather than take the time to compare one case to hundreds, as a kind of shortcut the lawyer groups an entire group of cases under a rule, which actually may be broader than the cases warrant, and then reasons in the deductive form. The lawyer's use of deduction to apply case law is made possible by the courts' willingness to follow dictum, that is, to treat nonbinding rules as if they were binding.

Analogy, nevertheless, is a heavily used method of legal reasoning. One typical setting in which the lawyer uses analogy is as an aid to completing a syllogism. As explained above, the lawyer often uses analogy to decide how to characterize the facts, thereby deciding which of several minor premises to adopt in order to complete the syllogism.

Analogy is also used in a novel situation for which there may be no general rules. The lawyer may search for cases that seem similar in at least a few respects and then analogize them to the novel situation.

IV. DEDUCTION AND ANALOGY IN A JURY SYSTEM

Although case law holdings are theoretically binding on subsequent cases, in a jury system a prior case often has little impact on subsequent, similar cases. This phenomenon occurs because a decision by one jury does not bind another jury. In other words, the jury's decision in the first case does not create a rule binding in the next case.

Assume that the jury in a case decides that a physician who failed to administer a particular diagnostic test was negligent. A jury in a later case involving identical facts would nevertheless be free to decide that the physician in that case was *not* negligent. The first jury's verdict does not bind the second jury, despite the similarity of the facts.

A jury verdict, however, can be "transformed" into a binding holding if the losing party challenges the verdict in some way, such as by moving for a new trial or for judgment as a matter of law,[12] or by appealing. As a result of the challenge, the trial or appellate court reviews the jury verdict and renders a decision, perhaps set forth in a written opinion. Assuming that the opinion is published, its holding becomes a binding precedent in future similar cases.

For example, let us assume that the losing party appeals. As explained in Chapter 1, the appellate court does not decide the facts de novo. Rather, it merely considers whether the jury's verdict was supported by substantial evidence.

This inquiry produces one of two possible results. First, the appellate court may hold that the jury's verdict is supported by substantial evidence. For the first time in the case, there is a judicial holding—a rule binding in future cases.

Consider carefully, however, the exact nature of the holding. The appellate court did not hold that a physician who fails to administer the test is

---

[12] The grounds for these various motions are discussed in Chapter 1.

always negligent but only that the jury had before it sufficient evidence to conclude that the physician in that case was negligent.

This holding is that certain facts *may* constitute negligence, not that they necessarily do. The holding, nevertheless, can influence the resolution of future similar cases. For example, if a physician's lawyer in a later case involving similar facts moves for summary judgment[13] on the ground that failure to administer the test cannot constitute negligence, the patient's lawyer may cite the earlier decision holding that failure to administer the test may constitute negligence and thereby defeat the motion. When the later case goes to trial, however, the jury will be free to decide that the physician in the later case was not negligent. Thus, the appellate court's holding essentially does little more than assure that patients in later, similar cases are entitled to a trial on the issue of whether the physician was negligent.

Of course, the physician's lawyer in the later cases may attempt to defeat even that limited use of the earlier case. The lawyer may attempt to distinguish the earlier case or, failing that, argue that it was wrongly decided.

The other possible result on appeal is that the appellate court could hold that the failure to administer the test cannot be considered negligence. This holding can also influence the resolution of future similar cases. Another physician sued for failure to administer the test could argue that the prior case established as a matter of law that failure to administer the test does *not* constitute negligence. The patient, the plaintiff, can attempt to distinguish the prior case or to persuade a court that it was wrongly decided. Should the patient fail in that argument, the prior holding will become controlling.

This is not to suggest that a jury trial never has an impact on future cases unless the jury's verdict is challenged. In a jury trial, the judge decides all questions of law. The judge's decisions on these questions along with the decisions of the appellate court reviewing those decisions, if published, also constitute binding precedents.

V. EPILOGUE: CHANGING CASE LAW

The description of the legal reasoning process in the preceding chapters has assumed that the common law never changes, except by an act of the legislature. If the law were subject to change at any time, then predicting the rights and duties of parties would be an impossibility. Further, conceding that a court is free to change the law at any time renders the principles of the rule of law and stare decisis meaningless.

---

[13] Summary judgment is discussed in Chapter 1.

Yet, the courts do have the power to modify the common law with sufficient justification. In this final section, the situations in which a court may be persuaded to modify case law rules and the techniques that the court may use are briefly discussed.

A. *Flexibility Without Changing Case Law*

As an initial matter, courts have considerable ability to reach the desired result without having to change the law. This flexibility exists because, as discussed above, common law rules are often indeterminate. First, prior cases applying the language are binding only to the extent of their narrow holdings, and thus the prior cases very often do not apply or can be distinguished. Second, even binding language may be too general to require only one result. Third, application of the policies may also support any of several results, depending upon the court's judgment about the relative weight of the policies and the relationship between the policies and the means used to further them.

Thus, except in the easy cases, the existing law does not really require a single result. Courts often have the ability to reach the result demanded by either party to a dispute. As long as the result can be reconciled with the language of the rules and any contrary precedents can plausibly be distinguished, the court has not "changed" the law. If anything, the court has merely created law where none existed.

B. *Justifications for Changing Case Law*

Occasionally, however, a situation arises in which the result the lawyer wishes to reach cannot plausibly be reconciled with the language of the existing rules. The rights or duties that the client wants to exist in some situation can arise only by changing one or more existing rules of case law.

The principle of stare decisis creates a strong presumption against overturning a prior decision but does not prohibit the practice. If the court is going to change the law, it will do so for reasons of policy.

Because the original rule was based on policy judgments, the lawyer must essentially persuade a court that the prior judgments can no longer be considered correct. Recall that applying policies to decide cases requires two types of judgments. The lawyer may argue that either or both of the judgments were wrong.

The first type of judgment pertains to the relative weight given to different policies. The prior court struck a balance between two policies, based on the perceived importance of each. The lawyer must now argue that the relative importance of the policies has changed. As a result, a new rule is necessary. Or, to put it another way, a new balance must be struck, a new line drawn.

For example, courts in the nineteenth century adopted a rule known as the "fellow servant rule," which held that an employee injured on the job could not sue his employer for negligence if the injury was caused by another employee. The courts essentially concluded that the policy of promoting economic development outweighed the policy of compensating the injured worker. In the twentieth century, however, courts began to create exceptions to the fellow servant rule, thereby allowing employees to sue their employers for injuries caused by the negligence of other employees. The courts had simply decided that the policy of compensating the injured was now entitled to greater weight.

The second type of judgment pertains to the relationship between ends and means. The prior court adopted a rule because it believed that such a rule would best promote certain policies. The lawyer now argues, without necessarily quarreling with the ends sought by the prior court, that the rule adopted simply does not promote those policies any longer, if it ever did. The rule, in other words, has not worked in practice and must be changed.

For example, the traditional common law rules governing the duties that landowners owe those who come onto the land categorized those who entered the land as trespassers, licensees, or invitees. The landowners' duties varied, depending upon the category into which the entrant fell. Some courts, however, came to believe that the various categories were difficult to apply and that the underlying policies could best be effectuated by adopting a single duty requiring the landowner to exercise reasonable care under the circumstances.[14]

Changes in the law of this type are perhaps easier for the court to adopt because, as noted above, the relationship between ends and means, in theory, is a matter that the court can decide empirically. Thus, in the example above, the court announced that the prior rule was "difficult to apply"—a conclusion that was ostensibly based on factual observation. By changing the law in this way, the court is not admitting that it has changed policies but only that it is "correcting" the law in light of new information. The underlying policies of the prior cases continue to receive the same weight.

C. *Techniques for Changing Case Law*

A court that has decided to change case law may use a variety of techniques, some of which may blunt the impression that it has departed from the principle of stare decisis. In this subsection, a few of these techniques are discussed.

---

[14] *See, e.g.,* Basso v. Miller, 40 N.Y.2d 233, 386 N.Y.S.2d 564, 352 N.E.2d 868 (1976).

1. *Confining a Case to Its Facts*

First, the court may confine a prior case to its facts. This is, in effect, a relatively weak form of overruling. The holding in the prior case is treated as correct, and yet the court refuses to generalize from that holding to any future case. The court has effectively repudiated any dictum in the prior case that suggested that the holding reflected a more broadly applicable rule.

For example, a case holding that to knock a cafeteria patron's dinner tray out of that person's hand is an offensive touching might be confined to its facts by a court. The court is now free to hold that it is not an offensive touching to knock a box of pizza, a deck of cards, a family heirloom, or anything else out of the hand. The holding in the prior case has been confined to the facts of that case. The court need not find some basis on which to distinguish later cases involving pizza or heirlooms. The law has changed, permitting the court to treat pizza and heirlooms differently from dinner trays, even though the court has not explicitly overruled the prior case.

2. *Overruling* Sub Silentio

Second, the court may overrule a prior case *sub silentio*. The court generally does this by articulating a set of policy judgments in a later case that, if applied to the earlier case, would have caused a different result. The court declines explicitly to overrule the prior case, and yet the lawyer understands that the prior case no longer controls future decisions.

For example, assume that a case holds that a court must give a consumer prior notice and an opportunity to be heard before authorizing the sheriff, who is acting on behalf of a store, to seize goods for which the consumer allegedly has failed to pay the store. Assume also that a later case permits seizure of the goods without prior notice and an opportunity to be heard, as long as the court at the time it authorizes seizure has adequate grounds to believe the store's claim to the goods is well founded and gives subsequent notice to the consumer. This may amount to a *sub silentio* overruling of the first case.[15] Nothing in the first case suggested that the court there did not have adequate grounds to believe that the store's claim was well founded, and thus the first case is arguably indistinguishable from the second. The second case reached a different result because the court changed its policy. The first case is not explicitly overruled, but future cases will apparently be decided differently.

---

[15] This example is based on Fuentes v. Shevin, 407 U.S. 67 (1972) and Mitchell v. W.T. Grant Co., 416 U.S. 600 (1974).

3. Creating Exceptions

Third, the court may create an exception. This is an explicit, but only partial, repudiation of the prior case. The prior case remains good law, but it no longer controls all of the situations it once did.

The last example could be used to illustrate this technique as well. Assume that, in the first case, there had *not* been adequate assurances that the store's claim was well founded. In that situation, the second case, rather than overruling the prior case *sub silentio,* might simply create an exception—holding that, although prior notice is generally required, subsequent notice is sufficient if the court has adequate assurances that the store's claim to a right of seizure is well founded.

Obviously, lawyers may differ at times over whether the second case represents an exception to the first case or an overruling of it *sub silentio.* To the extent that the two cases are truly different, the second case may well be carving out an exception to the general rule set forth in the first case. To the extent that the two cases seem indistinguishable, however, then the conclusion is almost inescapable that the first case has been overruled *sub silentio.* As has been seen, lawyers may differ over whether two cases are distinguishable, and thus they may differ over whether the second case created an exception to, or overruled *sub silentio,* the first case.

Any exception changes the law with respect to those situations embraced within the exception. Moreover, by defining the factual predicate of the exception broadly, the court can bring large numbers of cases within the exception. Eventually, the exception may become more widely applicable than the so-called general rule, with the result that the exception is said to "swallow the rule." At the time it was created, the exception seemed a minor change in the law, but over time it proved to be a virtually complete repudiation of the earlier rule.[16]

4. Legal Fictions

Fourth, the court may use a legal fiction to change the law. A legal fiction, in effect, is a declaration that the law regards something as true even though it is not. Generally speaking, a legal fiction is used to supply a missing element in a rule. By declaring the element to be present, the court permits the rule to apply to facts where it would otherwise not apply. To all appearances, the law has not changed. In reality, however, the court has rewritten the rule so that the missing element is eliminated or replaced.

---

[16] If no future cases follow the earlier rule, a lawyer may well conclude that the earlier case has been confined to its facts.

One of the most commonly used legal fictions is the technique of implication, in which a court declares that some element is implied to be present, even though in any meaningful sense it is not present.

For example, assume that a case holds that a corporation cannot be sued in a state unless that corporation consents to the jurisdiction of the courts. Assume now that a second case holds that a corporation, by doing business with a citizen of the state, implies consent to jurisdiction. Obviously, the corporation did not truly consent to jurisdiction, and yet it may now be sued. The law appears not to have changed because it still bases jurisdiction on consent. In effect, however, the element of consent has been replaced with the element of "doing business," which is converted to consent by a legal fiction.

Legal fictions can prepare the legal community for an explicit change in the law. Once the fiction has become well established, a court may decide to abandon the pretense and admit that the fiction is only that. By this point, however, the rule as modified by the use of the legal fiction is so sufficiently entrenched that the court will very likely not be criticized for having changed the law. If anything, it may be praised for candor in abandoning what had been an obvious fiction all along.

5. Explicit Overruling

Finally, a court may explicitly overrule a prior case. The policy justifications for changing the law are sufficiently compelling to override the presumption in favor of stare decisis, and the court simply changes the law.

PART TWO

Advanced Legal Reasoning

6

A Historical Perspective
on Legal Reasoning

The premises underlying the process of legal reasoning in the United States reflect deeper assumptions about the relationship among individuals and the community, about the possibilities of human understanding, and about the nature of reality itself. That is, assumptions that govern the realms of philosophy, religion, science, politics, literature, and other disciplines also shape our understanding of law and of legal reasoning.

The American Constitution was written in the late eighteenth century at the height of the Enlightenment and thus reflects the assumptions underlying Enlightenment thought. Two centuries later, however, developments in every area of human endeavor have challenged, often successfully, these same assumptions. The result has been to cast grave doubt upon the theoretical underpinnings of legal reasoning.

American lawyers, accordingly, have struggled continually to reconceptualize the law and the legal reasoning process in light of their changed understanding of the world. Legal reasoning today is thus a patchwork of ideas that have survived from earlier times combined with ideas borrowed from contemporary thought.

In this chapter, an attempt is made to explain American legal reasoning at the end of the twentieth century as the product of a historical process. The discussion begins with an investigation of the Enlightenment assumptions on which the American legal system was constructed and moves on to a description of how one of those assumptions, a belief in natural law, was successfully challenged in the early nineteenth century, leading to the emergence of a new synthesis, known as formalism, at the end of the nineteenth century. Formalism was itself successfully challenged in the early twentieth century by the Legal Realists. Legal thought in the late twentieth century has been dominated by attempts to reexplain the legal reasoning process in the wake of the Legal Realist critique.

I. The Enlightenment Origins of American Legal Thought

A. *The Emergence of Enlightenment Epistemology*

The eighteenth-century architects of the American legal system worked on the basis of the assumptions that characterized Enlightenment philosophy. The inquiry here thus begins with a brief summary of Enlightenment thought.

The roots of the Enlightenment are generally traced to the Renaissance, the Protestant Reformation and the Scientific Revolution. The fourteenth-century Italian Renaissance was sparked by the rediscovery of classical Greek writings and featured a return to secular concerns, in sharp contrast to the theological focus of medieval thought. The Reformation, which began with Martin Luther's posting of the ninety-five theses in 1517, challenged the traditional authority of the Roman Catholic Church, claiming that individuals could acquire religious truth through their own interpretation of the scriptures. The Scientific Revolution, which is usually dated from the sixteenth century as well, was an endeavor to ascertain truth through a scientific, that is, a rational and empirical, method.

The Reformation and the Scientific Revolution shared a commitment to the pursuit of truth by individuals who exercised reason rather than passively accepting traditional authority. To a considerable extent, then, both of these movements were concerned with epistemology, or the theory of how knowledge is obtained. They emphasized skepticism, individualism, and reason. In common with the Renaissance, they were primarily secular in orientation.

In the seventeenth and eighteenth centuries, these currents of thought produced two distinct schools of philosophy, which combined to form the Enlightenment. The first school, known as rationalism, began with the work of René Descartes. Descartes adopted a position of radical skepticism, questioning everything and accepting nothing on authority. He then attempted to determine whether there was anything that could be known with certainty and found only one thing: He could know for certain his own doubt. From the fact of his doubt, he deduced his own existence—a deduction sometimes referred to as the cogito, after the famous proposition *cogito, ergo sum* ("I think, therefore I am"). Descartes went on to develop an entire philosophy, including an explanation of the existence of God, by a series of deductions originating with the cogito. Descartes' model of epistemology was mathematics, a system that begins with certain intuitive truths and then arrives at further truths by a process of deduction. Descartes rejected as unreliable the information provided by one's senses because he found that appearances often deceive us—things are not as they seem.

In Cartesian philosophy, then, the pursuit of knowledge originates with the individual who refuses to accept any truth that cannot be established by his own exercise of reason. Cartesian rationalism dominated European philosophy in the seventeenth and eighteenth centuries and is represented, for example, in the work of Benedict de Spinoza and Gottfried Leibniz.

By beginning with his own self-consciousness, Descartes separated his mind from the tangible things of the world. He first proved the existence of his own thoughts, then reasoned from that to the existence of his body and the other objects in the world. Thus, built into Descartes' epistemology is a distinction between one's individual, subjective consciousness and the objective world existing beyond one's mind.

The other school of philosophy that arose out of the Reformation and the Scientific Revolution was empiricism, whose most important figures include three seventeenth- and eighteenth-century British philosophers, John Locke, George Berkeley, and David Hume. Locke, too, began with a skeptical posture. He believed, however, that knowledge came not through Cartesian introspection, but rather through the experience of the senses. In Locke's view, the only things we can know for certain are those that we can learn empirically. Berkeley and Hume each pushed the implications of Locke's empiricism a step further. Berkeley argued that to exist is to be perceived. Because abstract ideas cannot be sensed, they cannot exist outside the mind. Hume took the position that because we experience only isolated sensations, no principle can be known through induction and no causal link between phenomena can be established with certainty. All we can know is the particulars that we experience. Our notion that these particulars demonstrate a unifying principle or a chain of causation is merely a psychological predisposition, a habitual assumption that the particulars are related, not something we can definitely know.

Despite the disagreement between Descartes and Locke concerning whether intuition or sense impression are the starting points of knowledge, the rationalists and empiricists made certain common assumptions growing out of Descartes' work. Both Descartes and Locke subordinated metaphysics to epistemology, meaning that they started with a theory of knowledge from which they constructed their account of reality. Both began their inquiry with the individual. Descartes began with individual intuition, whereas Locke began with individual sense impressions. With both, however, the individual is at the center of their philosophy. Finally, in beginning with the individual, both the rationalists and the empiricists assume a distinction between the subjective mind of the individual and the objective world outside of individual consciousness.

Rationalism and empiricism represent the two strands of Enlightenment epistemology. Enlightenment thinkers believed that we can know only by reason or experience, the methods used by science, and turned away from tradition, authority, and revelation as a means of knowing the world. The Enlightenment thus represented an attempt to apply the scientific method to all forms of knowledge. The Enlightenment image of the natural world was inspired by Isaac Newton's laws of physics: The universe is an elaborate machine, like a clock, that operates in a regular fashion according to a natural law established by the Creator. The eighteenth-century Enlightenment has been called the Age of Reason and, at least at the time of the American Revolution, the Cartesian rationalist strand dominated the empirical strand, particularly in political philosophy.

Medieval philosophers had divided in their metaphysics between the realists and the nominalists. The realists believed that general concepts have a real existence and traced their lineage to Plato and his belief in the existence of "forms" that are the universal essences of particular earthly objects. The nominalists believed that only particulars actually exist and that general concepts are merely names that humans apply to groups of particulars. As early as the fourteenth century, William of Ockham had associated nominalism with empiricism in a way that anticipated Berkeley and Hume. Although the work of the British empiricists brought a nominalist strand to Enlightenment philosophy, the dominant metaphysic in the late eighteenth century was realist: The universe is governed by natural laws that reason can perceive.

B. *The Emergence of Liberalism*

Enlightenment developments in epistemology were accompanied by a parallel development in political philosophy: the emergence of liberalism. The challenges to the religious authority of the Catholic Church posed by the Reformation and the Scientific Revolution coincided with a challenge to the political and economic authority of the state. This challenge came from a rising middle class that rejected the mercantilist economic policies of the European monarchs. Liberalism, the political and economic philosophy of the middle class, shared with Enlightenment epistemology a belief in freedom for the rational individual—whether freedom of inquiry or freedom of economic enterprise.

Liberal political theory, particularly as expounded by its most influential theoretician, John Locke, held that individuals have natural rights to liberty and equality, that individuals through a social contract agree to form governments for the sole purpose of protecting those rights, and that the only legitimate government is based on the consent of the governed. Liberal economic theory asserted that an unregulated market economy allowing individuals the freedom to pursue their rational self-interest would produce greater wealth than the heavily regulated economies of mercantilism.

In Locke's view, the purpose of government was the protection of individual liberty. Locke also wrote about the form that government should take, arguing for a separation of powers among different branches of government so that no one branch would dominate. After studying the British constitutional system, Baron de Montesquieu refined Locke's separation of powers theory, calling for a division of government into the legislative, executive, and judicial branches.

The fundamental premise of Lockean liberalism was that individuals have rights based on natural law. A belief in natural law was traceable to the Stoics of ancient Greece and had been incorporated into medieval theology, which understood natural law to be law based on the will of God as revealed in scripture and to be binding on all people.

Belief in a natural law that governed human affairs also fit comfortably in the Enlightenment image of the universe as an elaborate machine governed by Newtonian laws of physics. People, like nature, were subject to a natural law. Thus, Thomas Jefferson in the Declaration of Independence could proclaim the existence of "self-evident" truths concerning the equality of men at birth and their natural right to life, liberty, and the pursuit of happiness. This natural law, however, was to be ascertained through the exercise of intuition and reason in the tradition of Descartes rather than to be derived from religious revelation. Natural law had acquired a basis in secular thought.

The epistemological and political theory of the Enlightenment converged in the late eighteenth century to produce the experiment of the American Constitution. Reduced to its essence, eighteenth-century American legal philosophy might be characterized as the use of reason to protect liberty. Through the exercise of reason, men could discern their natural rights, some of which they codified in the Bill of Rights of the U.S. Constitution.

So intense was the belief that these natural rights had genuine existence that many considered their codification in a Bill of Rights superfluous and even dangerous, because it could lead courts to assume that only the codified rights were enforceable. In the years following the Revolution, courts claimed the right to invalidate legislation that was contrary to natural law, even though not prohibited by anything in the Constitution.

Eighteenth-century American legal philosophy held that the common law was similarly based on principles that could be discerned by a court through the exercise of reason. These case law principles included the natural rights of men, and thus the common law posed no threat to liberty.

The institutional structure that ensured that reason would protect liberty was the separation of powers. Judges, who were guided by reason rather than political passion, would review the constitutionality of legislation or apply the common law. Judges as rational decisionmakers would guarantee the preservation of liberty.

Reason would thus protect liberty through the rule of law. Courts were not to decide cases in accordance with the individual preferences of the judge but in accordance with the dictates of law ascertained by reason.

C. *The Decline of Naturalism*

In the early nineteenth century, a number of forces delegitimated explicit appeals by judges to natural law. Jacksonian democracy, with its emphasis on popular sovereignty, favored a conception of law as something created by the consent of the people rather than discovered through the exercise of reason. The rise of the market economy demanded by liberalism undercut belief in objective value. Value was not eternally fixed but was reestablished daily by the consensus of those in the market.

Naturalism was also challenged by the utilitarian philosophy of Jeremy Bentham and John Stuart Mill. Bentham argued that a society should seek the greatest happiness for the greatest number, a philosophy that seemed congenial to majoritarian democracy because it argued for the welfare of the society as a whole rather than for the inalienable rights of individuals. The greatest happiness for the greatest number could be inconsistent with the interests of any particular individual, and thus utilitarian philosophy was deeply corrosive of any naturalist belief in individual rights. Individual rights would be protected, if at all, not because of the worth of the individual, but because to do so would benefit the society as a whole. Utilitarianism suggested that courts should not look backward to determine what preexisting rights were determinative of a dispute but should look forward to the consequences of each possible resolution of the dispute.

Gradually, naturalism in legal theory was supplanted by positivism, the belief that law is the command of a human sovereign, which in the case of the United States is the people. Individual rights were seen as merely the correlatives of duties, and thus rights, like duties, were simply the creation of law. Although natural law might continue to exist as a moral category, only laws adopted by a sovereign could form the basis of a judicial decision. Law no longer originated in God or nature, but in popular consent.[1]

II. LEGAL FORMALISM

In the late nineteenth century, the emergence of university-based law schools with full-time faculties spawned a body of theoretical writing on the subject of how lawyers and judges apply positive law to ascertain individual rights and duties. One of the most influential commentators on the subject

---

[1] Although the common law was created by judges and not by an elected legislature, it was explicitly incorporated into the law of most states by a constitutional or statutory provision adopted through democratic processes. Moreover, in all states, under the doctrine of legislative supremacy, the legislature has the power to modify or reject any part of the common law. Under these circumstances, early nineteenth-century theoreticians had little difficulty conceptualizing the common law as based on popular consent.

was Christopher Columbus Langdell, who was appointed dean of the Harvard Law School in 1870.

Langdell proposed the idea that law is a science, like biology or physics. The data on which this science is based are judicial decisions. Dean Langdell continued the analogy far enough to argue that the library is to a lawyer what the laboratory is to the chemist or physicist. As he explained in an 1887 commencement address at Harvard,

> [It] was indispensable to establish at least two things; first that law is a science; secondly, that all the available materials of that science are contained in printed books. . . . If it be a science, it will scarcely be disputed that it is one of the greatest and most difficult of sciences . . . We have also constantly inculcated the idea that the library is the proper workshop of professors and students alike; that it is to us all that laboratories of the university are to the chemists and physicists, all that the museum of natural history is to the zoologists, all that the botanical garden is to the botanists.[2]

Just as the scientist could discern the laws of nature by studying empirical data, the lawyer could discover the laws of society by studying cases. The method used by the lawyer was that of induction. After reading some number of cases articulating a particular rule, the lawyer could infer that this rule must be a general rule of law.

Langdell believed that the end result of this process of observation and induction would be the discovery of a small number of very general rules. All future cases could be decided by applying these general rules to the facts through the process of deduction. Those judicial decisions that did not adhere to these general rules could be dismissed as wrongly decided.

Langdell made this approach explicit in the preface to his 1871 casebook on contract law. He explained there that

> [l]aw, considered as a science, consists of certain principles or doctrines. To have such a mastery of these as to be able to apply them with constant facility and certainty to the ever-tangled skein of human affairs, is what constitutes a true lawyer . . . [M]uch the shortest and best, if not the only way of mastering the doctrine effectually is by studying the cases in which it is embodied. But the cases which are useful and necessary for this purpose at the present day bear an exceedingly small proportion to all that have been reported. The vast majority are useless, and worse than useless, for any systematic study. Moreover, the number of fundamental legal doctrines is much less than is commonly supposed; the many different guises in which the same doctrine is constantly making its appearance . . . being the cause of much apprehension. If these doctrines could be so classified and arranged that each should be found in its proper place, and nowhere else, they would cease to be formidable from their number.[3]

---

[2] Quoted in W. Twining, Karl Llewellyn and the Realist Movement 12 (1973).
[3] C. Langdell, A Selection of Cases on the Law of Contracts viii (1871).

Langdell's approach has often been called "legal formalism" or, simply, "formalism." The term refers to a process of deciding cases by the mechanical application of general rules.

Formalism in many respects represented the apotheosis of Enlightenment philosophy in American legal thought. Langdell's belief that law was a science was consistent with the Enlightenment endeavor to apply the scientific method to all forms of knowledge. The combination of induction and deduction in Langdell's method brought both the empiricist and the rationalist strands of Enlightenment epistemology into legal reasoning.

Formalism was also consistent with the political liberalism of the Enlightenment. Specifically, formalism affirmed the principle of the rule of law by insisting that all adjudication was the mechanical application of rules. The rules were either those enacted by the legislature or those already announced in prior cases. The judge, in effect, had no discretion; he was bound by preexisting law. Law restrained the courts and thereby protected liberty.

Formalism affirmed the liberal belief in the natural equality of men. In applying a relatively few very general rules to a large number of transactions, formalism denied the relevance of differences among the people involved in a transaction. That is, formalism denied the relevance of social or economic hierarchy.

Formalism also held, as did liberalism, that individuals in civil society were free to exercise their will. In its refusal to take account of social or economic hierarchy or many of the particulars of individual transactions, formalism was systematically blind to all but the crudest forms of coercion and thus saw human activity as predominantly free. Because individuals were free, as formalism defined freedom, judicial intervention in the private sector should be limited to acts that in some way enforced or ratified the will of the private parties rather than imposing the will of the state.

The mechanical application of rules brought predictability to adjudication, which promoted trade and investment among private actors. Formalist assumptions that individuals were free to exercise their will and to assume or decline legal obligations mirrored the assumption of market economics that market participants act as rational maximizers of their own utility. Judicial abstention from the imposition of the will of the state, in other words, was the legal analogue to laissez-faire economic policy. Formalism thus seemed consistent with liberal economic theory as well.

Formalism held an additional attraction for lawyers in particular because its ostensibly "scientific" character elevated the study and practice of law to a plane of specialized, technical expertise, equivalent to that required of physicists, chemists, and other scientists. Formalism, in short, seemed to promise a scientific legal system characterized by liberty, equality, economic prosperity, and political legitimacy.

Despite the consistency of formalism with much of Enlightenment philosophy, the political consequences of formalism in the late nineteenth century were quite different from those of Enlightenment philosophy in the late eighteenth century. Enlightenment epistemology and political theory had been revolutionary in their impact. Enlightment epistemology challenged centuries of established religious authority, while its political theory justified the overthrow of a feudal order that could trace its origins to the collapse of the Roman empire.

Formalism, by contrast, tended to legitimate the existing distribution of wealth and power. Its essential premise was that there is a single, correct rule of law that has been laid down in prior cases and the only task for the court is to discover and apply it. Such a system assumes implicitly that prior cases are correct and that the existing order is intrinsically just. Indeed, any decision that departed from the existing rules would be erroneous.

Formalism also departed from late eighteenth-century Enlightenment philosophy in its refusal to embrace naturalism explicitly. The positivist revolution of the early nineteenth century had progressed far enough so that Langdell could not have credibly argued that judges could find law through the exercise of Cartesian reason. Rather, law was to be found empirically, by reading actual decisions of the courts. Nor did the U.S. Supreme Court of the late nineteenth century claim the power to invalidate legislation that conflicted with natural law not expressly codified in the Constitution.

Naturalism, however, did survive in the sense that nineteenth-century courts often interpreted the law against a backdrop of Enlightenment assumptions about the inherent "nature" of liberty or property. Formalism, in other words, inherited from naturalism a realist metaphysics. Formalist thinkers assumed that concepts such as liberty or property existed in the abstract and had an established content. Once a judge had determined that a particular concept was applicable to the case under consideration, that judge could reason deductively from the nature of the concept to determine the correct result.

III. The Critique of Formalism

From its inception, formalism was under attack by a small, but growing, number of legal scholars. The assault on formalism was a challenge to both its methodological assumptions and its political consequences. In the ensuing sections, the methodological critique and then the political critique of formalism are outlined.

A. *The Methodological Critique*

Formalism was a vulnerable target methodologically because the assumptions upon which it rested were cast into doubt by developments in science and philosophy. The same skepticism that had undercut religious faith at the dawn of the Enlightenment now corroded belief in the existence of discernible a priori categories.

The skepticism was both epistemological and metaphysical. The epistemological skepticism questioned the ability of humans to perceive reality accurately. The metaphysical skepticism questioned whether there was a reality to be perceived. More specifically, the empiricist strand of Enlightenment philosophy began to dominate the rationalist strand and then was itself called into question, while nominalism in metaphysics displaced realism. The collective effect was a claim that there are no a priori categories, but even if there were, we could not know them. This claim evolved in the mid-twentieth-century into the philosophical perspective generally known as postmodernism and seemed to bring the modern era in philosophy to a dead end.

The skeptical stance that culminated in postmodernism was not a sudden break with the past, but rather a continuation of a process of critical inquiry that had begun with the Renaissance, the Reformation, and the Scientific Revolution. In the eighteenth century, Immanuel Kant had challenged both the rationalist and the empiricist strands of Enlightenment epistemology. He agreed with the empiricists that reason alone can teach us nothing and that knowledge must come from sense experience. At the same time, sense impressions, unless organized by some kind of a priori categories, were meaningless, and thus empiricism alone was inadequate. The result was that humans could never know the world as it actually exists. They could know only appearances.

In the realm of science, Charles Darwin's *On the Origin of Species,* published in 1859, placed humanity within the animal kingdom, thus calling into question whether men possessed a privileged position from which they could rationally perceive the world. Within a few decades, Sigmund Freud began to explore the workings of the unconscious mind, further challenging man's claim to rationality and freedom. The emerging social sciences of the late nineteenth century and early twentieth centuries, particularly behaviorist psychology, sociology, and anthropology, treated human behavior as biologically, socially, and culturally determined rather than as the product of reason or free choice. Karl Marx in particular proposed an enormously influential theory of economic determinism, in which human behavior was shaped by changes in ownership of the means of production. All of these developments coalesced to create a vision of humanity as consisting not of autonomous, rational actors in the Cartesian tradition but merely of intelligent animals responding to their environment.

Developments in linguistic theory further undermined man's claim to rational thought. Ferdinand de Saussure, a leading nineteenth-century linguist, argued that words refer to other words, not to objects in the world.

That is, language is a closed, self-referential system, not a mechanism that exactly represents reality. By the mid-twentieth century, Edward Sapir and Benjamin Lee Whorf proposed their hypothesis that language actually determines an individual's perception of reality. That is, rather than inventing words to reflect objects in the world, people perceive the world in terms of the words they know. Thus, knowledge is shaped by language, which is a cultural phenomenon. The beginning of knowledge is not individual introspection, but collective inquiry, because we think in socially constructed categories.

The methodological critique also drew strength from a Romantic, historicist tradition that emerged during the early nineteenth century in reaction to the mechanical world view of the Enlightenment. Whereas Enlightenment liberals envisioned societies of rational individuals governed by timeless and universal law, the Romantics placed greater emphasis on the historical, contextual, and nonrational aspects of human life. Individuals were to be understood not as autonomous citizens of the world but as members of a nation formed by, and sharing in, the myths and beliefs the nation held at a particular time. The historicist tradition was reinforced by Darwin's work, which demonstrated the evolving and contextual nature of human existence.

In the early twentieth century, Newtonian physics, the cornerstone of the Enlightenment vision of the universe, came under attack. Albert Einstein's theory of relativity asserted that time moves at different rates for observers moving at different velocities. Einstein also found that matter and energy, which had been understood as the irreducible minima of the universe, in fact could be converted into each other and that even time and space were on a continuum. Werner Heisenberg's Uncertainty Principle asserted that, at least at the subatomic level, phenomena are changed by the act of being observed, and the quantum mechanics of Max Planck and Niels Bohr found that subatomic phenomena could best be described for some purposes as taking the form of a wave and for other purposes as taking the form of particles. The discovery that the movement of subatomic particles at best could be predicted only with degrees of probability suggested that if nature at its most elementary level was indeterminate, the search for certain knowledge was futile.

The effect of these developments was to cast into doubt the Enlightenment assumption that humans could understand ultimate reality by either the exercise of reason or empirical observation. Instead, all knowledge was perspectival or situational—the world was understood differently by human observers according to their circumstances. Thus, judges could not be completely objective or rational observers.

The metaphysical element of the critique of Enlightenment philosophy raised the question whether there was an ultimate reality to be perceived. Enlightenment metaphysics had rested on its epistemology, and with the epistemology under attack, the metaphysics collapsed. The nineteenth-century philosopher Friedrich Nietzsche declared that God was dead and that there were no facts, only interpretations. Late nineteenth-century pragmatist philosophers, most prominently William James and John Dewey, influenced by the consequentialism of utilitarianism and the contextualism of the historicists, abandoned the attempt to determine whether propositions were a priori true and measured the truth of an idea only by its consequences. Early twentieth-century anthropologists who conducted ethnographic studies of primitive societies found cultures functioning successfully based on widely varying moral beliefs, which suggested that ethical principles were culturally determined and did not have ontological existence. Again, twentieth-century relativity theory and quantum mechanics called into question whether there was a "true" characterization of any phenomenon. The logical positivists of early twentieth-century philosophy denied that there were any a priori categories.

Early twentieth-century thought, in short, seemed to dismiss the possibility of a meaningful metaphysics. There were no fixed truths to be known. Further, the claims of rationalism and empiricism having been debunked, there appeared to be no privileged means of knowing. For the postmodernists, then, there was only endless critique.

Postmodern philosophy ultimately produced two principal movements. The existentialists, such as Martin Heidegger and Jean-Paul Sartre, following Nietzsche, argued that in the absence of God or truth, men are free to be what they wish and that they must choose the principles on which to base their actions. Existentialism is sometimes characterized by the proposition that "existence precedes essence"—meaning that the only thing certain about man is his existence and that his nature, his essence, is established only through his own actions.

The linguistic analysts, following Ludwig Wittgenstein, attempted to reduce philosophy to the analysis of propositions. Questions of philosophy, they argued, resulted from misunderstandings of language. The task of the philosopher, then, was to analyze language and to resolve questions by correcting linguistic errors.

B. *The Political Critique*

Formalism was subject to a political critique based on disagreement with both the formalist vision of society and the political consequences of formalist legal theory. This critique held that formalism was out of step with reality and that it led to judicial decisions that were inconsistent with majority rule.

The problem with the formalist vision of society was that it denied the relevance of social hierarchy. By bringing all cases under a few general rules, formalism treated all people the same. Thus, for example, consumer contracts, employment contracts, and commercial contracts were all governed by a single body of contract law. A laborer negotiating with his employer was governed by the same rules as two merchants negotiating with each other. Inequalities in wealth, knowledge, or power were irrelevant.

The formalist vision drew on the liberal conception of society as an aggregation of rational, autonomous individuals. In the Lockean concept, all persons were born free and equal. With that premise, there was no justification for narrowly drawn and detailed laws that attempted to distinguish among persons based upon their individual circumstances.

The industrialization of America in the nineteenth century seemed to many to destroy the plausibility of the Lockean vision. At the end of the century, American society was characterized by gross inequities of wealth, power, and opportunity, to the disadvantage of workers, farmers, women, and racial and ethnic minorities.

Formalist judicial decisions, such as *Lochner v. New York*,[4] voiding New York's maximum hour law for bakers on the ground that it interfered with the bakers' liberty of contract, were attacked by progressives as hopelessly blind to social reality. Bakers were not, in fact, equally free with their employers to negotiate their contracts.

Much formalist jurisprudence was also criticized as simply inconsistent with majority sentiment and thus undemocratic. Justice Oliver Wendell Holmes, Jr., began his dissent in the *Lochner* case with the observation that "[t]his case is decided upon an economic theory which a large part of the country does not entertain."[5] The Great Depression that began in 1929 solidified a substantial electoral majority against the political consequences of formalism and ushered in the New Deal of President Franklin Delano Roosevelt. By the end of the New Deal, the progressive opponents of formalism constituted a consistent majority of the U.S. Supreme Court and the term "Lochnerism," referring to the New York bakers' case, had become a term of opprobrium.

IV. LEGAL REALISM

The methodological attack on formalism was led by Oliver Wendell Holmes, Jr., a lawyer, Harvard Law School professor, and justice of both the Massachusetts Supreme Judicial Court and the United States Supreme Court. His incisive critique of formalism led to its eventual demise and established for him a reputation as America's greatest legal philosopher.

---

[4] 198 U.S. 45 (1905).
[5] 198 U.S. at 75.

The shift to legal positivism in the early nineteenth century had represented a shift from law as a divine creation or a natural occurrence to law as a human creation. Holmes understood the consequences of this shift: As human creations, the conceptual categories of the law, such as property or liberty, were not self-defining, but manipulable and thus often incapable of determining results.

Holmes, in other words, denied the central premise of formalism: that abstract rules could be mechanically applied to decide individual disputes. He summarized his view in one of his most famous epigrams, written in *Lochner v. New York*,[6] in which he said that "[g]eneral propositions do not decide concrete cases."

Holmes believed that judges actually decide cases not by formal deduction from rules but by reference to policy considerations. As he explained in his 1881 book, *The Common Law*:

> The life of the law has not been logic: it has been experience. The felt necessities of the time, the prevalent moral and political theories, intuitions of public policy, avowed or unconscious, even the prejudices which judges share with their fellow-men, have had a good deal more to do than the syllogism in determining the rules by which men should be governed.[7]

Holmes's work thus mixed the historicist, pragmatist, and positivist themes in nineteenth-century thought. Law was not a fixed body of rules having ontological existence but the evolving product of historical circumstances.

Over the course of the next half-century, an increasingly large number of lawyers and judges came to accept Holmes's view that formalism did not describe the actual process of adjudication. Roscoe Pound, the dean of the Harvard Law School, founded a movement known as Sociological Jurisprudence, which he regarded as a movement for pragmatism as a philosophy of law. Pound insisted that judges be sensitive to the actual facts of the world, to the issue whether, for example, laborers were truly equal to their employers and thus able to bargain freely, and emphasized the ways in which law in action could differ from the law in books. He proposed that judicial decisions be made through the weighing of policy interests and referred to judges approvingly as social engineers.

By the 1920s, a new school of jurisprudence, known as Legal Realism, had developed around the attack on formalism.[8] The logical positivists of

---

[6] 198 U.S. 45, 76 (1905) (Holmes, J., dissenting).

[7] O. HOLMES, THE COMMON LAW 5 (Howe ed., 1963).

[8] Among the most prominent realists were Karl Llewellyn, Jerome Frank, Walter Wheeler Cook, Arthur Corbin, Hessel E. Yntema, Underhill Moore, Herman Oliphant, and William O. Douglas.

early twentieth-century philosophy asserted that only propositions that could be empirically verified were true. Truth was accessible through science. In much the same way, the Legal Realists of that era believed that social science could rescue law from the collapse of conceptualism.

In looking to science, the realists might at first be thought to share the methodology of the formalists. In fact, however, whereas Langdell had seen in science primarily the deductive rationalism of Descartes, the Legal Realists were drawn to empiricism. Thus, the move from formalism to Legal Realism represented an epistemological shift from a deductive science to a more empirical one. Science would reveal for the Legal Realists how the law actually operated in practice and thereby provide a basis for sound decisions.

Legal Realism also represented a shift in the metaphysics of American legal thought. Despite the name, realism in fact represented a move from the realist metaphysics that dominated the Enlightenment to a nominalist metaphysics. The Legal Realists saw legal concepts as merely empty labels placed on phenomena by individuals. The concept of property, for example, had no intrinsic content. To declare that some legal interest was property did not necessarily say anything in particular about that interest. One could not deduce any specific conclusion from the designation of the interest as property.[9]

Indeed, some of the best known work of the realists consisted of attempts to ridicule the formalists' reification of legal concepts. Felix Cohen, for example, wrote a much discussed article, "Transcendental Nonsense and the Functional Approach,"[10] in which he posed questions such as "Where is a corporation?" His point was that a corporation is a concept, not a thing; it does not exist anywhere. A court may choose for policy reasons to treat a corporation for some purpose as if it were "present" in a particular location. Such a result, however, is justified on the grounds that it is sound policy to treat the corporation as present in the jurisdiction, rather than because the corporation is actually there.

The skepticism about the determinacy of rules was accompanied by a reconceptualization of the categories of the law. The formalists had conceived of the law as creating sharply defined categories into which factual situations could be placed. Each category was associated with a specific legal consequence. Thus, the placement of a situation in a particular category determined the rights or duties applicable to that situation. Drawing upon developments in twentieth-century science, the realists no longer believed that the phenomena of the world fell into natural categories, such as

---

[9] *See* Vandevelde, *The New Property of the Nineteenth Century: The Development of the Modern Concept of Property,* 29 BUFF. L. REV. 325 (1981).

[10] 35 COLUM. L. REV. 809 (1935).

matter and energy or space and time. The dominant model of reality was no longer categories, but continua. Coercion and free will, for example, defined opposite poles of a continuum, not two mutually exclusive categories. Thus, facts did not fall into a category, but along a continuum. Legal reasoning was not a process of categorizing distinct phenomena, but rather of drawing lines to create distinctions among essentially indistinguishable phenomena. Such a process could not be mechanical in the way that formalism imagined adjudication; it necessarily involved the exercise of judgment.

Legal Realism was characterized not only by skepticism about the technique of formalism but also by a disagreement with the political views of the formalists. The realists were sympathetic with Franklin Roosevelt's New Deal. They favored a legal system that was much more willing to regulate commercial activity to protect the weaker members of society against the strong.

The realists challenged the efforts of the formalists to state legal rules at a high degree of generality. Even apart from the emptiness of the categories, the realists contended that because there were inequalities within society, for the law to treat everyone the same was in fact to give preference to the stronger. For example, to treat a worker and an employer simply as two equals engaged in freely negotiating the terms of an employment contract was to deny the reality that the worker may have had little true bargaining power. Realists were more likely to evaluate judicial decisions according to their actual effect on society, rather than according to their consistency with prior cases or abstract rules.

If the realists were correct and judges were not deciding cases by the mechanical application of rules, then formalism was simply a fiction used by judges to legitimate decisions based on their own political views. Because judges were not elected, that method of adjudication seemed undemocratic. Moreover, if the judges were not mechanically applying rules, then adjudication was not the uniform, predictable process that formalism had promised.

The realist critique of formalism was devastating. All of the virtues of formalism had rested on the assumption that rules could be applied mechanically. Yet, the realists were unable to articulate a new theory of adjudication that avoided resorting to the judge's individual policy preferences. To advocate that judges simply decide cases based on their personal preferences seemed profoundly inconsistent with American democratic theory, under which the people make the laws and judges merely apply them. The realists had destroyed formalism, but they could offer no entirely acceptable theory with which to replace it.

The realists generally favored certain techniques. They believed that the process of applying a rule required an examination of the policy or purpose behind the rule. Their preferred method of adjudication was a case-by-case balancing of policies in light of the facts of the particular case, with consideration given to how the rule would operate in practice. They disfavored grand statements of abstract rules. Such rules offered a false hope of predictability and obscured the true nature of the policy judgments that were required.

Some realists proposed the use of social science techniques to study the operation of the law in practice. Realist law professors launched ambitious empirical projects to study social behavior, the functioning of the legal system, and the relationship between the two. Yale Law Professor Underhill Moore, for example, studied parking and traffic patterns in New Haven, Connecticut, during the 1930s in an effort to determine the extent of compliance with municipal ordinances under various circumstances. The hope was that social science could replace formal rules as the basis for structuring legal rights and duties. Realists particularly favored legislative reform and codification of the common law to remove obscurity and to place the law firmly on the pillars of scientific research. Karl Llewellyn, for example, a leading realist, was the principal draftsman of the Uniform Commercial Code during the 1940s.

Legal Realism thus had both a critical and a constructive strand. The critical strand within the theory emphasized the indeterminacy of law and was directed at debunking the claims of formalism and proving that general concepts could not conclusively decide specific disputes. The constructive strand attempted to use emerging social science techniques to guide the work of legislatures and courts.

By and large, however, the social science studies undertaken by the realists did not seem to accomplish much. The results were often inconclusive or trivial. Further, it was never clear how the descriptive project of studying the law in practice could perform the normative task of determining what the law should be.

The most important legacy of realism was its claim that the law was indeterminate and thus adjudication was a matter of politics, not reason. This essentially epistemological claim, however, had a profound political implication. If judges were not governed by reason, then it seemed that the rule of law as traditionally understood was at an end.

V. POSTREALIST LEGAL THOUGHT

Legal philosophy in the second half of the twentieth century has been dominated by efforts to respond to the realist critique. In this section, the impact of realism on mainstream legal thought is considered, followed by a discussion of some of the principal responses of the legal academy to realism.

A. *Contemporary Mainstream Legal Reasoning*

The result of the realist critique is that mainstream legal reasoning at the end of the twentieth century is a sort of modified formalism. Most lawyers today are neither formalists nor realists. Formalism is too discredited to provide a complete philosophy of legal reasoning. At the same time, realism never developed a suitable substitute and thus never entirely displaced formalism as the dominant mode of legal reasoning.

As modified formalists, mainstream lawyers do not think all cases can be decided by the mechanical application of rules, but neither do they think adjudication is entirely unconstrained. Sometimes the rules dictate the results, and sometimes they do not. Lawyers speak of cases as being "easy" or "hard." An easy case is one in which it appears that a rule seems to determine the outcome. A hard case is one in which the rules do not seem to require one specific result.

Where a case is easy, lawyers generally expect that the rules can be applied in the essentially mechanical way contemplated by formalism. Where a case is hard, the rule is applied so as to further the policies underlying the rules.

The extent to which policy judgments are an acceptable basis for adjudication in the modern world is reflected in the willingness of courts to overrule prior decisions on policy grounds. Whereas formalism, at least in theory, had required that new decisions be reconciled with prior cases,[11] contemporary American legal thought permits judges to change a rule if public policy requires it.[12]

The justification for judicial power in mainstream legal thought rests on the assumption that law is determinate enough so that most transactions never give rise to a dispute, most disputes are resolved without adjudication, adjudication in most cases is constrained by the law, and the limited judicial discretion exercised in comparatively rare hard cases is simply a function of the unique role assigned by the Constitution to the courts. Thus, the power of the judge to decide the occasional dispute in which the law is silent or unclear does not delegitimate the entire legal system.

Jurisprudential debates among legal academicians in the postrealist era, however, have been dominated by one question: Is the resolution of legal disputes on policy grounds consistent with democratic government or is it

---

[11] Formalists acknowledged that prior cases could be disregarded if they were incorrectly decided. The premise, however, was that the court was merely correcting a mistake, not changing its mind.

[12] *See, e.g.,* Sindell v. Abbott Laboratories, 26 Cal. 3d 588, 163 Cal. Rptr. 132, 607 P.2d 924 (1980). Some courts, however, do continue to insist that significant changes to the common law be made only by the legislature. *See, e.g.,* Martin v. Trevino, 578 S.W.2d 763, 772–773 (Tex. Civ. App. 1978).

an illegitimate usurpation of power by unelected judges? One important result of this debate has been the rise of several different schools of thought concerning how to address the problem of legitimacy. Just as Legal Realism began as an academic discussion that found its way into mainstream legal practice, the work of these modern schools is certain to have an impact on legal practice in the future.

B. *Law and Economics*

One modern school that has been predominantly conservative in its political philosophy is known as the "law and economics" movement. The beginning of the movement is often traced to an article written in 1960 by Professor Ronald Coase of the University of Chicago.[13] By the mid-1970s, the movement had become an important force in American legal education.

The most influential proponent of law and economics theory is Richard Posner, formerly a professor at the University of Chicago and now a judge on the United States Court of Appeals for the Seventh Circuit. It is in part through Judge Posner's judicial opinions that law and economics theory has begun to influence the development of legal doctrine.

The early practitioners of law and economics theory believed that they had an approach that eliminated the indeterminacy of policy judgments. Their premise was that the legal system, rather than referring on an ad hoc basis to various individual policy preferences, should adopt the rule in every case that would lead to the most efficient use of economic resources. On the assumption that the free market leads to the most efficient use of resources, some law and economics work concluded that the law should compel the same result that would be reached by the operation of a free market if there were no transaction costs.

For example, a proponent of law and economics theory might oppose publicly funded lawyers for poor plaintiffs.[14] If the case has any merit, goes the argument, a lawyer will be found who will take it, even if only on a contingent fee basis. If the case does not have merit, then it should not be brought in the first place and most certainly should not be brought at taxpayers' expense. In other words, the operation of a free market will guide lawyers to the meritorious cases. By appointing lawyers, the state wastes resources on meritless cases, contrary to the policy of wealth maximization.

Adherents to law and economics theory claimed that the policy of efficiency provides the principled basis for adjudication that, as it had turned

---

[13] Coase, *The Problem of Social Cost*, 3 J. L. & Econ. 1 (1960).

[14] *See, e.g.,* McKeever v. Israel, 689 F.2d 1315, 1324–1325 (7th Cir. 1982) (Posner, J., dissenting). I am indebted for this example to Robin Paul Malloy, who refers to the McKeever case in his Law and Economics: A Comparative Approach to Theory and Practice (1990).

out, formalism could not. At the same time, the theory generally had the same promarket bias as late nineteenth-century formalism and classic liberal economic theory.

In addition to making the normative claim that the law should promote efficiency, law and economics theoreticians also made a number of descriptive claims. One of these was the claim that the common law in fact embraced the value of efficiency, and thus legal rules, if their effects were analyzed, would be found to promote efficient results. For example, under Judge Learned Hand's well-known formula,[15] the law of negligence imposes liability on those who fail to take precautions to prevent accidents when the cost of prevention is less than the potential liability, discounted by the probability that the loss will occur, while exonerating those who do not take precautions when the cost of prevention is greater than the probable loss. In this way, the law of negligence imposes liability on an actor only when that actor behaves inefficiently. Another descriptive claim was that people actually behave as rational maximizers of their individual economic well-being. Again, the link between law and economics and classic liberal theory is clear.

Criticisms of early law and economics theory centered on both its political orientation and its methodological assumptions. Progressive critics of law and economics theory disagreed that wealth maximization should be identified as the primary goal of the law. They favored a system that, at times, may seek other goals, such as compensating injured victims or protecting the vulnerable against the more powerful.

They also observed that efficiency, as an essentially utilitarian value, is destructive of individual rights. For example, a negligence rule that exculpates an actor who declined to prevent an injury because the cost of prevention was greater than the potential loss may conserve the resources of the society as a whole, but it leaves the victim with an uncompensated injury. That is, the society prospers, though at the expense of those who have the misfortune of suffering the injuries for which the negligence rule does not require compensation.

Even assuming that efficiency is the primary goal, these critics also questioned whether the market, in fact, is the most efficient allocator of resources. Market economics rests on a number of assumptions, such as the availability of information, the absence of transaction costs, and the absence of barriers to entry, that may not be true in practice. For example, an indigent with a meritorious legal claim may not be able to obtain a lawyer through the free market because lawyers may be both unaware of the claim and unable to learn about it without incurring prohibitive costs. Thus, deference to the market may not yield the results promised by market theory.

In fact, critics charged that much law and economics scholarship is based

---

[15] The Hand Formula is discussed in Chapter 9.

not on empirical research but on deductions from unexamined assumptions, such as the premise that humans seek to maximize their economic self-interest and the premise that everything can be valued monetarily. This critique sees law and economics as having more in common at times with Langdellian conceptualism than Legal Realist empiricism.

Critics also challenged the conservative political bias of law and economics theory. A system that values individual choices according to the dollar amount that an individual is willing to pay for that choice necessarily gives preference to those who have the most money and can pay the most for the satisfaction of their whims. And to the extent that one believes in the diminishing marginal utility of money,[16] then in a society where some have more money than others, dollars do not represent a uniform or constant method of valuation. In this view, law and economics theory uncritically reinforces the existing distribution of wealth by disproportionately valuing the preferences of the wealthy.

By the 1990s, these early criticisms of law and economics theory, in combination with a growth in the numbers and thus the diversity of practitioners of that theory, had resulted in a moderation of some of the claims made by the early theorists. Increasingly, proponents of law and economics theory no longer saw efficiency as the only or as the central value of the law, but as merely one of many values to be promoted. The value of law and economics theory in this view was that when efficiency was the preferred value, it could provide a scientific basis for selecting the best result, and when other values were preferred, it could show how those values could be promoted in the most efficient way.

In this later incarnation, law and economics theory has lost some of its profoundly conservative coloration. Once efficiency is deprived of its privileged status among values, law and economics theory seems predominantly a claim that judges should use social science, more specifically economics, as an aid to reaching decisions. That is, deprived of its normative claim, law and economics theory appears more than anything else to constitute a revival of the Legal Realist tradition, without the progressive political agenda. More specifically, law and economics theory shares with Legal Realism a belief that, with the death of formalism, law can be resurrected as a social science.

C. *Critical Legal Studies*

If law and economics theory now appears to be the principal heir to the constructive, social scientific strand of Legal Realism, the modern successor

---

[16] This is the thesis that each additional dollar received by someone is of less value to that person than each of the dollars previously earned, so that a rich woman places less value on a dollar than a poor woman.

to its critical strand and arguably the keeper of its progressive political flame is a movement called Critical Legal Studies (CLS), confined at this point almost entirely to law schools. Among the most influential members of the movement have been Harvard Law School Professors Duncan Kennedy, Roberto Unger, and Morton Horwitz.

The origin of CLS as a movement is generally traced to a conference organized in 1977 by Professor Kennedy and University of Wisconsin Law Professor David Trubek. The conference brought together a number of scholars whom the organizers believed were engaged in similar kinds of work. By the mid-1980s, enough former students of the leading CLS scholars had joined law faculties around the country for the movement to have become a major presence in American legal education. Even those who were not proponents of CLS often found themselves defining their position in opposition to CLS.

At its core, CLS seems to combine a skepticism about the determinacy of textual interpretation with a leftist political orientation. Defined this way, CLS appears almost indistinguishable from Legal Realism. Indeed, one is tempted to see it as a continuation of the realist critique of formalism by people who in many cases are farther to the left politically than were the New Deal realists. Such a view, however, overlooks the fact that the CLS movement emerged a full half-century after Legal Realism and thus shows to a much greater degree the impact of postmodernism on legal thought.

In the postmodern view, there are no foundational principles that permit the derivation of other assertions. That is, certain knowledge cannot be obtained either by deduction from intuited first principles or by empirical observation. The individual is not an autonomous, self-generating entity, but rather a social creation. Thus, there is no knowledge, only belief—and that belief is socially constructed.

Much of the work of the CLS movement involves an analysis of the premises underlying various legal rules in an effort to demonstrate that the rules are the product of choices between various sets of inherently conflicting and irreconcilable values. This approach, generally referred to as structuralism, is often traced to the work of twentieth-century anthropologist Claude Levi-Strauss, who believed that human understanding rests on "deep structures" of binary opposites. Each member of the pair can be understood only in reference to the other.

A structuralist analysis of the law begins with the premise that a court deciding any given case must choose between different outcomes, each of which is justified by one of the opposing values. Because the American legal system assumes the validity of both opposing values, a coherent argument can be made in favor of either result. To choose repeatedly the results that favored one of the values would completely negate the other value, a consequence to be avoided because the other value has an assumed validity. Thus, each case presents anew the question of which value is to be preferred in that instance.

The courts avoid both extremes, choosing one policy in most cases but never ruling out the possibility that the opposing policy may prevail in the next case. CLS scholars claim that a conservative, market-oriented ideology will prevail most of the time because of the political preferences of most judges in American society. The larger point, however, is that the choice of which ideology prevails is not dictated by a rule but is a matter of the ideological preferences of the judge who hears the case. Law, in other words, is not neutral, but political.

The CLS movement has also attempted to describe how judges write their opinions in a way that obscures the political nature of adjudication and attempts to justify the decision as consistent with, or even compelled by, widely shared principles of justice or sound policy. CLS scholars view legal doctrine as constituting an elaborate facade of legitimacy and inevitability that masks the political and contingent nature of judicial decisions.

The CLS analysis of legal texts often draws upon a technique associated with the French literary critic Jacques Derrida, known as deconstruction. To deconstruct a thesis is to show that the arguments in favor of that thesis can also support an alternative or even a contrary thesis. The technique of deconstruction, as applied to the law by the CLS movement, consists of identifying the policies that allegedly justified a particular rule and then demonstrating that those policies are equally consistent with a variety of other rules, including perhaps those that are antithetical to the original rule. The technique is thus based on a strong view of legal indeterminacy.

Consider, for example, a hypothetical rule that the sheriff cannot repossess on behalf of a merchant an appliance from a consumer for failure to make an installment payment without first giving the consumer notice and an opportunity for a hearing before a judge. A simple deconstruction of this rule might begin by noting that the policy behind the rule is to protect consumers against merchants with greater bargaining power who impose one-sided agreements on consumers. It would go on to point out, however, that the rule may well have the effect of causing merchants to refuse to sell on an installment basis to consumers who are particularly bad credit risks (and hence have the least bargaining power) or to raise the price of the goods for those same consumers to cover losses incurred as a result of nonpayment. In either event, the rule may ultimately make certain goods completely unavailable to the very consumers whose access to the goods the rule was intended to protect. The policy of protecting the consumer thus seems consistent with any of a number of different rules, including a rule that no notice or opportunity to be heard must be provided, the opposite of the rule that the policy seemed initially to justify.

The CLS movement is also defined by its leftist political orientation. Although CLS adherents do not share a detailed political program, in general the movement is characterized by egalitarian and communitarian ideals; some members would characterize themselves as socialists. For the most part, however, CLS scholarship is not much concerned with practical reform in the realm of law or politics.

As has been seen, the effect of demonstrating that courts produce rules based on political preferences is to undercut the legitimacy of the judicial process in a democracy. The CLS movement has attacked the legitimacy of current mainstream legal thought in order to pave the way for change to a more egalitarian society.[17]

Like the Legal Realist movement, however, the CLS movement has been much more successful at critiquing mainstream legal thought than at proposing a coherent theory to take its place. And, indeed, those CLS scholars who are most heavily influenced by postmodern thought, sometimes referred to collectively as the irrationalist strand of CLS, believe that the construction of a coherent theory is impossible. In this view, any theory that one might propose is subject to a deconstructive critique.

It is this absence of an affirmative program that gives rise to perhaps the most powerful criticism of the CLS movement. Its members are sometimes denounced as nihilists because they press on with their efforts to delegitimate the American legal system without having a clearly defined alternative.

Indeed, opponents contend that CLS proves both too little and too much. On the one hand, the CLS opponents say, the CLS movement has greatly overstated the indeterminacy of the law. These opponents contend that, in common experience, the courts are controlled by precedent far more often than the CLS movement is willing to admit, that legitimate adjudication has never required absolute certainty of result, and that the movement can be regarded as much ado about very little. On the other hand, CLS opponents argue, the withering deconstructive critique of the CLS movement undercuts its own political program by leaving no basis upon which to prefer the egalitarian or communitarian values of CLS over any other set of values.

Legal Realism was subject to similar criticisms—arguments that, on the one hand, its indeterminacy thesis was overstated, and that, on the other hand, Legal Realism was ultimately nihilist. The criticisms persisted and in the 1940s eventually helped to destroy Legal Realism as a movement.

Such criticisms, however, did not prevent Legal Realism from having an enormous impact on American law, although much of that impact was felt only after the ideologically compatible New Deal won success at the polls. And, since the death of the movement, many of its insights have survived as elements of mainstream legal thought, while much of its methodology has been resurrected by proponents of law and economics or Critical Legal Studies.

---

[17] Most members of the CLS movement are law professors. Criticism of legal doctrine and the legal system thus is also their professional avocation, and any specific piece of CLS work may not and need not have an obviously leftist political orientation.

CLS has yet to claim the success enjoyed by the Legal Realists. Although the CLS movement has produced a creative and stimulating body of legal scholarship, its impact on law practice in the conservative political climate of the late twentieth century is difficult to discern.

D. *Rights Theory*

Several legal scholars, often grouped together as "rights theorists," have resisted the nominalist metaphysics of postmodern legal thought. These theorists have attempted to identify a set of fundamental rights or widely shared principles that can provide a basis for resolving disputes.

The rights theorists represent a return to rationalism because they find these principles not through researching the actual views of the citizenry or the holdings of the courts, but through the use of intuition and deduction. These theorists also generally reject the utilitarian ethics that have dominated American law since the nineteenth century in favor of an ethic grounded on preserving individual rights.

Among the most influential rights theorists has been Professor John Rawls of Harvard. In his 1971 book, *A Theory of Justice,* Rawls attempted to discern the basic principles of justice by imagining a hypothetical situation in which the members of society were asked to choose the principles that should govern the society without knowing what their own abilities or advantages in that society would be. Rawls argued that the result would be a broadly egalitarian ethic that would attempt to neutralize all natural advantages with which people were born and create the maximum opportunity for everyone.

In many respects, Rawls's theory is reminiscent of the social contract theories developed during the Enlightenment by writers such as John Locke. Just as Locke imagined presocial man in a state of nature creating a government that would protect a person's property against the incursions of others, Rawls imagines people in an "original position" shrouded by a "veil of ignorance" about their own situation devising an egalitarian set of principles to protect their opportunity for advancement.

The rights theorist who has written most extensively on the problem of legal reasoning is Professor Ronald Dworkin of New York University and Oxford University. Much of Dworkin's work explicitly addresses the problem of legal reasoning. In his 1986 book, *Law's Empire,* Dworkin developed a concept of law as representing the value of integrity. Dworkin argues that a judge can find the one right answer in a dispute by a process that involves, first, finding those results that can be reconciled with the body of existing legal doctrine taken as a whole, and then, second, choosing from among these results that which places the law in the best light as a matter of political morality.

The rights theorists have provoked a rich debate in the legal academy. Their work is both epistemologically and ethically provocative. It is epistemologically provocative because it seeks to restore the sense that the law can be known, that reason is distinct from power, and that knowledge can be distinguished from politics. It is ethically provocative because it re-claims a place for the dignity and worth of the individual in a legal culture that has been predominantly utilitarian for at least one hundred and fifty years. Rights theory, in other words, attempts to reestablish a place for lib-eralism in contemporary legal thought.

In both its epistemology and its ethics, the work of the rights theorists cuts against the grain of postmodern thought. When Dworkin argues that disputes can have one right answer, he rejects the postmodern belief that all knowledge is a matter of perspective. And in placing the individual at the center of law, rights theorists reject the postmodern tendency to treat the group as prior to, and constitutive of, individuals.

Yet, despite the attention that they have received, the rights theorists have not had much measurable impact on the courts, nor have they inspired a school of jurisprudence comparable to that of the law and economics or CLS movements. In pursuing a more rationalist epistemology, the rights theorists have attempted to avoid the nominalism to which empiricism seemed to lead, but they have also abandoned the empiricists' goal of link-ing the pursuit of knowledge with human experience. Thus, although the work of the rights theorists may be persuasive to those who share their ini-tial assumptions, it has been generally unsuccessful in convincing other scholars that they must or should share those assumptions.

If Critical Legal Studies is a movement without a vision, rights theory seems to offer a vision without a movement. The promise of rights theory is attractive and the ambitious nature of the work of men like Rawls and Dworkin is impressive, but most remain unpersuaded that these theorists have adequately described how the world is or can be.

E. *Pragmatism*

Pragmatism began with the philosophy of Charles Sanders Pierce, William James, and John Dewey in the late nineteenth century. Pragmatism and legal reasoning theory met very early in the person of Oliver Wendell Holmes, Jr., who was a member of the Metaphysical Club, a group of intellectuals, in-cluding James, who gathered periodically in Boston during the late nine-teenth century to discuss philosophy. Holmes appears to have influenced James, and contemporary legal pragmatists often claim Holmes as their in-tellectual forebear. Pragmatism slipped into dormancy with the passing of James and Dewey but was revived in the 1980s by the work of philosopher Richard Rorty, sometimes under the rubric of neopragmatism.

Pragmatism, as it is understood at the end of the twentieth century, rests on two core themes: antifoundationalism and instrumentalism. The former it shares with postmodern thought generally, including Critical Legal Studies, and the latter it shares with law and economics.

Antifoundationalism is simply the postmodern belief that there are no a priori truths. All knowledge is really socially constructed belief, although members of the society may experience the belief as true and act upon it. And, because societies differ, knowledge is perspectival.

Pragmatism differs markedly from CLS, however, in the consequences for legal thought that it draws from antifoundationalism. Whereas CLS adherents take the position that postmodernism has destroyed the last vestiges of an objective basis for law and has thus revealed the utter subjectivity of judicial decisions, pragmatists regard the dichotomy of objective and subjective decisionmaking (as those terms traditionally are understood) as representing a false choice. That is, pragmatists seek an alternative to the view that law must be either objectively true or completely subjective.

One strand of pragmatism has found this alternative in the concept of an interpretative community, which builds on the philosophy of Ludwig Wittgenstein. Wittgenstein argued that no reality exists apart from our observations. Words thus do not correspond to Platonic essences; they have no core meanings. They are given meaning, however, by the community of people that interprets them. A word is not completely indeterminate because the shared assumptions of the interpretive community about the meaning of the word limit the range of ideas that the word can communicate.

The meaning of legal texts, such as statutes or judicial decisions, is thus constrained by the society that interprets them. Although legal texts may not have an objective meaning in the sense that they represent a Platonic essence or some idea having ontological existence, neither is their meaning to be ascertained subjectively. The ability of an interpretive community collectively to give meaning to a text undermines the claim that legal reasoning is subjective. The text may be said to have "objective" meaning in the sense that the meaning is socially rather than individually constructed; that is, meaning is not subjective, but intersubjective. This meaning, however, is a culturally relative one. A different society might interpret the text differently.

The pragmatist movement in the law, in other words, attempts to find some basis for constrained judicial decisionmaking in a postmodern world. It abandons the Enlightenment quest for objective certainty as a false start and an impossible task and thus is untroubled that legal reasoning cannot resolve disputes mechanically. The pragmatism movement has also attempted to offer the constructive program that CLS is said by its critics to lack and that some CLS adherents say is impossible to create.

It is in this constructive program that the second theme of pragmatism—instrumentalism—is particularly evident. Pragmatic instrumentalism is the belief that actions should be judged by their results, rather than being judged according to consistency with first principles. Pragmatists do not attempt to maintain consistency with respect to any single principle or value. Thus, a value that may be given great weight in determining what action to take in one context may be given far less weight in determining what action to take in another context.

Some pragmatist scholars trace their methodology to the Aristotelian concept of practical reasoning. Aristotle's theory was that one can determine the correct solution in particular cases without having a universal theory of what is true. No single principle always prevails; no single approach always suffices. Rather, cases are decided individually, by studying the consequences of each possible result.

In pragmatism, there is a real echo of the kind of policy science reflected in the law and economics movement. And, indeed, Richard Posner is now regarded as both the leading exponent of law and economics theory and a pragmatist. Where pragmatism parts ways, however, at least with early law and economics theory, is in its refusal to accept as privileged any single value or approach. A pragmatist may choose the most efficient result in one case and a less efficient one in the very next case.

Pragmatism also features a marked compatibility with the case-by-case decisionmaking process of the common law. Much as common law judges decide only the precise dispute before them and treat as nonbinding dictum any pronouncement not strictly necessary to the decision of the single case, so too do pragmatists solve problems one at a time rather than trying to construct a universal theory. In the pragmatic view, knowledge is to be gained through attempts to solve specific problems as they arise and not to be constructed as a systematic theory in a vacuum.

Although pragmatists believe that their methodology justifies the results they reach, they generally do not claim that it compels those results. That is, a pragmatist judge could explain the result reached in a case by listing the relevant policies and explaining how that result furthered each of the various policies. The process is not mechanical, however, and other judges might have found that the same considerations led them to a different result. To a pragmatist, the law cannot be said to require a specific result, but it can be said to constrain and justify decisionmaking.

Many pragmatists claim for themselves a progressive political agenda. They argue that pragmatism's refusal to treat any single principle as unassailable or privileged and its willingness to try different approaches in different situations provides a methodological basis for social change. They further argue that pragmatism's instrumentalism is forward looking and thus corrosive of authority, tradition, and the established order.

Like the other schools of judicial reasoning, pragmatism has its critics. Some critics argue that pragmatism's refusal to privilege any particular value undermines any claim that it is a progressive political force. Pragmatism, they contend, can equally accommodate a wide array of leftist, centrist, and rightist political ideologies, as indicated by the fact that prominent pragmatists include scholars with quite different political orientations. Indeed, because pragmatism rejects grand theories in favor of a case-by-case approach, some have argued that pragmatism is an inherently conservative movement that will inevitably reject radical change in favor of incremental and contextual tinkering.

The pragmatist methodology has also been subject to criticism. Some critics see in its antifoundationalism the same postmodern nihilism that they find in Critical Legal Studies. Antifoundationalism is said by others to be self-contradictory because to claim that there are no a priori truths is to assert an a priori truth. Some point out that pragmatism does not have, and would reject as unpragmatic, any general theory of how various considerations are to be deemed relevant to deciding which result in a case is to be preferred or even how the case itself is to be defined. From this perspective, pragmatism is not so much a theory as a willingness to admit that one has no theory.

VI. CONCLUSION

The question of the place of legal reasoning in the American legal system began as a problem of political philosophy. The liberal political theory of the Enlightenment posits that the purpose of government is to protect the liberty of the individual. The means by which this is to be accomplished is the rule of law. Law will limit the power of government and thereby guarantee individual liberty. Liberal political theory thus places upon the courts the task of deciding disputes in accordance with law.

To decide in accordance with law necessitates that the court first ascertain the law. The political project of subordinating government to the rule of law thus entails an epistemological task: to find the law.

Enlightenment epistemology, as has been seen, had two strands: rationalist and empiricist. Both, however, shared the Cartesian dualism between subjective individual consciousness and the objective world beyond that consciousness. On this premise, the task of adjudication in accordance with law was equated with deciding on objective, rather than subjective, grounds.

Enlightenment metaphysics was predominantly realist in 1776 and thus the postrevolutionary judge was assured that objective law did exist. In the late eighteenth century, realist metaphysics in law took the form of a belief in natural law. Natural law, which could be ascertained through reason, would control the judge and provide an objective basis for decision in accordance with law.

The empiricist strand of Enlightenment epistemology, however, began to cast doubt on the authenticity of a natural law discernible only through reason. Jacksonian democracy, moreover, called for a more consensus-based theory of law, one in which the law was found in the consent of the governed rather than through the exercise of intuition. The result was the displacement of naturalism by positivism.

The late nineteenth century produced a new synthesis under the rubric of formalism: Positive law could be found through a process of induction and could be applied to individual disputes through a process of deduction. That is, the law was now to be found empirically by examining the statutes and the cases. Legal reasoning was a science that, like physics or biology, enabled the judge to find the law. The realist metaphysics had shifted from a late eighteenth-century naturalism to a late nineteenth-century positivist conceptualism.

The skeptical empiricism that had undercut naturalism, however, also began to undermine conceptualism. By the end of the first one-third of the twentieth century, at least in the academy and on many appellate courts, the dominant metaphysics was nominalist: Legal concepts did not really exist; they were merely names attached to groups of particular cases that appeared from one perspective to share some common attribute.

Without a metaphysics, lawyers were left with only epistemology or method. Members of the new dominant movement, the Legal Realists (who were philosophical nominalists), sought to reconceive law as an empirical process. Lawyers and judges would study how the law functions in practice. Disputes would be decided in a way that would promote sound public policy.

From the beginning, however, the Enlightenment task had been to decide cases objectively rather than subjectively. If decisions were to be based on policy, then the Enlightenment project seemed to require that policy be objectively ascertained. The dilemma was to find an objective basis for judicial decisionmaking.

The history of legal reasoning in the late twentieth century is the story of the different responses to this dilemma. Four have been considered here.

The first response, which characterizes contemporary mainstream legal thought, is simply to refuse to acknowledge the victory of nominalism. Most disputes, it is argued, can be decided by finding principles in the prior cases and reasoning deductively from them. This may not be true in a few hard cases or occasional cases of first impression, but these are exceptional and do not undermine the legitimacy of the system as a whole.

The second response has been to seek in a putative public consensus an objective basis for policymaking. Although such an endeavor would seem obviously empirical, this approach by and large has involved a resurrection of rationalism. By a process of intuition and deduction, legal scholars have attempted to identify those policies or principles that would seem necessarily to inhere in our legal system and thus to be at least implicitly the product of broad popular consent. This approach has given rise to the rights theorists, who have sought to rescue liberalism from empiricism. It also describes the early work of the law and economics movement, which found in efficiency the fundamental, unassailable value needed to decide cases. Although their accomplishments are impressive as an intellectual exercise, the rights theorists have served more as departure points for critics than as sources of guidance for courts deciding cases. The law and economics movement has had somewhat more influence on the courts but to some extent has abandoned the claim that efficiency is a privileged, fundamental value.

The third response, which characterizes much of the Critical Legal Studies movement, is to concede completely the victory of nominalist metaphysics and to declare dead the search for an objective basis for adjudication. In this view, adjudication is inherently subjective, and the Enlightenment conception of law is a failure. Liberal individualism is doomed and must be replaced with a more communitarian or egalitarian theory. The content of this alternative theory, however, remains largely to be explained.

The fourth response, which characterizes the pragmatists, is to reject the Cartesian dualism of subject and object as presenting a false choice. In this view, Descartes was wrong to place the individual at the center of knowledge. Knowledge is socially constructed; the truth is what a community believes at a particular time. Truth is not objective in the sense of being eternally fixed, but neither is it subjective in the sense of being individually constructed.

In pragmatism, the Enlightenment epistemological and metaphysical framework is thus abandoned entirely. Pragmatists endeavor to find solutions to particular cases as they arise, without first constructing a Newtonian body of laws to govern all cases.

Pragmatism has much in common with contemporary mainstream legal thought. Mainstream legal thought is in many respects antitheoretical. Having lost formalism and being unable to embrace realism, it proceeds without a single coherent theory. It is formalist in easy cases and realist in hard cases, attempting to use the best of both theories and unable fully to adopt either.

Further, the policy judgments that are pervasive in late twentieth-century judicial decisions, especially in hard cases, are methodologically indistinguishable from the practical reasoning advocated by contemporary legal pragmatists. Pragmatism thus provides a philosophical position for policy scientists operating in a postmodern world.

Enlightenment philosophy, of course, had been employed by legal theorists in pursuit of liberal political ends. If the epistemology and metaphysics are wrong, then what of liberal individualism? If pragmatism refuses to accept any particular value as privileged, then does it adequately protect liberty? Pragmatism as an approach would seem to be capable of reconciling the resolution of a dispute with various quite different political ideologies, a thought that should not be particularly comforting to liberals—or communitarians, Social Democrats, or Conservatives. If the dilemmas of contemporary legal reasoning began as problems of political philosophy, that would seem to be precisely where they end.

7

Policy Analysis, Synthesis, and Application

In this chapter, a systematic understanding of the manner in which lawyers analyze, synthesize, and apply policies in the legal reasoning process is developed. In the first section, the way in which a rule can be analyzed as a compromise among various pairs of conflicting policies is described; the discussion then turns to some of the more pervasive policy conflicts in American law. The second section concerns one method by which the policies relevant to a particular situation can be synthesized by identifying the relationship that each policy bears to the others in that situation. In the third section, the manner in which policies are applied to decide particular disputes is explored, a topic that was introduced in Chapter 5.

I. POLICY ANALYSIS

A. *The Dilemma of Choosing Among Opposed Policies*

Every legal dispute poses a conflict between at least two opposing policies. In adopting a rule to govern the dispute, the court strikes a compromise between these policies.

Indeed, policy conflicts are built into the structure of the legal system. That is, the American legal system seeks to further a multitude of opposing policies all at the same time. Thus, for example, the system attempts to adhere to majority rule while also protecting individual rights; it strives to be just, but also efficient.

The system cannot give equal weight to all of these policies at the same time. If the majority decides that all persons at the age of eighteen shall be subject to military induction, a court faced with an individual who refuses military service because of religious beliefs must choose between majority rule and individual religious freedom. One policy must give way to the other in specific cases.

Yet, all of the policies are important, and few would advocate that any one policy should always prevail. Indeed, as is discussed in the next section of this chapter, the fundamental paradox of the American legal system is that to pursue any one policy to the exclusion of the opposing policies would ultimately be destructive of the ends represented by that very policy. The task of the court in resolving disputes is to decide, under a particular set of facts, which policy to prefer in that case and how to strike the compromise with the opposing policies.

Because each of the policies receives preference in some cases, any set of rules embraces opposing policies simultaneously. The typical experience of the lawyer in synthesizing a body of rules is that during synthesis a general rule will be identified that represents the triumph of one policy but that is both defined and limited by more specific rules that give preference to an opposing policy.

Thus, no rule ever fully resolves the conflict between the opposing policies. At best, it merely relocates the conflict to some issue presented at a lower level of generality. Although the rule on its face may seem to further a particular policy, each time the rule is defined or qualified, the original policy conflict reemerges and must be resolved anew.

The fact that legal rules are compromises between opposed policies forms the basis of the lawyer's intuition that there are two sides to every case. No matter which policies appear to support a particular position, there are always competing policies to which the courts, on at least some occasions, have given preference. Thus, any set of rules embraces at various levels of generality conflicting policies that support diametrically opposed results. The lawyer who can identify the various combinations of opposed policies underlying the rules will understand instantly the nature of the argument that can be made on each side of the case.

This is not to say that every case as a practical matter can be decided either way. In a given context, factors such as history, precedent, individual judicial preferences, and the specific facts of the case may combine in such a way as to leave only one plausible result. Even in that situation, however, the existence of competing policies permits the lawyer to articulate a perfectly coherent argument in favor of the losing side. Indeed, the losing argument may be one that in a different time would have prevailed or perhaps at one time did prevail, but in the current setting it is unpersuasive.

B. *Specific Policy Conflicts*

Policy analysis is the process of identifying which policies support each possible result in a particular dispute. That process requires an understanding of the principal policy conflicts that underlie American law. In the remainder of this section, a number of the more pervasive policy conflicts are introduced. They are described in relatively general terms here and will be illustrated in more concrete terms in Part III.

These policy conflicts are by no means exhaustive of those that lawyers must resolve. For example, many disputes in constitutional law pose a conflict between a policy of centralizing power in the federal government or decentralizing it in the states. This policy conflict, like many others, is not discussed here because the discussion is intended to demonstrate a methodology rather than to provide any kind of comprehensive survey.

The policies discussed here can be characterized in a variety of ways. Some are more general than others. For example, the policy of paternalism, discussed later, is a very general term that embraces more specific policies, such as consumer protection. Judicial opinions refer to the policies at different levels of generality and thus do not necessarily use the terminology employed here.[1]

1. The Individual and the Community

A first basic tension in American law is essentially political in nature and centers on whether to grant primacy to the individual or the community (or its representative, the state). This tension, no matter at what level of generality it is resolved, always seems to reemerge at a lower level of generality. Thus, the same tension reappears in different contexts throughout American law.

At its most general level, this tension raises the question whether the will of the state or the will of the individual is to prevail in a given situation. The conflict between the will of the state and the will of the individual is discussed herein as the conflict between majoritarianism and individualism.

Assume that a rule exists providing that, in a particular situation, the state must give effect to the will of the individual. Such a rule, however, does not fully resolve the question of primacy between the community and the individual; it merely relocates it. Although the rule states that the individual's will is to prevail, the question of primacy reemerges as the question of how to define the individual's will. Because an individual may be coerced by circumstances into choices that are not truly free, deference to the will of the individual may require the state to intervene to protect the individual against private domination. Thus, the tension between the community and the individual reemerges as a tension between the policy of state evaluation

---

[1] The terminology is my own. Because there is no developed body of scholarship on the nature of policy analysis, there is no established terminology.

of the circumstances of individual choice and the policy of presuming conclusively that individual choices represent the uncoerced will of that individual. This tension is discussed further on as the conflict between the policy of paternalism and the policy of autonomy.

Now assume that the rule provides that the will of the state, rather than the will of the individual, shall prevail in a particular situation. Again, this does not fully resolve the question of primacy between the community and the individual but only relocates it. Because the law has authorized the state to impose its will, the state must decide whether to exercise its will in favor of its own welfare or the rights of particular individuals. This tension might be characterized in a number of ways but is discussed later as the tension between efficiency and justice.

If the state chooses in a particular situation to seek justice, for example, that choice again merely relocates the tension between the community and the individual. The tension reemerges as a choice between a utilitarian theory of justice, which gives primacy to the welfare of the community, and a rights-based theory of justice, which gives primacy to the entitlements of the individual.

As this discussion illustrates, the tension between the community and the individual is never fully resolved. It constantly reemerges at different levels of generality as different cognate policy conflicts, with courts often preferring one policy at one level of generality and the opposing policy at another.

a. Individualism and Majoritarianism

The framers of the Constitution understood that they were constructing a government based on two opposing values: democracy (as we now use the term) and individual rights. Democracy requires that the will of the majority as represented by the decisions of the state be obeyed, but individual rights theory subordinates the will of the majority to the will of the individual. The court must decide in particular cases whether to embrace a policy of majoritarianism and defer to the will of the majority or to embrace an individualist policy and defer to the will of the individual.

The conflict between majoritarianism and individualism exists most obviously where the legislature enacts a statute on behalf of the majority. Assume, for example, that a legislature enacts a law prohibiting the advocacy of communism as a form of government and the law is challenged as a violation of the Constitution's guarantee of freedom of speech. A majoritarian court generally believes that the people have the power to punish speech that they consider injurious and is likely to uphold the law. An individualist court generally attempts to protect the right of individuals to express their political views and is likely to invalidate the law.

Because the common law is presumed to represent the popular will,[2] the conflict between majoritarianism and individualism also pervades common law adjudication. For example, under the legal doctrine of defamation, the court may force a speaker to compensate another individual whose reputation was injured by the speaker's remarks. The majority's wish to impose liability for defamatory comments thus conflicts with and prevails over the speaker's right to say what he believes.

One can distinguish between a policy of majoritarianism and the more specific policies in support of which the majority may exercise its will, just as one can distinguish between a policy of individualism and the more specific decisions made by a given individual. A majoritarian takes the position that the will of the majority should prevail, whether that will is to prohibit nudity at the beach, ban smoking in restaurants, or impose an implied warranty on the sale of a house. An individualist takes the position that the will of the individual should prevail, whether the individual wishes to criticize the president, agree to mine coal for $1 an hour, or practice animal sacrifice as a religious rite. Thus, the policies of majoritarianism and individualism may be linked in a particular situation with any of a countless number of other policies, ranging from the protection of the tobacco industry to the prevention of cruelty to animals.

American law does not consistently favor either majoritarianism or individualism. In some situations, one policy prevails, whereas in other situations the opposing policy does. The law of a particular community, for example, may allow smoking in a restaurant, but not nudity on the beach. Which policy prevails often depends upon the nature of the other policies with which each is linked in a particular situation. Thus, the lawyer can predict the choice between these two policies only within specific contexts.

If majority rule prevails in every case, then democracy will harden into the totalitarian state. If individual will prevails in every case, then the democratic society will collapse in anarchy. Majority rule and individual rights each act as a check on the other. The conflict between majoritarianism and individualism can never be fully resolved.

---

[2] As noted in Chapter 6, since the early nineteenth century the common law has been assumed to represent the popular will, even though it is made by judges rather than elected legislators. This assumption of popular consent is based on the fact that in many states the common law of England was accepted by a state constitutional provision or a legislative enactment and that in all states the legislature may change the common law at any time. One can readily question whether the common law truly represents the popular will. Given the power of special interest groups, the large sums needed to campaign for office, and other failures of the legislative process, however, one can raise the same question about enacted law.

Further, the policies of majoritarianism and individualism are so general that even the choice of one or the other in a particular situation may not resolve the dispute. For example, as is discussed in the next subsection, individual will may be defined in more than one way. The choice of individualism thus leaves the conflict unresolved, merely shifting it to the more specific issue of how to define the will of the individual.

b. Autonomy and Paternalism

Where the law seeks to give effect to the will of the individual, it confronts a choice between a policy of paternalism and a policy of autonomy. Under a policy of paternalism, the law protects the weak from domination by the strong. Under a policy of autonomy, the law avoids regulating individual choices.

The conflict between paternalism and autonomy is rooted in two competing views of the possibility of individual freedom. The policy of autonomy assumes that the government is the primary threat to individual freedom and thus holds that the law should facilitate rather than regulate individual choice. The policy of paternalism assumes that the primary threat to individual freedom is powerful individuals or private organizations that dominate others, whether for economic or other reasons, and thus the law should regulate private transactions to prevent domination and to ensure that individual exercises of will are truly free.

Assume, for example, that an illiterate man has purchased a refrigerator from a department store and has signed a finance agreement permitting the store, whenever it believes he has missed a payment, to repossess his refrigerator without prior notice. If the court prefers a policy of autonomy, it will probably conclude that the consumer freely signed the agreement without having someone read it to him and he should be bound by his choice. Indeed, continues the argument, invalidation of the repossession provision could force the store to adopt more expensive remedies, such as suing the consumer to obtain return of the refrigerator, thus raising the cost of doing business, a cost passed on to consumers. The store might even decide not to sell on an installment basis to individuals who are bad credit risks, thereby eliminating entirely their ability to purchase expensive appliances. In this view, refusal to enforce the contract would very likely lead to fewer choices for future consumers. The policy of autonomy, in other words, assumes that government interference in private arrangements is ultimately destructive of freedom.

If the court prefers a policy of paternalism, it will question whether the consumer freely chose a contractual arrangement that he did not understand. The court may also question whether he could realistically have found anyone who could have adequately explained the provision to him, whether any store would have sold him a refrigerator without such a term in the contract, and whether he had any real choice other than to sign the contract or forgo owning a refrigerator entirely. If the court enforces the provision, then all vendors will insert such provisions in their financing agreements. Thus, enforcing the agreement could effectively limit the freedom of consumers to obtain on favorable terms goods considered virtual necessities in the modern world. The policy of paternalism, in other words, assumes that real freedom requires the state to police private arrangements to ensure that those with less power are not coerced by circumstances into agreements to which no person with equal bargaining power would consent.

Private domination is a greater threat to individual freedom in some situations, whereas state coercion is a greater threat in others. The lawyer can thus predict the choice between paternalism and autonomy only in specific contexts.

The conflict between autonomy and paternalism, moreover, is persistent and can never be fully resolved. If autonomy were to prevail in every case, the court would enforce all private arrangements, including contracts induced with a gun to the head. The threatened party, having freely chosen to sign rather than die, should be held to the agreement. If paternalism were to prevail in every case, then no individual decision would be free from judicial intervention. Every transaction that resulted in disappointment or injury would lead to litigation over claims that the transaction was not the result of a truly free, informed choice.

Even where the choice between paternalism and autonomy is made in a particular situation, that choice may not resolve the dispute. The policies of paternalism and autonomy are so general that they may be indeterminate. For these policies to be determinate, one must have a relatively specific conception of what constitutes coercion or domination in a particular situation and what means would be effective in reducing or eliminating coercion or domination.

For example, assume that a woman complains to her employer about a male coworker who reads, at his desk during lunchtime, magazines that feature nude photographs of women. The supervisor then fires the male employee for sexually harassing the woman, whereupon the man sues the employer for wrongful termination and the woman for intentional interference with economic relations. A paternalistic court determined to intervene in the workplace to prevent private domination of the weak by the strong needs more than its commitment to paternalism to decide the dispute. It must decide whether the man, by reading the magazine, is forcing the woman to endure sexist denigration or whether the woman, by trying to stop the man from reading the magazine, is forcing him to defer to her vision of proper gender relations. Only by deciding what coercion means in this very specific situation can the paternalist court resolve the dispute.

c. Justice and Efficiency

Where the will of the state prevails, the conflict between primacy for the community and primacy for the individual is not completely resolved. The state must make a series of choices about the ends for which it will exercise its will, choices that resurrect the same conflict. Thus, for example, the conflict between the community and the individual often reemerges as a conflict between a policy of social efficiency and a policy of justice for the particular individuals involved in a transaction.

A good example of the conflict between justice and efficiency involves the procedural doctrine of res judicata. That doctrine precludes a party from relitigating a previously adjudicated claim against the same party. The doctrine prevents wasteful relitigation and thus is based on the policy of efficiency. It can lead to injustice in particular cases, however. Assume, for example, that a worker receives a slight burn injury as a result of his employer's negligence. The worker sues the employer and receives minor compensation. Ultimately, the burn does not heal properly, becomes cancerous, and causes severe injury.[3] Most people would probably agree that because the employer's negligence caused the injury, justice requires that the employer fully compensate the worker. Yet, the doctrine of res judicata precludes the worker from filing a new suit to recover additional compensation for the unforeseen severity of the injury. In that case, the policy of efficiency would prevail over the policy of justice.

If it is to retain the support of the people, the American legal system can never abandon its aspiration for justice. At the same time, a legal system that squanders its own resources and those of the society that it serves will lose the respect and support of that society and may ultimately impoverish itself to the point where it no longer can function. The legal system must be both just and efficient. The conflict between these policies can never be fully resolved. The lawyer can predict the choice between efficiency and justice only in specific contexts.

Even where the choice between efficiency and justice is made in a particular case, that choice does not necessarily resolve the dispute. The concepts of efficiency and justice are so general that they are often indeterminate. For example, a decision that the court will seek the most just result does not resolve the dispute because there are many different conceptions of justice. And in selecting a particular conception of justice, the lawyer will again confront the tension between the community and the individual. That is, as discussed in the next subsection, the desire to seek the just result shifts the tension to the more specific question of how to define justice.

---

[3] This example is based very loosely on the facts of Smith v. Leech Brain & Co., 2 Q.B. 405 (1962).

d. Rights Theory and Utilitarianism

Even where the state decides to pursue a policy of justice for the individual, the tension between the individual and the community remains unresolved. Rather, it reemerges as a conflict between rights-based theories of justice and utilitarian theories of justice.

Rights theory posits that individuals have certain rights that the law should protect and enforce because it is just to do so. A court that held a strong conception of individual rights, for example, might hold that the manufacturer of a product that injured a consumer must compensate the consumer because the consumer has a "right" to be free of physical injury caused by others. Rights theory can generally be traced to the natural law assumptions of Enlightenment thinkers like John Locke and has been reinforced by the deontological ethics of Immanuel Kant.

Utilitarianism generally posits that justice requires the result that affords the greatest happiness for the greatest number. That is, a just result is one that is beneficial for society as a whole, regardless of its impact on particular individuals. Utilitarianism is often traced to the work of Jeremy Bentham.

In utilitarianism, the importance or even the existence of individual rights is essentially denied. Under a utilitarian theory of justice, the court must do what is best for the community in general, even if that severely limits the rights of individuals. Individuals may be protected by utilitarianism, but only to the extent that their protection benefits the society as a whole.

The pursuit of the just result often poses a choice between a utilitarian theory of justice and a rights-based theory. For example, a motorist who is sued by a bicyclist for accidentally striking the bicyclist on a crowded city street may base the defense on having taken every reasonable precaution to avoid hitting the bicyclist, claiming therefore that the only way to guarantee the safety of the bicyclist would be to ban traffic from the streets, which would be injurious to the welfare of the society. The bicyclist may base the claim for compensation on a person's right to use the street free of injury caused by others. Thus, the motorist has adopted a utilitarian theory of justice, whereas the bicyclist relies on rights theory.

Even making the choice between these two theories of justice, however, often does not resolve the dispute. The concepts of rights and utility are both so general that they can be highly indeterminate.

Deciding that individuals have rights, for example, does not determine which rights they have. And, even assuming that there were broad agreement that people have certain rights—such as the right to property, the right to privacy, or the right to free speech—the nature of the rights must still be defined.

Defining rights as absolute is unworkable because two absolute rights will eventually conflict.[4] For example, a newspaper that wishes to publish the name of a rape victim who desires anonymity raises a conflict between the right of free speech and the right of privacy. If both rights are absolute, the case cannot be resolved. One or both rights must be limited in some way. But the simple statement that there is a right of free speech or a right of privacy provides no guidance as to how to limit the rights or which to prefer.

Because of the indeterminacy of the concept of rights, in many disputes the position of each party may be supported by a different conception of the nature of their respective rights. The musician, a man who wants to play the tuba in an apartment house late at night, will talk about his "right" to use his property, whereas the neighbor, a man who wishes to sleep at that hour, will talk about his "right" to peaceful enjoyment of his home. The court cannot decide the case merely by deciding that it wishes to protect individual rights. It must adopt a very particular conception of specific individual rights.

Utilitarianism poses a problem analogous to that of rights theory. The concept of the greatest happiness for the greatest number is so general that it can be highly indeterminate. To find the utilitarian result, one must first decide what forms of happiness are to be counted, how they are to be measured, and whether some forms are entitled to more weight than others. One person may believe, for example, that the greatest happiness for the greatest number requires closing down a factory that pollutes the air, whereas another person may believe that the greatest happiness for the greatest number requires permitting the factory, which employs a large segment of the community, to continue to operate. One needs to believe not merely in utilitarianism but in a particular conception of the greatest happiness before utilitarianism can be of assistance in resolving a dispute.

Individualism is a deeply rooted value in American society, and thus arguments based on individual rights have strong intuitive appeal. Indeed, most utilitarians at some level incorporate a notion of individual rights into their theory. For example, most utilitarians would probably recoil from a psychopath's argument that he should be allowed to murder a comatose patient because he would obtain great pleasure from the act, whereas the comatose patient would suffer nothing, and thus the murder would increase the aggregate happiness in society. In effect, utilitarians would regard individual rights, in this case the right of the patient to life, as setting some kind

---

[4] For a discussion of how the belief in absolute rights of property proved unworkable, *see* Vandevelde, *The New Property of the Nineteenth Century: The Development of the Modern Concept of Property*, 29 BUFF. L. REV. 325 (1981).

of limit on the application of the utilitarian calculus. At the same time, a complete rejection of utilitarianism in favor of individual rights could allow the single, unreasonable individual to undermine the welfare of the entire community.

Thus, utilitarianism tends to be limited in extreme cases by individual rights, and extreme assertions of individual rights are usually limited by some utilitarian calculus. Few, if any, of us would be prepared to accept either theory without some limitation from the other. The tension between these different theories of justice can never be fully resolved. The lawyer can predict the choice between these theories of justice only in specific contexts.

2. Positivism and Naturalism

A second basic tension in American law, between positivism and naturalism, is essentially metaphysical. This tension occurs between two different conceptions of the source and nature of law, each of which justifies a series of specific policy choices. The following discussion concerns the general conflict between these two theories, while alluding to some of the policy choices associated with a positivist or naturalist theory of law.

Naturalism generally holds that universal laws exist that are applicable to all persons at all times and that these laws are based on the will of God or the nature of the universe. Naturalism is often traced to the Stoic philosophers of ancient Greece, who found natural law through reason. In the medieval period, Catholic theologians found the source of natural law in the will of God, which was revealed through the scriptures. The religious skepticism triggered by the Renaissance, the Reformation, and the Scientific Revolution shifted naturalism back to secular grounds so that by the time of the eighteenth-century Enlightenment, naturalists referred more often to reason than revelation for the source of law.

Naturalists generally take the position that human laws inconsistent with natural law are not truly law. Naturalism was an important element of American legal thought at the time of the Revolution, and in the early years of the republic, courts claimed the right to void legislation that was inconsistent with natural law.

Positivism regards law as the command of a sovereign. Law is thus the creation of human society; it is not the product of God's will or inherent in nature. Positivism is commonly traced to the work of Jeremy Bentham and John Austin in the eighteenth and nineteenth centuries and is represented in the twentieth century by the work of H.L.A. Hart.

As discussed in Chapter 6, positivism displaced naturalism as the dominant theory of law in the United States during the early nineteenth century, thus bringing an end to the practice of voiding legislation that was inconsistent with unwritten natural law. Because sovereignty in the United States resides in the people, positivism seemed more consistent with democratic theory than naturalism, which found the source of law outside the will of the people.

Positivism has never entirely displaced naturalism, however. First, positivism seems an incomplete theory of law because it does not explain why the will of the majority should prevail. For that, one must resort to a naturalist explanation, such as the explanation that it is in the nature of things that the majority should rule or that democracy is the only morally just form of government. Thus, the legitimacy of positive law seems to rest ultimately on naturalist assumptions. The result is that positivist justifications of a particular rule or result inevitably lead back to naturalism.

Second, because positivism looks only to the commands of the sovereign, it seems not to provide an adequate basis for deciding disputes when the sovereign is silent or unclear. Naturalism thus offers a source of guidance when, as often occurs, positive law is indeterminate. For example, a court attempting to interpret a vague statute may interpret the statute in a way that seems reasonable or just. In so doing, the court has eschewed an interpretation based on the will of the people and found one based on natural law.

Third, because positive law in the United States is based on popular consensus, it may be inconsistent with deeply held notions of justice. As this suggests, courts have adopted various rules that permit them to invoke naturalist considerations to override positive law in certain cases. For example, assume that the legislature enacted a statute providing that the beneficiary of a life insurance policy may sue the insurance company directly to enforce the policy. Subsequently, the beneficiary of a policy murders the insured and sues to collect the proceeds. Although the language of the statute may direct the court to order payment of the proceeds to the beneficiary, most would find that result reprehensible. A court would likely refuse to reach the result, despite the clear language, perhaps invoking a rule that allows it to interpret statutes so as to avoid manifestly unjust or absurd results.[5] Naturalism thus provides a moral basis for evaluating the content of positive law.

Naturalism, then, coexists with positivism, providing the theoretical underpinnings for positivism, supplementing positive law where it seems inadequate to resolve a dispute and, in extreme cases, countermanding the results required by positivism. Positive law, without naturalism, seems undesirable, if not theoretically impossible.

At the same time, naturalism can never displace positivism entirely. First, as noted above, the idea that law is based on any source other than the will of the people seems to many profoundly undemocratic.

---

[5] This example is based on the facts of Slocum v. Metropolitan Life Ins. Co., 245 Mass. 565 (1932), discussed in H. HART & A. SACKS, THE LEGAL PROCESS: BASIC PROBLEMS IN THE MAKING AND APPLICATION OF LAW 76 (1994).

Second, natural law as unwritten law introduces tremendous discretion and indeterminacy into the legal system. Without an authoritative codification of the tenets of natural law, naturalism threatens to undermine the uniformity and predictability of the law. To the extent that a judge may confuse his or her personal preferences with divine revelation or the dictates of reason, naturalism undercuts the rule of law.

Third, much law in the modern world governs mundane, trivial matters that could be regulated in any of a number of ways. It is simply implausible that the thousands of minute regulations applicable to daily life are rooted in God's will or the nature of the universe. Naturalism thus provides an unconvincing justification for the content of much of contemporary law.

For these reasons, American law contains strands of both positivism and naturalism. The court must determine in specific situations which issues to resolve in accordance with rules adopted by the sovereign and which to resolve with reference to naturalist notions of justice or reasonableness. The tension between naturalism and positivism can never be fully resolved. It reemerges throughout American law in different contexts and at different levels of generality.

3. Instrumentalism and Formalism

a. In General

A third basic tension in American law, between formalism and instrumentalism, is essentially epistemological. Formalism and instrumentalism are competing theories about the way in which courts ascertain the law, that is, about the nature of adjudication. Each of these theories entails a number of more specific policy choices.

Formalism conceives of adjudication as the mechanical application of general rules to particular situations. Formal rules specify facts that give rise to rights or duties. Application of the rules consists of an examination of the evidence to determine whether the specified facts are present.

Formalists believe that the formulation of law as a set of rules brings uniformity and predictability to the law. Predictable rules put everyone on notice about their rights and duties, one aspect of justice, and permit the parties to rely on a stable legal regime, another dimension of justice, reflected in the popular notion that it is unfair to change the rules in the middle of the game. By permitting individuals to anticipate how the law will apply, rules facilitate the making of enforceable private arrangements necessary to a modern market economy. At the same time, they simplify the adjudication of disputes, thus leading to a more efficient judicial system. Indeed, by allowing parties to predict which claims are likely to be successful, rules discourage frivolous, wasteful litigation. Uniform rules treat like cases alike, another aspect of justice.

Formalists endeavor to state rules at the highest possible level of generality. The more general the rules, the more cases they embrace and the greater the uniformity of application.

Instrumentalism conceives of adjudication as deciding a dispute in the way that will further the relevant policies. Under this view, a rule must always be interpreted so as to effectuate the underlying policies. If a literal reading of the terms of the rule would not serve those policies, the terms should be read more broadly. Additionally, implicit terms might be inserted in the course of interpretation under the theory that these terms must be treated as present if the rule is to promote the policies that led to its adoption.

One question facing the instrumentalist is the source of the underlying policies. Naturalism and positivism offer theories about the source of the law, and instrumentalism has been associated with both. Theories of interpretation that look to the intent of the framers of a law, for example, are essentially instrumentalist and positivist, because they attempt to effectuate the policy behind the law and find that policy in the will of the sovereign. Theories of interpretation that apply a law in a way that is just or reasonable are instrumentalist and naturalist.

Instrumentalists sometimes prefer to express the intention of the court or legislature with flexible standards, such as "good faith" or "reasonableness," which then must be applied to the facts of each individual case. Such standards differ from rigid rules in that they do not specify all of the facts necessary or sufficient to create a right or duty. Rather, they characterize the facts that will produce the legal consequence and leave it to the court to determine which facts satisfy that characterization in a particular situation.

Instrumentalists do not claim that their approach to adjudication produces the same degree of uniformity or predictability that formalism does but argue instead that much of the predictability attributed to formal rules is illusory in any event because the language of the rules is often indeterminate. Indeed, they argue that the formalist penchant for generality produces indeterminacy. The more general the rule, the less determinate it is.

As for the uniformity associated with formalism, instrumentalists argue that it is often undesirable. They claim that flexible standards are more likely to yield the most just result in particular cases. Rules are likely to be overinclusive or underinclusive. That is, a rule may be overinclusive in applying to situations where that result is not demanded by the policy underlying the rule. It may be underinclusive in failing to apply to situations where the policy underlying the rule requires that it apply. Overinclusive rules are undesirable because they limit freedom unnecessarily, whereas underinclusive rules are undesirable because they fail to solve fully the problem that they are intended to address. Rules are inevitably overinclusive or underinclusive because of the difficulty of crafting a rule that anticipates every circumstance that will arise and of finding words that precisely correspond to the exact situations in which the rule should apply. Further, the more general the rule, the more likely it is to be overinclusive or underinclusive.

Thus, the instrumentalist contends that the formalist effort to formulate law in terms of general rules is inherently flawed because it nearly always leads to disjunctions between the language and the policy of the law. Flexible standards permit the court to take account of special circumstances not contemplated by a more rigid rule and thus avoid overinclusiveness or underinclusiviness.

The difference between formalism and instrumentalism may be illustrated by a hypothetical rule that requires all persons to walk on the left side of the road.[6] Formalism would require that the rule be applied so as to find that one who walked on the right side was in violation of the rule, regardless of the reason. In this way, all persons are treated uniformly and everyone can act on the assumption that pedestrians will walk on the left side of the road. If a pedestrian is found on the right side of the road, the court can determine without a difficult inquiry that the pedestrian was a wrongdoer.

A problem arises, however, in the case in which traffic is extremely heavy on the left side of the road and very light on the right, with the result that it is actually safer to walk on the side prohibited by the rule. The rule is overinclusive because it requires walking on the left side of the road when the policy underlying the rule, public safety, does not demand that result.

The formalist position is that to allow the pedestrian to deviate from the letter of the rule would defeat the advantages of a uniform and predictable rule. The instrumentalist position, by contrast, is that it is absurd for a so-called safety rule to require the pedestrian to take the unsafe action and to punish the pedestrian for furthering the policy underlying the rule. It is for this reason that instrumentalists often formulate the law as a flexible standard rather than a rigid rule. For example, an instrumentalist might propose that the law be reformulated as a standard that requires all pedestrians simply to walk safely. Thus, the pedestrian could always act so as to promote the policy behind the law, whether that meant walking on the left or the right side of the road.

Such a flexible standard, unlike a rigid rule, does not prescribe the exact facts under which a right or duty arises but permits the court to consider any facts relevant to the underlying policy of safety. By allowing the court to take account of special circumstances, standards permit a just result in particular cases. Standards may make it more difficult, however, for motorists to anticipate the side of the street on which pedestrians will be walking and

---

[6] This example is suggested by the cases of Martin v. Herzog, 228 N.Y. 164, 126 N.E. 814 (1920) and Tedla v. Ellman, 280 N.Y. 124, 19 N.E.2d 987 (1939).

for pedestrians to determine on which side of the street the law requires them to walk. It also requires a more complex inquiry to determine whether the pedestrian was acting in accordance with the law than in the case of a rigid rule. Thus, standards may lead to the perception that the law is neither uniform nor predictable.

If formalism is subject to the charge that rigid rules are overinclusive and underinclusive, instrumentalism is subject to the opposite criticism: that it undermines uniformity and predictability in the law, permitting judges to decide cases in accordance with personal preferences, rather than as prescribed by law. Thus, instrumentalism is said to effect injustice by departing from the norm of equal justice under the law and by defeating the parties' reliance on a stable legal regime. Its unpredictability discourages investment, increases transaction costs, and encourages litigation, all of which result in the inefficient use of resources.

Formalists tend to respond to problems of overinclusiveness or underinclusiveness—to situations in which the language and policy of a rule are not coextensive—in several different ways. One is to generate a series of subrules creating exceptions to the general rule. For example, the rule requiring pedestrians to walk on the left side of the street could include an exception for rush hour, when there may be heavy traffic in one direction and light traffic in the other. The creation of an exception, however, undercuts any claim that the rule must remain absolute and leads to demands that other exceptions be created to address other problems of overinclusiveness or underinclusivness. The endless proliferation of exceptions undermines the predictability of the rule because people can then never be certain when a new exception may be created and because, as the structure of rules becomes more complex, the probability that someone will misunderstand the complex edifice or that the elaborate structure will create unintended gaps or conflicts becomes greater. The existence of numerous exceptions also prevents uniformity in the application of the rule.

Further, the exceptions themselves will be overinclusive or underinclusive, with the result that the problems created by the general rule are merely shifted to the subrule. For example, the exception for rush hour traffic would be overinclusive on holidays, when traffic does not follow the usual rush hour pattern. One could create an exception to the exception for holidays, but certain holidays are not widely observed and other days that are not legal holidays may be observed by large numbers of people, with the result that the exception to the exception could itself be overinclusive or underinclusive.

As the exceptions and qualifications proliferate, the advantages of formalism are lost. That is, a body of rules that seeks to address narrower and narrower categories of cases begins to take on the characteristics of an instrumentalist approach—rejecting predictability and uniformity in favor of reaching the correct result in each particular case. Indeed, if the body of rules becomes too complex and detailed, there may ultimately be a reaction leading to the abandonment of the entire structure in favor of a single standard that, like the complex body of rules, permits the best result in each case.

Another way to address the disjunction between the language and policy of the rule is to interpret the rule so that it does not apply in the way that most people would expect. This prevents the rule from defeating the underlying policy, but it undercuts the predictability and the uniformity of the rule by disregarding its plain meaning and breeds cynicism about a legal system that appears to manipulate rules.

In the end, the core formalist position is that rules are defensible if they yield the best result in most cases. Some degree of overinclusiveness and underinclusiveness, although regrettable, is justified by the uniformity and predictability attributable to rules. In contrast, instrumentalists seek to obtain the best result in every case, even at the cost of uniformity and predictability.

Formalists, then, organize phenomena in broad categories, the members of which are subject to general rules. That is, formalists seek to universalize phenomena, to regard each situation as representative of a general type, requiring that it be treated like situations of the same type.

Instrumentalists, by contrast, place phenomena in categories of one. That is, they seek to particularize phenomena, to regard each situation as unique, requiring that it be treated individually in the way that will further the relevant policies. Inasmuch as they regard situations as unique, instrumentalists may conceptualize situations as falling along a continuum rather than into large, sharply defined categories.

Because of its abstraction and the accompanying tendency toward overinclusiveness and underinclusiveness, formalist reasoning is often criticized as both artificial and superficial.

The artificiality is attributable to formalism's divorce from policy, such that in extreme cases its rules or categories may serve little purpose other than their own existence. Thus, distinctions are sometimes referred to as formal when they seem unrelated to furthering any relevant policy. Or, lawyers will refer to some act or situation as existing in form (but not substance) when the mechanical rules defining the act or situation have been complied with, but the policy that attaches significance to the act or situation has not been furthered.

For example, assume that a governor signs legislation by mistake, believing that the bill is a different piece of legislation. A lawyer might characterize the governor's approval as formal because the governor complied with all the mechanical requirements for approval, although the policy that justifies requiring the governor's approval (the policy that a bill should not become law unless both elected branches of the government concur) was not furthered by the signature. Lawyers will say, in such a circumstance, that to give effect to the governor's signature is to exalt form over substance, which means to apply the rules without regard to the underlying policies.

The superficiality of formalism is attributable to its level of abstraction, such that legal consequences turn on fewer and fewer facts and thus may be divorced from reality. For example, the concept of equality is sometimes referred to as formal equality when the persons in question are equal in only superficial ways, as where a rich man and a poor man are said to be equal in a court of law. At its extreme, formalism may ultimately produce a regime of law separated from values or facts, consisting merely of self-referential rules and categories that are neither good nor true.

Instrumentalism, because of its unstructured examination of consequences, is often criticized as a political rather than a legal method of reasoning. At its extreme, instrumentalism produces a series of ad hoc decisions that seem merely to accomplish the purposes of the individual decisionmaker. The distinction between adjudication and legislation vanishes, and with it, the concept of the rule of law.

Whereas formalists must address the over- and underinclusiveness of rigid rules, instrumentalists must address the unpredictability and ad hoc nature of flexible standards or policy-driven interpretations of rules. Instrumentalists often attempt to bring some degree of uniformity and predictability to adjudication by developing sets of presumptions or maxims that reflect the manner in which past cases have been decided and that provide some guidance to the lawyer. As these presumptions and maxims proliferate and are applied with some frequency, they may begin to take on the character of rules—becoming more conclusive and hence more rigid in their application. Thus, just as formalism's need to avoid over- and underinclusiveness may push it toward instrumentalism, instrumentalism's need to provide uniformity and predictability may push it toward formalism. Neither theory alone seems to offer a completely adequate method of adjudication.

Formalism is associated with objectivist theories of intrepretation, whereas instrumentalism is associated with subjectivist theories. Objectivists interpret a rule or situation from the perspective of some generalized or ideal person, whereas subjectivists interpret it from the perspective of actual, particular individuals. That is, objectivists (like formalists) generalize phenomema, and subjectivists (like instrumentalists) particularize it. Thus, for example, an objectivist would interpret a word in a contract from the perspective of a hypothetical "reasonable person," whereas a subjectivist would interpret the word from the perspective of the particular parties to the contract.

The arguments for and against objectivism and subjectivism thus mirror the arguments for and against formalism and instrumentalism. Objectivism provides uniformity and predictability but may be over- or underinclusive, whereas subjectivism presents the opposite situation.

Although formalism is associated with rules and objectivism and instrumentalism is associated with standards and subjectivism, in practice these different theories or approaches may appear in a variety of permutations. Formalism, like rules and objectivism, seeks to universalize phenomena, whereas instrumentalism has in common with standards and subjectivism the aim to particularize phenomena. The same desire for uniformity and predictability that pushes the law toward formalism also pushes it toward rules and objectivism, and the same desire for the correct result in each case that pushes the law toward instrumentalism also pushes it toward standards and subjectivism.

Yet, just as the law alternates between giving primacy to the community and giving it to the individual and alternates between naturalism and positivism in different contexts and at different levels of generality, so too it vacillates between approaches associated with formalism and those associated with instrumentalism in different contexts and at different levels of generality. Rigid rules may be qualified by subrules that incorporate flexible standards. Standards may be defined by objective tests in some situations and by subjective tests in others. The policy conflicts associated with formalism and instrumentalism are never fully resolved.

b. Application to Statutory Interpretation

The tension between formalism and instrumentalism has been of particular significance in the development of theories of statutory interpretation. Formalism is generally associated with a textualist theory of interpretation, that is, interpretation by examination of the text alone.

The use of a textualist theory of interpretation is defended on the ground that the text of a law is all that was adopted by the drafter. In this view, attempts to discern some underlying intent are speculative and permit the interpreter to introduce personal preferences under the guise of enforcing the underlying intent. Because it links interpretation to concrete language on a page, textualism is often regarded as the most certain method of interpretation. Textualist interpretations also ensure that those to whom the law applies will not be penalized for having relied on the law's apparent meaning.

Textualism is criticized on the ground that the pure language of a rule is often, if not always, indeterminate and that interpretation is not possible without making at least some minimal assumptions about the underlying policy of the law. Thus, the critique continues, the certainty of textualist interpretations is an illusion that masks the fact that the court has supplied meaning to the terms of the text. Textualism may limit the range of possible interpretations, but it cannot assist in choosing among those that are permissible. Textualism thus does not provide a complete theory of interpretation. Some recourse to nontextualist theories of interpretation must be made in at least some cases.

Textualism nevertheless currently appears to enjoy a greater degree of legitimacy among courts than other theories. Courts commonly begin their interpretation of a statute with its text, and a much cited rule states that if the meaning of the text is clear, the interpretation of the statute is at an end. Even when a court relies on nontextual sources, it often minimizes the role of those sources or treats them as merely confirming the text.

Instrumentalism is generally associated with a number of different theories of interpretation, which are distinguished by the source of the underlying policy. These theories are identified here as intentionalism, purposivism, and nonoriginalism.

Intentionalism, the theory that a statute should be interpreted so as to further the intent of the drafters, is subject to a number of criticisms. First, there is the problem of determining the actual intent of a lawmaker who may have explicitly adopted only the words of the statute. Intentionalist interpretations usually require examining the history of a law in an attempt to infer the intent from the circumstances of its enactment. The problem of inferring intent is compounded by the fact that the statute was probably a compromise among conflicting interests and thus among competing intents. Some legislators may have had no intent at all, only motives, such as getting reelected or repaying a favor from another legislator. Other legislators may have voted for a law that they opposed, hoping to avoid enactment of a more extreme measure or, if this law was the extreme measure, hoping to prompt a popular backlash or constitutional challenge that a less extreme measure would not have triggered. The history may be partial, because complete records of every relevant incident leading to enactment of the law do not exist, or it may be misleading, because some expressions of legislative intent may have represented the position of only a few of those voting on the statute. The record may be silent because the issue was not anticipated (and thus the drafters had no intent with respect to it) or because the only way to obtain a consensus was to remain deliberately vague about the statute's intended effect. And, of course, under even ideal circumstances, all historical accounts are shaped by the perspective of the historian.

Because of these difficulties, some instrumentalists proposed a purposivist theory of interpretation in which a law is interpreted so as to promote its ostensible purpose. Purposivism is distinguished from intentionalism in that purposivism avoids inquiry into the minds of the drafters and looks at the apparent object of the law. For example, the purposivist may ask simply what the mischief was that existed when the law was adopted, on the assumption that the purpose of the law was to remedy the mischief. In a sense, purposivism is an objectivist theory of intent, whereas intentionalism is a subjectivist theory. The purposivist eschews all the difficult empirical questions that arise concerning the actual thoughts of the legislators and looks simply at the language and setting of the law to determine the purpose it appears to serve.

Purposivism, too, has been subject to criticism, however. By divorcing interpretation from the actual intent of the framers, purposivism seems to license the interpreter to infer almost any purpose that can be reconciled with the language of the statute. Moreover, the broader the range of circumstances from which the interpreter may infer purpose, the less constraining purposivist interpretation is. At the same time, if purposivism seeks to constrain interpretation by limiting the range of circumstances from which the purpose may be inferred to the text of the law, then purposivism seems to add very little to textualism. That is, under a text–bound version of purposivism, the interpreter will infer that the purpose of the statute is to do whatever it is that the statute appears to do. Determining what the statute does, however, is the very issue to be resolved. Thus, in using the language of the statute to determine its purpose, one ends up where one began: with the language of the statute.

Purposivism is also flawed in its assumption that a law has a single purpose or a set of consistent purposes. In fact, statutes represent compromises among multiple conflicting purposes. In applying a statute, a court must decide which of these purposes to further at the expense of the others. Given that the statute was drafted, however, so as to accomplish all of the purposes in some measure, the court has no basis on which to decide to what extent one of the purposes shall prevail over the others in future applications of the statute to unforeseen circumstances.

Nonoriginalism is a theory of interpretation that draws its name from the fact that it does not rely on the original intent or purpose behind the law. Rather, it interprets a rule in accordance with some other source of policy, such as contemporary community values. The merit of nonoriginalism is that it avoids all of the empirical problems associated with attempting to identify an authentic intent or purpose underlying a law.

Nonoriginalism, however, is perhaps the least legitimate method of interpretation in the minds of contemporary judges. The principal criticism is that it seems to grant to the interpreter virtually complete discretion to choose the policy to be furthered. Critics charge that nonoriginalism is, in fact, not interpretation at all, but judicial legislation under the guise of interpretation.

Defenders of nonoriginalism point to all of the indeterminacies associated with textualism, intentionalism, and purposivism and argue that all forms of interpretation permit lawmaking by the interpreter. They assert that nonoriginalism has the virtue of authorizing explicitly an interpretation that is desirable on substantive grounds. They also contend that it is the most candid method of interpretation because it does not seek to hide the interpreter's policy choices behind a facade of the plain meaning of the text, the intent of the framers, or the purpose of the law.

II. POLICY SYNTHESIS

After the lawyer, through policy analysis, has identified the policies supporting each possible result, the lawyer may attempt to develop a more sophisticated or convincing argument by synthesizing the policies. This requires determining the relationship that each policy has to the others.

The relationship between two policies may be determined by examining their relationship in theory or their relationship in their consequences. Depending upon which criterion is used, theory or consequences, the policies may have a different relationship. Thus, discussion begins with consideration of how policies might be related in theory, followed by considering how they might be related in their consequences.

A. *The Relationship in Theory Among Policies*

As was discussed in Chapter 6, the American legal system rests on a set of dualisms that were characteristic of Enlightenment liberal philosophy. In political philosophy, the dualism was the community (or its organ, the state) and the individual. In metaphysics, it was realism and nominalism. In epistemology, it was rationalism and empiricism.

Each of these three dualisms can be restated at a higher level of generality as a basic dualism of the universal and the particular. The universal is represented by realism, rationalism, and the community. The particular is represented by nominalism, empiricism, and the individual.

Many of the policy conflicts in American legal policy are simply more specific cases of one of these three dualisms or, at a very high level of abstraction, of the basic dualism of the universal and the particular.

The first four policy conflicts discussed in the first section of this chapter, for example, are specific cases of the political dualism of the community and the individual, which poses the question of the relationship between the community and the individual. Policies of majoritarianism, paternalism, efficiency, and utilitarianism all afford relative primacy to the community, whereas individualism, autonomy, justice, and rights theory all afford relative primacy to the individual. Majoritarianism gives primacy to the will of the community, whereas individualism gives primacy to the will of the individual. Paternalism, although it claims to protect individual freedom, reserves for the community the prerogative to define the conditions of freedom. Autonomy, by contrast, rejects community supervision of private choice. The law seeks justice out of concern for individuals, while seeking efficiency to ensure the prosperity of the community. Utilitarianism defines justice according to the welfare of the community, but rights theory favors the welfare of the individual. The political dualism of the community and the individual thus reappears pervasively in almost every aspect of American legal doctrine at multiple levels of generality. Adherents to each of the policies that grants primacy to the community seek to universalize the exercise of power, whereas proponents of the policies that grant primacy to the individual seek to particularize it.

The conflict between naturalism and positivism is a specific case of the metaphysical dualism of realism and nominalism. The metaphysical dualism thus addresses the question of the nature of law. Naturalism, as a form of realism, holds that laws have ontological existence. It universalizes law as a phenomenon that is true for all societies at all times. Positivism, as a form of nominalism, holds that laws are merely human creations. It particularizes law as a phenomenon that is the product of a particular society at a particular time.

The conflict between formalism and instrumentalism is a specific case of the epistemological dualism of rationalism and empiricism. The epistemological dualism addresses the question of the nature of adjudication. Formalism, like rationalism, rests on the method of reason and functions by deducing conclusions from universal principles. Instrumentalism, like empiricism, rests on the method of experience. Thus, cases are decided individually rather than categorically, through the attempt to determine which means in a particular situation would best serve the relevant ends. In other words, instrumentalists seek to particularize each case, to treat each case as belonging uniquely to a category of one.

In short, various policy conflicts, at moderately high levels of generality, represent choices among political, metaphysical, and epistemological theories. Further, the competing political, metaphysical, and epistemological theories, at an even higher level of generality, represent the opposite poles of the dualism of the universal and the particular.

This thesis provides a basis for evaluating the theoretical relationship among many different policies. Any two policies may be consistent in that they represent the same pole of a dualism, or they can be opposed in that they represent opposite poles of a dualism.

Utilitarianism and majoritarianism, for example, are consistent in theory because they give primacy to the community rather than the individual; that is, they represent the same pole of the political dualism. Formalism and naturalism are consistent in theory because they both represent the universal pole of the basic dualism.

Utilitarianism and rights theory, however, are opposed in theory because the former gives primacy to the welfare of the community and the latter gives primacy to the welfare of the individual. That is, they represent opposite poles of the political dualism of the community and the individual. Naturalism and positivism are opposed in theory because the former represents the universal pole of the basic dualism (it assumes a universal law originating in the will of God or the nature of the universe), whereas the latter represents the particular pole of the basic dualism (it assumes that law is the creation of particular societies under particular circumstances).

The relationship among the various sets of opposed policies discussed in the first section of the chapter may be diagrammed as follows:

Basic Dualism	Universal	Particular
Politics	Community	Individual
	(Majoritarianism)	(Individualism)
	(Paternalism)	(Autonomy)
	(Efficiency)	(Justice)
	(Utilitarianism)	(Rights Theory)
Metaphysics	Realism	Nominalism
	(Natural Law)	(Positivism)
Epistemology	Rationalism	Empiricism
	(Formalism)	(Instrumentalism)
	—Rules	—Standards
	—Objectivism	—Subjectivism

Any given judicial decision may be based on policy choices that are consistent at low levels of generality but inconsistent at higher levels. For example, a court may adopt a consistently utilitarian theory of free speech but then adopt an individualist stance in holding that a law prohibiting advocacy of communism is unconstitutional. The opinion is internally consistent at a low level of generality because its theory of free speech is consistently utilitarian. The opinion, however, is internally inconsistent at a higher level of generality because in adopting a utilitarian theory, it preferred the communitarian pole, whereas in adopting an individualist stance and voiding the law, it preferred the individualist pole.

The theoretical inconsistency may exist only at a very high level of generality. For example, imagine a decision that was completely consistent as a matter of political theory, such as one that consistently chose the individualist pole of each policy conflict but then relied on a naturalist theory of law. The combination of individualism and naturalism is a common one, reflected, for example, in the liberal theory of John Locke, who relied on naturalism to justify individual rights. Our hypothetical decision would be internally inconsistent at a very high level of generality because in its political theory it rests on the particularist pole of the basic dualism, whereas in its metaphysical theory it rests on the universalist pole. That is, as long as one looks only at its political theory or its metaphysical theory, the decision is consistent. When one moves, however, to the highest level of abstraction, the level of the dualism between the universal and the particular, it is inconsistent.

Inconsistency at that level of generality is not uncommon. The eighteenth-century philosopher Jeremy Bentham is treated as the modern founder of utilitarianism, but he was also a positivist. Bentham regarded natural law as "nonsense" and the allied notion of natural rights as "nonsense on stilts." There nevertheless is a theoretical inconsistency in his position because utilitarianism represents the universalist pole of the basic dualism and positivism represents the particularist pole.

Inconsistencies at such high levels of generality, however, are of little, if any, concern to a court. Indeed, to go one step further, it is virtually inevitable that a judicial decision will be inconsistent in theory at some level of generality. Or to restate the assertion, judicial decisions cannot make every policy choice in favor of the same pole of the basic dualism.

For example, the Lockean political theory just described was particularist in its political theory but universalist in its metaphysics.[7] Benthamite utilitarianism was universalist in its political theory but particularist in its metaphysics. In the late nineteenth century, the dominant judicial ideology was individualist and positivist, but also formalist.[8] That is, it embraced the particularist pole in its political and metaphysical theory but then chose the universal pole in its epistemology. The Legal Realists of the 1920s and 1930s were positivist and instrumentalist, but they shifted to a more communitarian political philosophy.[9] Thus, they were particularist in their metaphysics and their epistemology, but moved toward the universal pole in their political theory.

The phenomenon whereby judicial decisions cannot rest consistently on the same pole of the basic dualism is a consequence of a fundamental paradox underlying Enlightenment liberalism. The paradox is that either pole of these three dualisms, if pursued to its logical conclusion, is ultimately destructive of itself.

In politics, individual freedom, if taken to its extreme, leads to anarchy and the tyranny of the strong over the weak. Individual freedom can be guaranteed only by the power of the state. State power, by contrast, if taken

---

[7] For further discussion, *see* Chapter 6.

[8] Actually, the dominant ideology was not even internally consistent at the level of political theory because it often favored utilitarian theories of justice while rejecting paternalism; that is, its political theory embraced the communitarian (utilitarian) and individualist (autonomy) poles simultaneously.

[9] Like the late nineteenth-century formalists, the realists were not consistent even at the level of political theory. They moved toward paternalism while moving away from utilitarianism, thus reversing the preferences of the formalists.

to its extreme, leads to a completely totalitarian society in which individuals have no liberty or value and thus no stake in preserving the state.

In metaphysics, to be an extreme realist and claim that every rule is eternally fixed and absolute eliminates the possibility of change or of resolving conflicts between apparently conflicting absolutes. To be an extreme nominalist, however, and claim that every rule is contingent and constantly mutable reduces law to a set of arbitrary ad hoc whims. In either case, law loses the capacity to function as law.

In epistemology, to be an extreme formalist and state rules at the highest possible level of generality renders the rules incapable of determining any situation and thus ineffective. To state every rule at the lowest level of generality, however, would preclude any rule from governing more than the precise situation for which it was formulated and similarly render it incapable of determining any future situation.

This paradox has been reflected in each of the policy conflicts described in the prior section. Tensions between rights theory and utilitarianism, for example, or between naturalism and positivism or formalism and instrumentalism were described as incapable of full and final resolution. Courts choose rights theory one day and utilitarianism the next. They decide one case on purely formal grounds without any reference to policy and decide the next case entirely on grounds of policy.

The fundamental paradox restated is simply that to adhere to policies or ends that are completely consistent as a matter of theory produces consequences that are contrary to those same ends. Total freedom leads to anarchy and domination. Complete control leads to collapse. Extreme formalism as well as extreme instrumentalism yields complete indeterminacy.

The paradox is addressed as a practical matter through compromise. The legal system does not pursue any policy consistently or to its logical extreme. Rather, legal doctrine is the product of a series of compromises that produce the consequences desired but that are theoretically inconsistent. They cannot be otherwise.

The inconsistencies discussed in this subsection for the most part were at very high levels of generality—at levels that would be of little or no concern to a court. Theoretical inconsistency, however, is not uncommon at very low levels of generality. In Chapters 8 and 9, for example, the discussion concerns a number of areas of law in which courts have favored one policy in adopting a rule but have preferred the opposite policy in adopting definitions of or limitations to that same rule. Any body of rules is very likely to embrace simultaneously policies that are in direct conflict, as a matter of theory, at very low levels of generality. The point here, however, is that if the conflict does not appear at a low level of generality, it is virtually certain to appear at a high level.

That is, judicial decisions inevitably rest on theoretical inconsistency at some level of generality. They simultaneously embrace policies that represent contradictory poles of the various cognate dualisms.

B. *The Relationship in Consequence Among Policies*

Deciding cases through policy judgments is an inherently consequentialist practice. In other words, the lawyer is concerned primarily with finding the result that has the best consequence, meaning that it yields the most policy benefit, rather than the result that is internally consistent as a matter of theory.

In making policy judgments, lawyers are concerned principally with consequences. Thus, deciding the relationship among policies requires that the lawyer determine the extent to which two policies push toward consistent or opposite results. In other words, the lawyer must determine their relationship in their consequences.

Although the theoretical relationship among policies is fixed, the relationship among policies as measured by their consequences is not. Some policies may be consistent in their consequences in one case but opposed in the next. For example, promoting efficiency in one situation may require an individualist policy, whereas in the next situation it may require a majoritarian one. Thus, the process of synthesizing policies requires determining the relationship in consequence among various policies in a given situation.

In a particular situation, any two policies may have any of three relationships. They may be consistent, opposed, or independent in their consequences.

1. *Consistent Policies*

Two policies may be consistent with each other in their consequences in a particular situation; that is, both policies may be furthered by the same result. Thus, both policies support an argument that that result is correct.

For example, a lawyer for an appliance store attempting to decide whether a court will enforce a harsh sales contract between the store and a consumer may perform a policy analysis and determine that at least three policies support his client's position that the harsh term ought to be enforced. First, enforcement of the contract would further the policy of autonomy, because it would give effect to the choices made by the parties when they entered into the contract despite their unequal bargaining power. Second, enforcement of the contract would further the policy of efficiency, because any other result would encourage litigation by consumers seeking to avoid agreements they later regretted and could require the store to raise prices to all parties to pay for the litigation. Third, enforcement of the contract would further the policy of textualist interpretation (formalism), because it would honor the language of the agreement as written without inquiry into what the parties might secretly have intended or thought.

All three of these policies are consistent in their consequence in this case. In arguing this client's case, the lawyer can rely upon the standard arguments that typically support each of these policy choices.[10]

Lawyers find that certain policies seem to be consistent in their consequence in the great majority of cases, or at least are widely perceived as such. For example, many lawyers believe that formal rules are more certain and thus more efficient than instrumentalist standards. That is, formalism and efficiency are thought to be generally consistent in their consequences. Arguments for either of these policies thus overlap with arguments for the other. Similarly, individualism is often said to be consistent in its consequences with efficiency. This view is based on the assumption that allowing private individuals to work out their own arrangements through the market usually leads to the most efficient result.

The usefulness of this insight is that it can facilitate the process of developing arguments in favor of a particular position. Once the lawyer realizes that the client has adopted a formalist position, the awareness that formalism is often thought to be consistent with efficiency will lead the lawyer to think immediately of that policy as lending potential support to his client's position.

2. Opposing Policies

Two policies may be opposed in their consequences in a particular situation. That is, the result that furthers one policy would impede the other policy. Thus, one policy would support a determination that a particular result is correct, whereas the opposing policy would support a determination that it is incorrect.

Lawyers find that certain policies seem to be opposed in their consequences in a great number of cases, or at least are widely perceived as such. This phenomenon can facilitate the process of anticipating arguments against a particular position. After identifying the policies supporting the client's position, the lawyer can anticipate that the commonly opposed policies are very likely, if not certain, to support the position of the adversary.

The lawyer for the appliance store, for example, having identified autonomy, efficiency, and formalism as policies supporting the client's position,

---

[10] Note that the position taken by the lawyer for the appliance store is inconsistent as a matter of theory. Although the lawyer cited policies of autonomy and efficiency to support the position, these policies are inconsistent in theory. The policy of autonomy gives primacy to the individual, whereas the policy of efficiency gives primacy to the community. At an even higher level of generality, autonomy is also inconsistent with formalism in that the former represents the particular pole of the basic dualism, whereas the latter represents the universal pole.

can anticipate that the standard arguments based on paternalism, justice, and instrumentalism are likely to be raised by the adversary. For instance, because the opposing policy of paternalism is based on the assumption that private parties dominate each other, the lawyer can anticipate that the adversary may question whether the consumer freely and knowingly entered into the contract.

One mark of a creative lawyer is the ability to marshal as many policy arguments on the side of the client as possible. A particularly strong argument is one that demonstrates that two policies that often are opposed in theory or in their consequences—such as efficiency and justice—both lead to the same result.[11] This argument is especially strong because the lawyer, by finding support in both policies, in effect has neutralized one of the potential arguments against the client's position.

3. Independent Policies

Two policies may operate independently of each other in consequence in a particular situation. That is, the result that furthers one policy would not necessarily further or impede the other policy.

For example, assume that a lawyer represents the neighbor of a tuba player who insists on playing the tuba in an apartment house late at night. Through policy analysis, the lawyer determines that the client's position is supported by a policy of utilitarianism—the greatest happiness for the greatest number would result from restricting the hours during which the tuba player can play.

In that situation, the policy of utilitarianism may operate independently of the policies associated with formalism and instrumentalism. The neighbor's chances of prevailing are thus the same regardless of whether the court is inclined in this case to take a formalist or an instrumentalist approach. A formalist court, persuaded by the lawyer's utilitarian argument, might impose a rigid rule, such as a rule that the tuba player could not play after 9 P.M. An instrumentalist court, persuaded by the lawyer's utilitarian argument, might fashion a flexible standard, such as a requirement that the tuba player not play at an unreasonable hour of the night.

Sensitivity to independently operating policies can strengthen or add to the sophistication of the lawyer's argument. First, an awareness that there are sets of competing policies that in their consequences operate independently of the issue to be resolved allows the lawyer to generate a variety of ways in which to fashion a result favorable to the client. The lawyer does

---

[11] *See, e.g.,* Doe v. Miles Laboratories, Inc., 675 F. Supp. 1466 (D. Md. 1987) (requiring a manufacturer to compensate a consumer injured by the manufacturer's product, even when the manufacturer was not negligent in any way, is both just and efficient).

this by considering the various permutations that are produced by different combinations of independently operating policies. The lawyer can thus present the court with several different ways in which it can rule in favor of the client.

For example, the lawyer for the neighbor, realizing that there is a choice between formalism and instrumentalism and that the choice is essentially irrelevant to the issue of whether the tuba player should be restrained, can propose two different ways in which a court can rule in favor of the client. The court in ruling in favor of the client may adopt a formalist stance and impose a rigid rule (no tuba playing after 9 P.M.) or may adopt an instrumentalist stance and impose a flexible standard (no tuba playing at an unreasonable hour). In either case, the lawyer's client prevails.

Second, once the lawyer is aware that there is more than one way to prevail, then discussion can begin with the client on whether one form of victory would be preferable to another. Perhaps the client would prefer a rigid rule over a flexible standard. Each time an alternative presents itself, there is a potential question concerning whether the alternative is preferable. Knowledge of the alternatives allows the lawyer to identify issues that might otherwise be overlooked and to determine whether the resolution of the issue matters to the client.

Third, if the lawyer is aware that a particular judge is predisposed toward certain independently operating policies, the lawyer can appeal to that predisposition by adopting that policy. For example, if the lawyer is aware that a particular judge generally favors rigid rules, the lawyer may argue not only that the client should prevail, but that the relief should be cast in the form of a rigid rule, with the request for a standard as a fallback position. In that way, the lawyer identifies the client's claim with policies that the court is known to favor, even though as a practical matter those policies are irrelevant to the merits of the claim.

C. *The Significance of the Relationships*

The assertion in the prior discussion is that policies may be consistent in theory or in their consequences, but rarely are all the policies favoring a particular decision or set of rules fully consistent in both theory and consequence. If the lawyer must choose one form of consistency over the other, the question arises as to which form of consistency is more significant.

Recall that adjudication may be either formalist or instrumentalist. Formalism assumes complete theoretical consistency but claims to be blind to consequences. Rules are formulated at very high levels of generality and then applied mechanically to resolve disputes. Instrumentalism, on the other hand, resolves disputes on the basis of their consequences, that is, on the basis of the policies that each result would further.

Thus, the mere fact that the lawyer is engaged in making policy judgments means that the decision will be made on fundamentally instrumentalist grounds. In making policy judgments, then, the purpose of synthesizing policies is first and foremost to find the policies that support each of the various results, meaning that they are consistent in their consequences.

As noted above, the fact that certain policies are often believed to be consistent in their consequences facilitates the process of identifying additional policies that may support the result sought by the lawyer. It also makes more plausible the lawyer's argument that these policies support the result being sought because other lawyers are accustomed to seeing the policies associated. The claim that individualism and efficiency lead to the same consequence, for example, is an article of faith among those who believe that the market produces the most efficient result. Thus, the lawyer may need to do little more than demonstrate that a particular result is consistent with individual choice, and the argument that the same result is consistent with market economics and the promotion of efficiency will be instantly apparent and persuasive to many other lawyers.

Yet, theoretical consistency is not irrelevant. No court is entirely instrumentalist in its approach. Formalism, which assumes theoretical consistency, remains an important, even dominant, part of legal reasoning. As shown in Chapter 6, the formalist claim that general rules can determine results is a crucial part of contemporary mainstream legal theory.

For this reason, no court wishes to be accused of theoretical inconsistency. In a formalist world, theoretical inconsistency is fatal to the legitimacy of a court's decision. Indeed, the assertion that a judge is "result-oriented" (as opposed to theoretically consistent) is often taken as an epithet. The decision that has traditionally commanded respect is one that appears wholly consistent in theory and that is made without regard to consequences. In a sense, formalism remains the ideal and instrumentalism the grubby reality of adjudication.

Because theoretical inconsistency is incompatible with formalism, it provides the lawyer with an argument against a particular result. Further, even a purely consequentialist court could believe that theoretical coherency was desirable as a matter of policy. Thus, the judge, in choosing among results, has to consider among other things the fact that a given result would be theoretically inconsistent with other rules or decisions that the court has previously embraced as correct.

For example, assume that an appellate court has held unconstitutional a litter control statute restricting the distribution of political campaign literature on public sidewalks on the grounds that (1) the policy of free speech is entitled to great weight, (2) because many poorly funded candidates could not afford any other means of communication, the statute greatly impeded their exercise of free speech, and (3) the statute did not further any equally important policy sufficiently to justify this infringement on free speech. Thus, the court chose individual rights over majoritarianism and, in effect, helped somewhat to level the playing field between poorly funded and well-financed candidates. Assume further that the legislature next enacted a statute limiting the dollar amount of campaign contributions to prevent a few wealthy donors from "buying" an election through the financing of massive advertising. In upholding the statute, a trial court observes that although campaign contributions are a form of speech, its decision upholding the limitation is consistent (in consequence) with the prior case because, like the prior decision, the statute was intended to maintain a level playing field between poorly funded and well-financed candidates.

A lawyer for a candidate seeking to void the contribution limitation would argue on appeal that the trial court's decision is inconsistent (in theory) with the prior decision because it failed to give the same weight to the individual right of expression. This argument may prevail because the two decisions are inconsistent in theory at a fairly low level of generality. The prior decision by the court of appeals expressed a strong preference for individual rights in free speech cases, whereas the decision by the trial court favored majoritarianism in free speech cases.

One cannot conclude that this argument is certain to prevail, however, because the judgment about the relative weight of policies is not the only judgment. The court must also make judgments about the relationship between ends and means. The appellate court in the second case could conclude, for example, that the campaign contribution limitation was sufficiently high to allow ample opportunities for speech, and thus the statute did not impede more than slightly the policy of free speech. The court might ultimately conclude that once one took into account the relationship between ends and means, the greatest policy benefit would result from upholding the statute. Nevertheless, the inconsistency in theory between the trial court's decision and the appellate court's prior decision provides the lawyer with an argument for reversal of the trial court.

In assessing the potential significance of a theoretical inconsistency, the lawyer must determine the level of generality at which the inconsistency exists. The doctrine of stare decisis requires that like cases be decided in a like way. The distinction between holdings and dictum, however, rests on the premise that precedents are binding only on a narrow category of cases: those that fall within the terms of the holding. Thus, stare decisis demands consistency only at very low levels of generality. A later case that is like a precedent in all relevant particulars should be decided the same way. A later case that is like a precedent only at a high level of generality may not be decided the same way on the ground that the later case falls outside the terms of the holding, meaning that it is factually distinguishable and, accordingly, is not controlled by the precedent.

In short, theoretical inconsistency at a low level of generality is a stronger argument against a particular result than theoretical inconsistency at a high level of generality. A court may be very impressed by an argument that a decision to uphold a statute restricting free speech is inconsistent with many prior decisions giving great weight to free speech. Although none of the holdings in those cases controls the current case because the facts are different, the court understands that to move from strongly preferring the individualist position in the prior cases to favoring the majoritarian position in the current case is inconsistent in theory. At the same time, a court very likely would not be persuaded by an argument that the formalist epistemology underlying a proposed result is inconsistent in theory with the individualist political preferences of prior cases and thus the result must be rejected. The argument would probably be unpersuasive because the inconsistency is at a very high level of generality.

Theoretical inconsistency also provides the lawyer with a basis for critiquing the internal coherence of an opposing lawyer's argument. For example, if the adversary is relying on policies of individualism and efficiency to support the argument that a contract should be enforced as written, the lawyer can point out the inconsistency of efficiency with individualism and thus call into question the ultimate consistency of the adversary's position with individualism. If the court is more committed to individualism than efficiency as a philosophical matter, the lawyer's ability to characterize the adversary's position as efficiency-based and anti-individualist may result in the court's rejection of the adversary's argument.

Theoretical inconsistency may thus be used as a way to attack the consistency of a proposed result with precedent or as a way to expose the internal inconsistency of a particular position. In the former case, the court may decide that stare decisis requires rejection of the proposed result. In the latter case, the court may conclude that certain policies do not in fact support the proposed result, thus making it easier to reject that position on consequentialist grounds.

III. POLICY APPLICATION

A. *The Technique of Deciding*

It was explained in Chapter 5 that courts use policies to resolve cases in the way they believe will yield the greatest policy benefit. Determining how to achieve this result requires that the lawyer make two types of judgments—the first about the relative importance of policies and the second about the relationship between ends and means.

As an initial matter, the lawyer, through policy analysis and synthesis, identifies the policies supporting each result. The lawyer then attempts to determine the benefits that each possible result would produce through furthering the supporting policies, at the same time attempting to determine the cost that each possible result would produce through impeding the opposing policies. If a result would further the supporting policies more than it would impede the opposing policies, then, assuming that all of the policies were equally important, the result would be desirable.

The problem, however, is that all policies are not equally important. At any given moment in history in any given court, certain policies are preferred. Thus, the court is very likely to decide that the result that furthers the preferred policies is correct, unless that result is enormously costly in terms of the opposing policies.

For example, many courts prefer individual rights over majority rule in freedom of speech cases. Thus, those who demand impeachment of the president or display paintings of nude men and women are likely to find that their right to engage in these activities will prevail over the power of the majority to prohibit them. Because the right of free speech is preferred, the result supported by that policy usually prevails.

Yet, the man who attempts to incite a riot or reveal the position of troops in time of war would probably find that the majority's power to prohibit those instances of speech prevails over his right to engage in them. A riot or a defeat in battle could deal a serious blow to democratic government. The cost of permitting individual rights to prevail in these cases is considered too great.

In the end, there is nothing truly mathematical or mechanical about the process of making these judgments. In general, lawyers can sense that if a preferred policy supports their position, they are likely to prevail—just as they are likely to lose if a preferred policy supports their adversary's position.

At the same time, if the result lawyers seek seems only remotely to further the policies supporting their position, their argument is considerably weakened. For example, a woman who demands the right to deliver a speech over a loudspeaker at 3 A.M. in a residential area is in a weak position (even though the preferred policy of free speech supports her case) because permitting her to deliver the speech at that time and place and in that manner is only distantly related to the policy of free speech. As long as she is permitted to give the same speech to the same audience at other times and places, there is very little cost to free speech in denying her the permission she seeks. The relationship between the preferred ends and the means she seeks to employ is simply too attenuated for her to prevail, even though the policy of free speech is given great weight and supports her position.

B. The Indeterminacy of Policy Judgments

Policy judgments are often indeterminate for three reasons. First, there is not always a general consensus concerning the relative weights that should be assigned to policies. Thus, a lawyer cannot be certain whether, for example, a court will weight justice more heavily than efficiency or weight majoritiarianism more heavily than individual rights.

Second, judgments about the relationship between ends and means, although ostensibly empirical in nature, in fact are usually based on speculation. For example, one lawyer may believe that the regulation of sexually explicit films will further the end of reducing crime, whereas another lawyer may believe that it will not. Because often neither lawyer in a dispute can prove the nature of the relationship between ends and means, the lawyer cannot be confident of the court's ruling on that issue.

Even apart from these difficulties, however, there is a third source of indeterminacy in policy judgments, which arises from the fact that policies can be stated at multiple levels of generality. Thus, the problem of generality that creates indeterminacy in rules and forces courts to resort to policy judgments reemerges in the realm of policy.

As will be seen, the problem of generality poses the same dilemma for policies that it does for rules. A rule must be general if it is to control more than a single situation, and yet as it becomes general it also becomes indeterminate. Similarly, a policy must be stated at a certain level of generality if it is to assist in interpreting a rule, and yet, as a policy becomes more general, it also becomes indeterminate.

The discussion of this problem begins with consideration of the relationship between policies and rules. The relationship between policies and rules essentially is the same as that between ends and means. As noted in Chapter 1, the American legal system assumes that rules do not exist for their own sake, but rather are adopted as the means to ends. The ends, of course, are the underlying policies.

In general, policies and rules are both structurally and functionally different. The structural difference is that policies are typically stated as abstract absolutes, whereas rules are typically stated in more limited, concrete, and contingent terms. Policies by their terms are to be pursued in all circumstances, whereas rules apply only to the limited circumstances described in the factual predicate.

The structural distinction between ends and means blurs, however, when ends are stated at a sufficiently low level of generality. For example, one may be in pursuit of the end of maintaining a clean home. Ends stated at a high level of generality can often be furthered in a very large number of ways. One of the many possible means to the end of a clean home would be to dust the middle figurine on the top shelf in the parlor. One also could claim as a much more specific *end*, however, keeping the middle figurine on the top shelf in the parlor dusted. Thus, dusting the middle figurine could be characterized as either a relatively specific end or a means to a more general end. Note that, as the end becomes more specific, the range of possible means narrows until, at some point, the distinction between the end and the means vanishes.

Restated in legal terms, as policies are articulated in more specific terms they take on the character of rules, and the structural distinction between policies and rules dissolves. For example, one might begin with the very general policy of protecting free speech. This policy could be restated in more specific terms, such as repealing all statutes regulating speech, providing free desktop publishing software to every adult citizen, or insulating newspapers from liability for defamation. Each of these three ideas may be characterized as either a more specific statement of the general policy of promoting free speech or a means to the general end of promoting free speech.

The policy of insulating newspapers from liability for defamation can be stated more specifically still as the policy of requiring that public figures prove as an element of a defamation claim against a newspaper that the newspaper published the defamatory statement with actual malice. At this low level of generality, the policy is readily characterized as a rule. It is relevant to a quite narrow range of circumstances: defamation suits by public figures against newspapers. It has lost the character of an absolute end to be pursued in all circumstances.

The functional difference between rules and policies is that rules create legal consequences, whereas policies do not. Policies provide the justification for the rules but have consequences only to the extent that they are given effect in rules.

Because they are part of the context in which the rules are adopted, policies do provide a basis for interpreting the rules when the rules are unclear. The housekeeper who has been given a rule—the duty to dust the middle figurine on the top shelf in the parlor—may wonder whether the rule requires brushing it with a feather duster or using some more painstaking method. The act of dusting the middle figurine on the top shelf may serve a variety of ends, such as improving the appearance of the figurine or reducing the amount of dust in the room. If improving the appearance is the end, then quick use of a feather duster may be sufficient. If reducing the dust in the room is the end, then it may not be sufficient. By understanding the context in which the rule requiring the dusting of the figurine was given, including the end that the order was intended to further, the housekeeper is better able to interpret the rule.

Thus, policies function to provide an interpretive context for rules. To do so, however, they must be stated at a higher level of generality than the rule itself. That is, the functional role of policies depends upon maintaining the structural distinction between policies and rules. As has been shown, if a policy is permitted to drop to the same level of generality as the rule it underlies, the policy will collapse into the rule.

For example, a statute exempting a newspaper from the sales tax may rest on a policy of promoting the sale of newspapers. Stated this narrowly, the policy adds no context to the rule and would not aid in deciding, for example, whether a local shoppers' guide should be considered a newspaper within the meaning of the rule.

If the policy is stated more generally as protecting the economic viability of newspapers threatened by competition from broadcast media, then one might conclude that a local shoppers' guide was not a newspaper within the meaning of the rule because it operated in a market not served by broadcast media. The broader context provided by the more general policy supplies additional information that permits the lawyer to determine which interpretation would further the underlying policy. The policy is able to supply an interpretive context, but only if it is stated at a higher level of generality than the rule itself.

The dilemma, however, is that stating a policy at a higher level of generality makes it less determinate. Greater generality creates indeterminacy in two ways.

First, stating a policy at a higher level of generality renders the policy less determinate because this expands the range of means that might further such a broad end. For example, assume that the court favors a policy of protecting individual liberty. Achieving this end could require that a court enforce all contracts as written in order to avoid imposing its own will on the parties or could require the court to scrutinize every contract for indications of unequal bargaining power in order to avoid enforcing domination of one party by another. The general goal of protecting liberty might be furthered in one situation by judicial deference and in another situation by judicial scrutiny. By stating the policy at such a high level of generality, the lawyer permits the argument that even diametrically opposed means could serve to further the end.

The problem of indeterminacy has been illustrated by examining a number of the policies discussed in the first section of this chapter. Application of the policy of paternalism, for example, required first determining whether the man reading the magazine with the nude photographs was coercing his female colleague or whether she, in objecting to the magazine, was coercing him. A mere commitment to opposing private coercion cannot settle the question.

Second, by varying the level of generality at which policies are stated, lawyers vary the context within which the rule will be interpreted, which in turn affects the interpretation of the rule. For example, if the policy underlying the sales tax exemption described earlier is stated still more broadly as encouraging the free flow of information, then the shoppers' guide would seem to be a newspaper because it includes information, the flow of which could be stifled if the guide were subject to a sales tax. The ability of lawyers to manipulate the generality of policies, like their ability to manipulate the generality of rules, creates indeterminacy in the policies.

Note in this illustration that stating the policy behind the sales tax exemption at a high level of generality actually renders it less determinate. If the policy is to encourage the free flow of information, then providing a sales tax exemption for some forms of communications media and not for others could ultimately result in a state subsidy of certain points of view at the expense of others. Thus, depending upon various assumptions that the lawyer may make about the relationship between ends and means, promoting the free flow of information may require that the sales tax exemption either be eliminated or be construed as narrowly as possible, in order to avoid the potential for indirect censorship of views disfavored by the state. In other words, the policy of promoting the free flow of information that seemed initially to support the widest possible application of the tax exemption could also support a narrow construction or even abolition of the same tax exemption. A policy stated at a high level of generality can be indeterminate, and in fact can support diametrically opposed rules, unless the lawyer provides additional assumptions about the relationship between ends and means drawn from the factual context in which the policy will be applied.

C. Predicting the Decision of the Court

In nearly every case in which the law is indeterminate, most lawyers nevertheless have an opinion about the most likely result. The opinions are based on informed speculation concerning the way in which courts will resolve the relevant policy judgments—both the judgments about the relative weight of policies and the judgments about the relationship between ends and means. The speculation is informed by the lawyer's knowledge of the context in which these policy judgments will be made. The context includes a number of factors.

One important factor is the historical setting. Specific policies are given greater weight in one era than in another. Courts in the late nineteenth century, for example, favored a laissez-faire policy in which they intervened very little in market decisions, whereas in the mid-twentieth century courts rejected that policy in favor of more closely regulating market decisions. As discussed earlier, all else being equal, the result supported by the favored policy is likely to prevail.

Another factor influencing policy judgments is the philosophy of the individual judge deciding the case. Specific judges accord greater weight to some policies than to others and, in doubtful cases, are likely to decide the dispute in the way that furthers the policies they prefer. This is most visibly illustrated by the United States Supreme Court, which has typically comprised blocs of liberal and conservative justices, the members of which vote together a very large percentage of the time.[12] Judges on less prestigious courts, however, are no less influenced by personal preferences. Although at any given time there may be a dominant judicial ideology, specific judges differ in the degree to which they adhere to that ideology. Again, all else being equal, the result supported by the policy favored by the court is likely to prevail.

The precise facts of the situation giving rise to the dispute also affect which result will prevail. This is so because the relationship between ends and means varies with the situation. Accordingly, as the circumstances change, the total policy benefit derived from each result changes. Different results thus seem preferable under different circumstances.

For example, a court is much more likely to adopt a laissez-faire attitude toward the interpretation of a contract between two large corporations than it is if the contract is between a large corporation and an uneducated consumer. In this example, the choice is between a policy of enforcing private contracts and a policy of supervising the contracts to ensure voluntariness, that is, the choice is between autonomy and paternalism. Where the two contracting parties are large corporations with equal bargaining power and competent legal counsel, the contract is unlikely to be the result of coercion. Thus, enforcing the contract in that situation furthers the policy of autonomy at very little cost to the policy of paternalism. That result yields the greatest policy benefit.

However, if the contract is between a large corporation and a consumer, the likelihood of unequal bargaining power is much greater. The court may therefore decide that enforcing the contract in that situation is too costly in terms of the policy of paternalism. Thus, as the facts change, the relationship between the end of promoting genuinely voluntary contracts and the means of scrutinizing their terms also changes. As the facts change, the likely result changes.

A final factor included within the context is the existence of binding precedent and, to a lesser extent, persuasive authority from other jurisdictions. In the great majority of cases, courts decide disputes in a way that they can plausibly describe as consistent with applicable precedents. If the precedents have regularly given preference to one policy over the other in a given situation, it becomes more difficult for the court to reverse the preference in a similar situation and still maintain that it has followed the law.

For example, a court's decision that an outdoor movie theatre has a constitutional right to exhibit a film involving nudity would seem to require a

---

[12] The HARVARD LAW REVIEW publishes annually a table that indicates the percentage of the time that each justice voted consistently with each other justice in the prior term.

decision in a later case that an individual has a right to exhibit the same film in his own home. In the earlier case, the court concluded that the policy of free expression outweighed the policy of protecting individuals from being inadvertently offended while on the public street. Because passersby can avert their eyes, allowing the film greatly furthers free expression, while only slightly impeding the policy of avoiding offense. In the later case, the policy of free expression seems equally strong. Because the film is being shown in a private residence, however, allowing the film to be shown impedes the policy of avoiding offense *even less* than in the earlier case. Thus, to be consistent with the policy judgment made in the prior case, the film should be permitted in the later case as well.

Note in this example that the two cases are distinguishable. Open-air exhibition and private exhibition are sufficiently different factually that no one could suggest that the two cases are identical in all relevant respects. If the earlier case seems to control the later case, it is only because we recognize that the policy judgments in the prior case, if they are followed, require the same result in the later case.

Yet, if different policies had been involved, the two cases might have seemed to require different results. For example, imagine that one of the policies that supported the result in the earlier case was permitting the government to monitor the viewing habits of the population, particularly with regard to sexually oriented materials. Allowing an open-air exhibition would further that policy, whereas allowing private home screening would impede it. The court would likely allow the open-air exhibition but would shut down the private screening. The first set of facts, in other words, would not control the second set of facts. Whether a first case "controls" a second case thus depends upon which policies are affected by the results.

PART THREE

Applications

Part Three illustrates some of the ways in which the ideas set out in the first seven chapters can be applied to four varied and important areas of the law: contracts, torts, constitutional law, and civil procedure. The central thesis of Part Three is that the process of legal reasoning is the same, regardless of the subject to which it is applied. The same basic problems recur in every area of the law, and lawyers use the same techniques for resolving them.

Part Three does not contain a comprehensive, or even a summary, discussion of the important rules in the four subject areas but is merely illustrative and suggestive. There is no attempt here to apply all of the ideas contained in the first seven chapters or to apply any one idea consistently to all four subject areas. The intent is merely to demonstrate how the process of legal reasoning is applied to a wide variety of subjects.

Chapter 3 suggests that in synthesizing a body of law, the lawyer must determine the relationship of each rule to one or more other rules. But the various subject areas of law do not exist in a vacuum. Each subject also fits into a still larger framework. Lawyers have developed a conventional way of organizing this larger framework, which it may be useful to summarize here.

The basic division of the law is between substantive and procedural law. Substantive law is the body of rules and policies that defines the rights and duties that exist between persons, between persons and the state, or between public entities. Procedural law is the body of rules and policies that governs litigation in the courts.

Substantive law is traditionally organized into two bodies: private law and public law. Private law defines the rights and duties that exist between persons. Among the most important private law subjects are contracts and torts, which are discussed in Chapters 8 and 9, respectively.

Public law defines the rights and duties that exist between state entities and between the state and individuals. Public law includes, for example, constitutional law, criminal law, and administrative law. Constitutional law is discussed in Chapter 10.

Procedural law generally includes civil procedure, criminal procedure, and evidence. Civil procedure is discussed in Chapter 11.

8

Contracts

The law of contracts defines those duties that individuals or organizations assume through agreements. Contractual duties may arise in either of two general situations: under the doctrine of traditional contract and under the doctrine of detrimental reliance, also known as promissory estoppel.[1]

Contract law is generally said to based on the policy of individualism. A person is bound if, but only if, that person consents to the duty. The idea that one should be bound only through consent grew out of a naturalist conception of legal obligation. As will be seen, however, in the course of constructing the specific rules of contract law, the courts have often seemed to embrace a more positivist conception of law and have given preference to policies other than individualism, including majoritarianism, paternalism, efficiency, and those policies associated with formalism.

I. TRADITIONAL CONTRACT

One situation that gives rise to contractual duties exists where two or more persons form a traditional contract. The rule defining traditional contract provides that a contract is formed where two elements are present: (1) an offer is accepted, and (2) the contract is supported by consideration.

---

[1] Arguably, there is a third situation: under the doctrine of quasi-contract. A quasi-contract is a legal duty to pay compensation for goods or services imposed on the recipient of those goods or services in order to prevent unjust enrichment. For example, assume that an automobile mechanic repairs a car under the mistaken belief that the car owner has requested the service. Even though the parties never actually reached an agreement, the court nevertheless may impose on the car owner a duty to compensate the mechanic. Otherwise, the owner would be permitted unjustly to retain the benefits of the service provided.

Quasi-contract is often said to be more like a tort duty than a contract duty because it is imposed by a court to prevent injustice and because it is not based on an agreement. For reasons of space, quasi-contract is not considered further here.

A. *Offer and Acceptance*

The first element is an offer by one party that is accepted by the other party. The offer or the acceptance may occur by the express words of the parties or by their conduct. An example of an acceptance by conduct occurs where the first party sends a letter to the second party offering to purchase one lot of widgets for $300 and the second party ships the widgets.

1. *The Objective Test*

One of the rules defining the element of an offer and acceptance states the test to be used to interpret the meaning of the parties' words or conduct. This rule, usually called the objective test, provides that words or conduct shall be interpreted in the way that a hypothetical "reasonable person" would interpret them.

For example, a man who is negotiating to buy a car from his neighbor, upon hearing the neighbor's proposed terms, may exclaim, "Sounds good!"—which could be interpreted either as an expression of acceptance or merely as comment that the offer appears favorable. A jury applying an objective test would decide whether a reasonable person would interpret "Sounds good!" as an acceptance of the offer or as the expression of an opinion about the offer.

One of the policy considerations supporting the objective test is that it leads to predictability and uniformity in the law. It does so by allowing both parties to assume that words and conduct have a reasonable meaning. It also does so by encouraging parties to deal with each other in the normally expected manner, because parties who choose an unusual way of expressing themselves do so at their own peril. Another policy consideration underlying the objective test is that it promotes efficiency in adjudication because it allows the jury to avoid determining what the parties really meant. It may also diminish the frequency of frivolous litigation because it discourages parties from filing suit in the hope that they can persuade a jury that they attributed their own special meaning to the terms of the contract. Finally, because the objective test permits the court to supply its own definition of a term under the banner of the reasonable person, the objective test is also supported by the policy of majoritarianism.

In using an objective test, a jury may give the speaker's words a meaning that the person never intended them to have. In this sense, an objective test imposes on parties those obligations that they will be deemed to have assumed based on a reasonable interpretation of their words or conduct, whether they actually intended to assume them or not. By finding an offer or acceptance where it does not truly exist, the objective test, like formalism generally, is subject to the charge that it produces artificial results, that it treats as a contract something that is not a contract at all. The objective test thus seems inconsistent with the policy of individualism, under which courts are expected to enforce the will of the parties.

And, indeed, there is a theoretical inconsistency at several levels of generality. First, to the extent that the objective test enables the court on behalf of the community to supply its own meaning to terms, it is based on a policy of majoritarianism, which is directly opposed to the policy of individualism. Further, as will be explained shortly, the objective test is also supported by a policy of efficiency, which is inconsistent with individualism at a somewhat higher level of generality. Finally, the objective test is a formalist doctrine in that it attempts to treat specific instances of words or conduct as representative of general types. Thus, under an objective test, "Sounds good!" does not have as many meanings as there are speakers but always means what a hypothetical reasonable person would think it means. The objective test, like formalism, attempts to universalize situations. Individualism, on the other hand, represents the particular pole of the basic dualism. The use of an objective test to measure individual meaning is, at a high level of generality, inconsistent as a matter of theory.

The use of the objective test illustrates the phenomenon in which a general rule is defined by a more specific rule that is based on a policy inconsistent with the policy underlying the general rule. The general rule is based on a policy of individualism, whereas the more specific rule is based on majoritarianism, efficiency, and policies associated with formalism. Despite the theoretical inconsistency, however, the objective test for interpreting expressions of individual will is well established in contract law.

2. *The Subjective Test*

The alternative to an objective test is a subjective test, which interprets a party's words or conduct to mean what that party actually intended them to mean, no matter how idiosyncratic.

A subjective test in theory assures that no party is required to assume a contractual obligation that that party did not actually intend to assume. But it leads to uncertainty and some degree of inefficiency. The hearer cannot assume that the words mean what might be reasonably thought; thus the hearer must attempt to probe the speaker's true intent.

Another objection to the subjective test is that the true intent of a party can never be known with confidence. The speaker may not have consciously considered the disputed issue at the time, and even if the speaker did, time and the pressure of a dispute may have changed that recollection. The greater uncertainty inherent in a subjective test might encourage frivolous litigation because a party would always have the hope of persuading a jury that the words spoken had a special meaning.

If the naturalist and individualist conception of contract were to prevail, the court would embrace a subjective test. In fact, however, subjective tests are rare in contract law. Predictability and efficiency are of such great importance in contract law that the courts almost uniformly use an objective test to interpret the meaning of a contract.

B. *Consideration*

The second element of a contract is that both parties must have given consideration. A more specific rule defines the element of consideration as a benefit conferred or a detriment incurred by a party in exchange for a benefit from or a detriment to the other party. An even more specific rule defines the phrase "in exchange" to mean that consideration must be bargained for as part of the contract.

The requirement of consideration renders some agreements unenforceable under traditional contract doctrine. For example, if an aunt offers to give her nephew $1,000 and the nephew accepts, no enforceable contract has been formed even though there has been an offer and acceptance. No contract exists because the nephew did not confer a benefit or incur a detriment in exchange for the promise.

At one time, the requirement of consideration seems to have had an evidentiary function: It was more plausible that the parties actually had entered into a contract if both were seen to be exchanging something of value. Thus, it was sometimes said that contracts under seal did not require consideration because the signed and sealed document provided sufficient evidence of an agreement.

In more recent times, the requirement of consideration appears to rest on a policy of limiting contractual liability. Courts apparently did not wish to enforce what, in effect, were promises of gifts—promises for which the promisor received nothing in return. The doctrine seems to have achieved its modern form in the late nineteenth century and reflects the individualist policy of the courts of that era, which sought to limit government intervention in the private sphere.[2]

The doctrine is internally inconsistent, however, because although justified by a policy of individualism, it does not enforce individual will.[3] An individual may wish to be bound to give a gift and yet cannot effect that result under contract law. The court, in the name of limiting government involvement in private affairs in order to maximize private choice, refuses to enforce what is in fact the private choice of the parties. In its consequences, then, the doctrine is consistent with a majoritarian policy.

Although the consideration doctrine seems majoritarian in its consequence, the existence of the doctrine does not fully resolve the conflict

---

[2] *See, generally,* G. GILMORE, THE DEATH OF CONTRACT (1974).
[3] *See, e.g.,* C. FRIED, CONTRACT AS PROMISE (1981).

between the community and the individual. The conflict reemerges as the issue of how to define a benefit or detriment. An individualist policy would support a rule that the court will not inquire into the value of a purported benefit or detriment but will accept the parties' characterization of it, even if the supposed benefit or detriment appeared to be completely worthless. A majoritarian policy would support a rule that the court will inquire into whether the purported benefit or detriment is in fact that.

To adopt an individualist definition of consideration would subvert the majoritarian policy underlying the doctrine. By divorcing the doctrine from its underlying majoritarian policy, such a definition would convert the doctrine to a merely formal requirement. On the other hand, to adopt a majoritarian definition of the doctrine would only further deepen the community's involvement in scrutinizing a contract that was supposed to represent the will of the parties. That is, the law not only would require that there be consideration on both sides of the contract (even though the parties wished to make a contract unsupported by consideration on both sides) but would reserve for the community the prerogative to decide what consitutes consideration.

The law of contract has struck a compromise between the competing values and adopted a rule that the court generally inquires into the adequacy but not the sufficiency of consideration. This means that the court requires that some minimal benefit or detriment actually exist but does not examine very carefully the value of the consideration. Thus, the doctrine of consideration is all but formal. The consideration must be adequate, but this is not a demanding requirement.

II. DETRIMENTAL RELIANCE

A second situation where a duty based on a promise may arise occurs where the parties satisfy the elements of the doctrine of detrimental reliance. Under the rule that creates that doctrine, a party has a duty to perform a promise upon which another party has reasonably and foreseeably relied, at least to the extent necessary to prevent injustice. Thus, the elements are (1) a promise, and (2) reasonable and foreseeable reliance upon the promise.

For example, assume that after an aunt promised her nephew that she would give him $1,000, the nephew signed up for $1,000 worth of mambo lessons that he otherwise could not afford, relying on the promised money to pay for the lessons. Unless the promise is enforced, the nephew will have to default on his debt, with potentially severe consequences. If the court believed that the nephew's reliance on the promise was reasonable and foreseeable, it would enforce the promise to the extent necessary to prevent injustice.

Under the theory of detrimental reliance duties are created in situations where the elements of a contract are not present. First, a duty arises even though the promisee in no way indicated to the promisor that an offer was being accepted. Second, the element of consideration is also unnecessary. The detriment incurred by the promisee, although foreseeable, may be one for which the promisor did not bargain.

Thus, the rule creating a duty under traditional contract and that creating a duty under detrimental reliance are "cumulative," as that term was used in Chapter 3. Either duty may arise, regardless of whether the other one does.

Detrimental reliance has different elements than traditional contract because it rests on somewhat different policy considerations. In general, traditional contract rests on the policy of individualism: A duty arises only as a result of individual choice by a party. Imposition of a contractual duty is thought to be just, because no party is bound without consent. It is thought to be efficient, because it facilitates the allocation of resources through private choices made in the market.

Detrimental reliance, by contrast, is a relatively more majoritarian doctrine under which the state intervenes to protect a party against unjust loss caused by reliance on a promise. The duty that arises under detrimental reliance has been compared to a tort duty because it is imposed by the court out of considerations of policy, rather than as a result of an agreement between the parties. At the same time, the requirement that the reliance be foreseeable reintroduces an individualist element into the doctrine.[4]

III. THE NATURE OF THE CONTRACTUAL DUTY

A. *The Duty to Perform the Express Promise and Any Implied Promises*

The discussion thus far has summarized two situations in which duties arise under contract law. It has not, however, defined the exact nature of the duty. In this section, the nature of the contractual duty is discussed, although for brevity's sake, the discussion is limited to duties imposed by traditional contract.

A legal relationship, including a duty, is typically defined by three characteristics: the subject matter of the relationship, the nature of the relationship (whether permissive or mandatory), and the persons included within the relationship.[5] How each of these characteristics defines traditional contract duties is considered here.

---

[4] The link between foreseeability and individualism is discussed later in this chapter and again in Chapter 9.

[5] *See* Chapter 2.

The duty imposed by traditional contract law is to perform the promises that were contained in the accepted offer and, in some cases, certain additional implied promises not explicitly set forth in the offer. The subject matter of the duty, in other words, is to perform the express and implied promises.

The implied duties are often referred to as implied-in-law because the law will imply them in a contract regardless of whether they were included in the offer.[6] For example, contract law generally imposes on a merchant entering into a contract for the sale of a good an implied warranty of merchantability, or a duty to ensure that the good is fit for the ordinary purposes to which people put such a good. Such implied-in-law contractual duties closely resemble tort duties because they are implied by the law for reasons of policy, rather than because the parties agreed to them.

Contracts may create mandatory or permissive relationships. Consider, for example, bilateral, unilateral, and option contracts.

In a bilateral contract, each party promises to perform in exchange for the other party's promise of performance. For example, one party may promise to pay $300 for widgets, and the other party may promise to sell the widgets for $300. Both parties are required to perform. The relationship is mandatory for both.

In a unilateral contract, one party promises to perform if the other party takes some voluntary action. For example, a party may promise to ship the widgets if the other party pays $300. The other party, however, has not promised to pay the $300. Thus, only the first party is under a duty to perform (and that duty is conditioned on the other party's prior performance). Put another way, the relationship is mandatory only for the first party.

In an option contract, one party has a right to take some action and the other party has a duty to perform if the first party exercises his or her right. For example, a party may have an option to buy widgets, meaning that the legal relationship created by the contract permits (but does not require) that party to buy the widgets. If the party chooses to exercise the right to purchase, then the other party has a duty to sell.

Finally, contracts usually create a relationship only between the parties to the contract: the promisor and the promisee. The promisor has a duty to the promisee to perform the promises and that duty extends to no other person. An exception exists, however, in some situations where the parties intend that a third person receive the benefit of the promise. In such a situation, the promisor's duty may extend to this third person—called a third-party beneficiary—as well as to the promisee.

---

[6] These implied-in-law promises should be distinguished from promises that are implied-in-fact. The latter are promises that the parties actually do make to each other, although they do so through conduct rather than by explicit language.

B. *Liability for Breach of the Duty to Perform*

Where a promisor breaches a contractual duty, contract law may impose on the promisor liability to pay compensation to the promisee. Alternatively, where compensation would be an inadequate remedy, the court may order the promisor to perform the promise (generally referred to as ordering "specific performance.") In some cases, the breach may give the promisee the right to terminate the contract. For the sake of simplicity, only the situation in which the promisee seeks damages from the promisor is considered here.

The general rule is that a promisor is liable in damages for breach of contract if the promisor materially fails to perform the promise and the failure causes loss to the other party. That is, the elements of the rule creating liability are (1) a material breach of a contractual promise (2) with loss to the plaintiff (3) as a consequence of the breach.

1. *Material Breach of a Contractual Promise*

The first element necessary to establish liability is a material breach of the contractual promise by the promisor. Contract law includes a more specific rule defining the term "material breach." In the late nineteenth century, a common rule was that a breach occurred if the promisor did not perform the promise according to its exact terms, a rule sometimes known as the "perfect tender" rule because it required the promisor to tender perfect performance. In more recent times, however, the majority rule has provided that a promise is materially breached if the promisor does not substantially perform the promise.

The shift to a substantial performance rule represents a move toward a positivist and utilitarian theory of contract and away from a naturalist, rights-based theory. A naturalist, rights-based theory regards a contract as having moral force. The promisor by the promise confers on the promisee a right to performance. The promisee thus is entitled to a perfect tender. Such a conception of contract law is also supported by a policy of individualism, under which the court gives effect to the will of the parties.

A positivist, utilitarian theory of contract, by contrast, does not regard a contractual promise as having moral force. Rather, a contract is simply a promised but unexecuted exchange of goods or services that should not be completed if to do so would not benefit society as a whole. The substantial performance rule excuses minor deficiencies in performance in order not to require the economic waste involved in exacting strict performance from the promisor. It is a majoritarian policy because the court is declining to enforce the parties' will as set forth in the contract in order to further the state's policy of avoiding waste.

Assume, for example, that a builder constructs a house with a load-bearing wall located a few inches away from the position designated in the design, with the result that the house is structurally sound but that a room is slightly smaller than promised. Under a perfect tender rule, the promisee would be entitled to treat the contract as breached because the promisor had not delivered that which was promised. Under a substantial performance rule, however, the law does not require that the builder engage in the wasteful task of tearing down a portion of the house to relocate the wall, nor does the law allow the promisee to terminate the contract on the ground that it was breached.[7]

2. Loss by the Promisee

The second element of this rule is that the promisee must have suffered a legally cognizable loss, that is, an injury recognized as such by the law. Although one can imagine a variety of injuries that could result from a contract breach, usually only certain pecuniary losses are regarded by the courts as satisfying the element of an injury. For example, the promisor's failure to perform may have disappointed or even distressed the promisee. This emotional injury, however, almost certainly will not constitute an injury within the meaning of the rule imposing liability for breach of contract.

This result represents a choice of efficiency over justice. The promisee may have suffered genuine emotional injury from a breach, but such injuries are easy to allege and difficult to prove. Permitting recovery for them could turn every contract dispute into a lengthy litigation over claims of speculative validity. The rule assumes that it is better to deny recovery in the occasional instance where it is deserved than to invite endless, wasteful litigation. Moreover, the policy of encouraging breaches when to do so is economically efficient militates against awarding damages for noneconomic injury attributable to the breach.

Losses are legally cognizable only if they are certain, that is, not speculative. This rule is consistent with a utilitarian theory of contract law. Under a utilitarian theory, a party should not be discouraged from breaching a contract if a breach would result in the most socially advantageous use of resources. The promisor, however, can determine whether a breach would be efficient only if it is possible to calculate the cost of a breach. By excluding speculative damages, the courts facilitate the promisor's attempt to determine whether a breach would be utilitarian.

To avoid the effect of the rule requiring that damages be certain, the parties to a contract sometimes include a liquidated damages clause. Such a

---

[7] I have somewhat oversimplified the substantial performance rule. Where there is a minor breach, as in the example, the promisee is generally entitled to reduce the payment to the promisor by some amount as compensation for the breach. The court, however, does not order specific performance by the promisor or allow the promisee to terminate the contract for breach.

provision states the amount of damages that shall be payable in the event of a breach. That is, the parties establish the amount of the loss in advance by agreement.

Although a policy of individualism would suggest that these clauses should be enforced as the expression of the will of the parties, courts in fact often decline to enforce them if they require a payment so unreasonably high as to appear to be a penalty. A liquidated damages provision that imposes damages on the promisor disproportionate to the promisee's actual loss could force the promisor to perform a wasteful promise simply to avoid the penalty. Under the positivist, utilitarian conception of contract, promises should not be enforced if performance would use resources inefficiently. Thus, in this situation, the policies of individualism and efficiency, which are often assumed to be consistent in their consequences, appear to be potentially opposed. Recall that the same opposition between individualism and efficiency appeared in the choice between an objective and a subjective test.

3. Loss as a Consequence of the Breach

The third element of this rule is that the breach must have caused the promisee's injury. That is, damages are recoverable only if they are a consequence of the breach.

Additional rules, however, limit the consequential damages recoverable by the promisee.[8] The additional rules are needed because every act has an infinite number of consequences. Without these additional rules, a breach of even the most trivial contract would lead to infinite liability.

Assume, for example, that a taxi company breaches its promise to drive an accountant to a job interview. The result is that the man is late for the interview and is denied the job. He therefore takes a less desirable job in a different building, where he is physically attacked one evening three years later while in the parking garage. Because the accountant would not have been attacked but for the taxi company's breach of contract, the physical injury would seem to be a consequence of the taxi company's breach, thus requiring that the taxi company compensate the accountant for the injury.

Yet, there are policy reasons for regarding such a result as undesirable. Holding one liable for losses that occur years later could result in the imposition of staggering liability for even the most trivial promise, which would discourage economic activity. Further, if the justification for enforcing a contractual duty is that the promisor voluntarily assumed the duty, then it

---

[8] Courts sometimes award what are known as incidental damages. These damages must also be attributable to, or the result of, the breach, but they are not technically referred to as consequential damages.

seems inconsistent with that individualist policy to hold the taxi company responsible for a loss it could not have foreseen and thus could not knowingly have agreed to compensate. Based on these policy considerations, the courts have adopted a further rule under which the promisor is liable only for those consequential damages foreseeable at the time the contract was formed or actually foreseen because of special circumstances communicated to the promisor.[9]

Another rule, known as the doctrine of mitigation of damages, further limits the promisor's liability. This rule imposes on the promisee, in the event of a breach by the promisor, a duty to take reasonable steps to minimize the loss. If the promisee fails to take such steps, no part of the loss that would have been prevented by such steps can be recovered. In effect, the rule treats the avoidable loss as if it were caused by the promisee's failure to mitigate damages rather than being caused by the promisor's breach of the promise.

Assume, for example, that a factory owner enters into an employment contract with a manager whereby the owner agrees to pay the manager to run the factory for five years. The evening before work is to begin, the owner breaches the contract by firing the manager on a whim. That same evening, however, the manager receives an offer of an equally desirable job from a different employer. For some reason, the manager declines the offer and sues the owner for five years' lost salary.

Although the manager's salary loss is clearly a consequence of the owner's breach, it is also a consequence of the manager's refusal to accept the alternative employment. The loss, in other words, was jointly caused by the owner's breach and the manager's refusal of the other position. Under the doctrine of mitigation of damages, the loss is treated as if it were caused by the manager's refusal, and thus the owner is not required to compensate the manager for the latter's lost salary.

The mitigation of damages doctrine is another reflection of the modern positivist, utilitarian concept of contract law. It requires the promisee to prevent unnecessary injury, that is, wasteful injury. A naturalist, rights-based view of contract might hold that the manager, having entered into an agreement for five years with the owner, was entitled to the job and should not be required to work elsewhere simply to spare the owner the consequences of the wrongful act. That same view might regard the second offer of employment as an undeserved "windfall" to the owner, which unfairly spared the owner the consequences of the wrongful act. The positivist, utilitarian concept, in contrast, regards promoting the socially beneficial use

---

[9] *See* Hadley v. Baxendale, 9 Exch. 341 (1854).

of resources as more important than enforcing the moral content of the contract.

As this last example illustrates, a promisor's breach of contract may not be the sole cause of a loss. Indeed, there is no result that has only one cause. Every event has an indefinite number of causes.

For example, the assaulted accountant's loss can be attributed to a number of causes. Had the accountant's prospective employer been more sympathetic, the accountant would have been given the first job and thereby spared the injury. Thus the loss was caused in part by the prospective employer's attitude. At the same time, had the building been better guarded, the accountant would not have been attacked and thus the building owner's poor security was also a cause of the accountant's loss. Or, viewing the situation yet another way, had the accountant allowed himself enough time to get to the job interview in the event that the taxi company failed to perform, he would not have been late, and in this respect his loss was ultimately caused by his own imprudence.

The law does not contain any general rule that singles out one cause to which consequences should be attributed. If the accountant can demonstrate that his prospective employer or the owner of the building breached some duty to him, he may in fact have a right to compensation from both. In other words, various cumulative rules of contract and tort law may give an injured party the right to compensation from a large number of persons whose conduct constituted a cause of the injury.

Under a rule that limits the amount of compensation, however, the injured party may recover the total amount of the injury only once. Thus, if one of the wrongdoers who caused the accountant's injury compensates him, his right to compensation from the others is extinguished.

9

Torts

The law of torts defines certain duties that the law imposes upon persons in the absence of a contract. A tort is a violation of one of these duties. One who commits a tort is sometimes called a tortfeasor.

I. THE NATURE OF TORT LAW

No single principle determines under what circumstances tort law will impose a duty. Rather, the history of torts shows a gradual accumulation of duties newly imposed whenever policy considerations appeared to the courts to justify that result. Tort law is an intrinsically majoritarian body of law because tort duties are based not on the will of the parties involved in a situation but on the will of the state.

The distinction between tort and contract law illustrates the manner in which policy conflicts resolved at one level of generality reemerge at another level of generality. In theory, the law of contracts concerns duties that parties voluntarily assume, whereas the law of torts concerns duties that the state imposes on persons. In other words, the conventional understanding is that in contract law the court enforces the will of the individual, whereas in tort law the court enforces the will of the state.

Although the decision about whether a subject is to be governed by the will of the individual or by the will of the state initially appears to have been resolved by the allocation of that subject to contract or tort law, in fact the issue reemerges within each of these two fields of law. In contract law, the issue of whether to give primacy to the will of the state or to the will of the individual reemerges, for example, as the issue of whether to impose an implied warranty on a party. An implied warranty, although part of contract law and thus in theory a duty voluntarily assumed, is in fact, like a tort duty, imposed by the state for reasons of policy. Similarly, in tort law, as will be seen later on, the issue of whether to give primacy to the will of the state or to the will of the individual also reemerges repeatedly, in such form as the issue of whether to allow a tortfeasor to plead as a defense the fact that the victim consented to the injury or voluntarily assumed the risk of injury. Consent and assumption of risk, although part of tort law, are doctrines that allow the will of the individual, in this case the victim, to limit the general duty imposed on the basis of the will of the state.

II. THE STRUCTURE OF MODERN TORT LAW

Modern tort law, following the lead of Oliver Wendell Holmes, Jr., organizes tort duties according to the defendant's state of mind at the time the duty was breached. This has resulted in three categories of torts: those in which the tortfeasor intentionally caused injury (intentional torts), those in which the tortfeasor negligently caused injury (negligence), and those in which the tortfeasor caused injury without fault or intent (strict liability).

This organizational scheme illustrates the way in which a policy conflict reemerges in a body of legal doctrine at differing levels of generality but is resolved differently at alternate levels. Tort law is in theory a body of rules based on the will of the state, and yet the central organizing principle is the nature of the tortfeasor's act of will causing the injury. Although the concept of tort liability is majoritarian, the more specific rules imposing liability reflect at least limited deference to individualism in that they condition liability on some act of will by the tortfeasor.

A. Intentional Tort

Intentional torts are generally categorized according to the type of injury caused. They include interferences with the person, such as assault, battery, and false imprisonment; interferences with property, such as trespass to land, trespass to chattels, and conversion; and interference with economic relations.

The rules creating the intentional torts all have essentially the same generic elements. As a general matter, liability for an intentional tort arises where the defendant (1) performed some voluntary act (2) with intent that the act cause an injury, and (3) where the act causes (4) an injury.

The basic conflict in tort law between imposition of a duty based on the will of the state and an imposition of duty based on the will of the individual reemerges within intentional tort in the form of the issue of how to define the concept of intent. The conflict is reflected in the contrasting definitions of intent adopted in two well-known cases: *Garratt v. Dailey*[1] and *Cleveland Park Club v. Perry*.[2] Under the *Garratt* definition, which is the

---

[1] 46 Wash. 2d 197, 279 P.2d 1091 (1955).
[2] 165 A.2d 485 (1960).

more commonly accepted of the two, intent exists where the tortfeasor acts with either the desire to bring about the injury or the knowledge with substantial certainty that the injury will occur. Under the *Cleveland Park* definition, however, intent exists where the tortfeasor intended to perform the act causing the injury. That is, under the *Cleveland Park* definition of intent, the only exercise of will necessary for the imposition of liability is a voluntary muscular contraction. Thus, if the requirement of intent pushes the majoritarian concept of tort liability toward individualism, the *Cleveland Park* definition pushes the individualist concept of intent back toward majoritarianism. Indeed, under the *Cleveland Park* definition, intentional tort, which is the most individualist of the three forms of tort liability (because it generally requires the strongest act of will), seems to collapse into strict liability, the least individualist of the three forms.

The difference among the intentional torts rests primarily on the type of injury involved. An intentional infliction of offensive bodily contact, for example, is a battery, whereas an intentional restraint on another's freedom of movement is a false imprisonment.

Additional rules limit the scope of liability under the intentional torts by creating defenses to those torts. One common rule, for example, provides that one is not liable for an intentional tort if the injured party consented to the infliction of the injury. Thus, a boxer who is injured fighting in the ring would probably find that any claim for a battery against an opponent is barred by his consent to the fight.[3]

Although tort law is generally majoritarian, the consent defense reflects a judicial decision to favor the policy of individualism over the policy of majoritarianism in certain instances. That is, the will of the individual is weighted so heavily that the law may sometimes give effect to an agreement to allow the infliction of injury. Were majoritarianism accorded greater weight, a court might refuse to permit individuals to consent to their own destruction.

The consent defense again illustrates the situation in which a policy choice resolved at some level of generality simply reemerges at another level of generality. The tension between majoritarianism and individualism that underlies the general issue of whether to impose liability for a battery reemerges as the issue of whether to permit the defense of consent. In permitting a defense of consent, tort law gives preference to individualism in those circumstances to which the defense applies.

Yet, the doctrine of consent does not represent a complete victory of the policy of individualism even in those circumstances in which it does apply. This fact is reflected in the rule that measures consent with an objective test.

---

[3] *See* McAdams v. Windham, 208 Ala. 492, 94 So. 2d 742, 30 A.L.R. 194 (1922).

Under that test, a person is held to have consented to something if a reasonable person would have interpreted the words or conduct of that person as indicating consent, even if that person believed consent had not been given. For example, a boxer who puts on his gloves and climbs into the ring still carrying mental reservations about whether he wishes to fight may be found to have consented because his external conduct suggested to a reasonable person that he had consented. Thus, consent may be found where it does not really exist. In finding consent where it does not truly exist, the objective test, like formalism generally, is subject to the charge that it produces artificial results, that it treats as consent something that is not consent at all. In short, the majoritarian policy underlying the battery rule is limited by an individualist policy underlying the consent defense, which in turn is subverted by the objective test used to interpret expressions of individual will.

As in the case of the objective test in contract law, the objective test in tort law is based on a policy of efficiency, because it permits the world to take a person at his or her word without the need to engage in time-consuming and uncertain inquiries concerning that person's actual state of mind. Although individualism and efficiency are often thought to be consistent in their consequences,[4] the objective test reflects a situation in which courts promote efficiency by *limiting* individual freedom. In the case of the objective test, then, the two policies of individualism and efficiency are opposed.

Again, as in the case of the use of the objective test to interpret expressions of individual will in contract law, the use of an objective test to interpret consent in tort law is theoretically inconsistent. The objective test reflects policies of efficiency, majoritarianism, and formalism, all of which represent the universalist pole of the basic dualism, whereas consent is an individualist concept that represents the particular pole. Indeed, the policy of majoritarianism is directly opposed in theory to the policy of individualism. To state the inconsistency more concretely: The doctrine of consent in theory represents deference to the will of the victim, yet the objective test does not measure the victim's actual will. Rather, it measures only the community's interpretation of the victim's conduct. By divorcing consent from its underlying individualist policy, the objectivist test threatens to reduce consent to an empty formality.

B. Negligence

The rule that imposes liability for negligence generally requires that four elements be present: (1) the defendant owed a duty of reasonable care to the plaintiff, (2) the defendant breached the duty, (3) the plaintiff was injured, and (4) the breach was the actual and proximate cause of the injury.

---

[4] *See* Chapter 7.

The distinguishing feature of negligence is that the duty imposed is usually one to exercise reasonable care. One who fails to exercise reasonable care is commonly said to be "at fault." Thus, liability based on negligence is often referred to as liability based on fault.

Some legal historians argue that the creation of the tort of negligence represented a conscious policy choice to limit liability.[5] According to this view, prior to the mid-nineteenth century, one who injured another was very often liable even if not at fault.[6] The industrial revolution in the nineteenth century brought about increasing numbers of injuries that would have been expensive to compensate. In order to limit liability for these newly emerging industrial enterprises and promote economic growth, courts modified the existing rules so that liability would arise only in situations where the defendant had failed to exercise reasonable care.

Negligence was thus based on a utilitarian theory of justice, under which courts concluded that society as a whole would benefit more from having trains and factories than from compensating the victims. The courts chose utilitarianism over the rights of the injured and decided that the injured would not receive compensation if the defendant had acted reasonably. A rights-based theory of justice, by contrast, would have supported the conclusion that a railroad company that had set fire to crops on farmland adjacent to the railroad or a factory owner whose faulty equipment had mangled a worker should compensate the injured.

Although tort duties are generally majoritarian, the substitution of liability based on fault for strict liability reflects a limited move toward an individualist policy. Under negligence, at least in theory, one is not liable unless one acted with an improper state of mind. Liability is thus linked with the exercise of individual will.

The rule imposing liability for negligence, like those imposing liability for intentional torts, is limited by various rules creating defenses to liability. For example, in many jurisdictions the defendant is not liable for negligently caused injury if the victim assumed the risk of the injury, such as in situations where a person rides in a car with an obviously intoxicated driver. The defense of assumption of risk in negligence cases is analogous to the defense of consent in intentional tort cases. Like the defense of consent, it is based on an individualist policy under which the victim's expression of will in encountering a hazard limits the liability that the state would otherwise impose on the tortfeasor.

---

[5] *See* M. Horwitz, THE TRANSFORMATION OF AMERICAN LAW, 1780–1860 85–108 (1977).

[6] Although the term "negligence" appears in pre-nineteenth-century decisions, Professor Horwitz has argued that negligence in those cases referred to a failure to perform a specific duty imposed by statute or contract rather than to a failure to exercise reasonable care. Negligence, in other words, meant nonfeasance rather than misfeasance.

This illustrates the phenomenon in which a general rule based on one policy is limited by a more specific rule based on an opposing policy. Again, although tort duties are generally majoritarian, the assumption of risk defense reflects the opposing policy of individualism.

Let us now consider some of the rules that define the elements of the tort of negligence.

1. *Injury*

The element of an injury was limited for many years by a rule that restricted liability largely to cases of physical injury to persons or property. Thus, for example, one was not liable for negligence where the only injury was emotional distress or lost future profits. This rule was based in part on a policy of efficiency. Courts wished to avoid time-consuming litigation over claims that were difficult to prove.

In the twentieth century, courts shifted their policy preferences toward justice for the injured, with the result that lost profits and emotional distress are sometimes considered to constitute an "injury," as that term is used in the tort of negligence. Courts seem to regard the opposing policies as almost evenly balanced, however, and thus they define emotional distress or lost profits as a compensable injury in only certain limited circumstances.[7] Courts have preferred to weigh the policies almost on a case by case basis, rather than laying down a broad rule for or against liability.

2. *Causation*

The element of causation is satisfied where the defendant's breach of the duty of reasonable care is the actual and proximate cause of the injury. As a general rule, actual causation exists where, but for the defendant's breach, the injury would not have occurred.

This "but for" test has proven inadequate where two defendants jointly cause an injury that would have occurred even if only one of them had acted. For example, if two men negligently discharge firearms, both of which fire fatal shots into the heart of the victim, in a lay sense of the term both men "caused" the injury. Yet, by applying the "but for" test, neither man can be shown to have caused it. If the first man had not fired his weapon, the victim would still have been killed by the second shot. Thus, one cannot say that but for the first man's negligence, the injury would not have occurred. The same reasoning exonerates the second man as well. The

---

[7] *See, e.g.,* Union Oil v. Oppen, 501 F.2d 558 (9th Cir. 1974) (permitting commercial fishermen to recover lost profits caused by an oil spill); Dillon v. Legg, 68 Cal. 2d 728, 69 Cal. Rptr. 72, 441 P.2d 912, 29 A.L.R.3d 1316 (1968) (permitting a mother to recover for emotional distress inflicted by the death of her child, who was killed by a negligent automobile driver).

"but for" test, in other words, would absolve both gunmen of liability for the shooting.

Accordingly, many courts have adopted a rule that provides an alternative definition of actual causation. Under this rule, a defendant's breach of duty is considered the actual cause of an injury if it was a substantial factor in bringing about the injury, even though the breach may not have been the but for cause. The outcome of applying this test to the shooting circumstances would be that either of the two gunmen would be considered the cause of the death.

A major difficulty encountered in defining causation is that an act has an infinite number of consequences. Tort law has dealt with this problem in much the same way as contract law: by using the concept of foreseeability.[8] To avoid the imposition of infinite liability, courts have defined the element of causation to require that the defendant's breach be not only the actual, but the proximate, cause of the injury. One common rule defining proximate causation holds that an act is the proximate cause of an injury if it was foreseeable that the act would cause that type of injury to that class of persons.

The rule limiting liability to foreseeable injury seems to be contradicted as a matter of policy by another rule that defines the extent of damages recoverable. That rule provides that the defendant takes the plaintiff as the latter is found. That is, if the defendant performs an act that would cause only a very minor physical injury to the ordinary person, but that, because of a peculiar sensitivity, causes grievous injury to the victim, the defendant will be liable for the entire injury. Thus, the type of injury must have been foreseeable, but not the degree of injury.

These inconsistent rules are the result of a series of deliberate policy choices in which the courts alternate between a rights-based theory of justice, which requires compensating the victim, and a utilitarian theory of justice, which seeks to promote productive activity by limiting liability. In limiting proximate causation to foreseeable consequences, the courts lean toward a utilitarian policy of limiting liability. In requiring the tortfeasor to take the victim as found, the courts lean toward a rights-based theory of justice. Neither policy prevails in every case, and thus the rules, from a policy perspective, are inconsistent in theory. The two rules illustrate the phenomenon in which one rule is limited by a second rule that is based on a policy inconsistent with the policy underlying the first rule.

The foreseeability rule can also be justified on individualist grounds. To the extent that liability is based on individual will, the courts may wish not to impose liability for consequences that were unforeseeable and thus could

---

[8] *See* Chapter 8.

not have been willed by the tortfeasor. In this situation, then, efficiency and individualism, which are often opposed in their consequences, seem to support the same rule.

3. Breach

The rule that defines the breach of the duty of reasonable care adopts an objective test. Specifically, the defendant will be held to have breached the duty if the defendant failed to exercise that degree of care that a reasonable person would have exercised in the same circumstances. As in other situations where it applies, the use of the objective test to measure negligence reflects formalism and policies of efficiency and majoritarianism. Under the objective test, the standard of care required is not particularized to the individual but is generalized for everyone. It thus promotes uniformity and predictability in the application of the law. The objective test promotes efficiency because parties and juries are spared the task of inquiring into what reasonable care is for specific individuals. It also promotes efficiency to the extent that reasonable care is equated with conduct that conserves resources. It is a majoritarian doctrine in that it permits the court on behalf of the community to define reasonable care in accordance with its own views of sound policy.

Like formalism generally, the objective test is likely to be overinclusive and underinclusive. That is, the objective test may require conduct by some individuals that for them would be an extraordinary, or even impossible, exercise of care. Negligence as measured by an objective test does not mean that the individual acted less carefully than that individual normally does, but only that the individual failed to exercise the degree of care that some hypothetical reasonable person would have exercised.

The use of an objective standard to measure negligence may impose on some persons what amounts to liability without fault. No matter how much effort such a person exerts, liability cannot be avoided because that person is not capable of the level of care required by the reasonable person standard. This illustrates again how a specific rule defining a more general rule may be based on a policy that subverts the policy underlying the general rule. Although tort liability is generally majoritarian, the move to a negligence standard, by its focus on individual will, pushed tort law toward a policy of individualism. The objective standard, however, to the extent that it imposes liability on a particular defendant regardless of his or her state of mind, shifts tort law away from individualism and back toward a majoritarian policy—indeed, to such an extent that negligence under an objective standard may collapse into strict liability in specific cases.

The term "reasonable care" illustrates the indeterminacy of many legal rules. The term is so general that it is often almost impossible to determine whether the element of a breach of duty is satisfied.

Courts have addressed the problem of indeterminacy with efforts at greater specificity. For example, some courts have adopted a rule defining reasonable care in accordance with the well-known Hand Formula, named after Judge Learned Hand. Under that formula, reasonable care requires the defendant to prevent an injury only if the burden of prevention is less than the potential injury, discounted by the probability that the injury will occur.[9]

The Hand Formula reflects a preference for a utilitarian theory of justice over a rights-based theory of justice. Under the Hand Formula, if preventing the injury will consume more resources than allowing the injury to occur, then it is reasonable to allow the injury. A defendant may engage in conduct that is enormously destructive to others, as long as that conduct is beneficial to the society as a whole. The Hand Formula also represents an acknowledgment by the court that the term "reasonable care" should be applied, not by formal logic, but by determining whether the defendant's conduct furthers the underlying policy.

Like the objective test generally, the Hand Formula tends to subvert the individualist policy underlying negligence. Although the concept of negligence is generally individualist, the Hand Formula, because of its underlying utilitarian theory of justice, favors the communitarian pole of the political dualism. Negligence as measured by the Hand Formula is thus both individualist and utilitarian. It seeks to promote simultaneously policies that are diametrically opposed in theory. Negligence law, in other words, contains within itself arguments for both expanded and contracted liability.

4. Duty

The element of duty is usually defined by a very general rule that states that the court shall determine whether a duty exists based on considerations of policy. Because the existence of a duty is determined by the court rather than a jury, whether a duty exists is said to be a question of law.

Note that the rule defining when a duty exists does not prescribe any specific facts that must be present for a duty to exist but simply authorizes the court to consider any fact relevant to what it considers a legitimate policy consideration.

This does not mean that the law is completely indeterminate on the issue of whether a duty exists. In fact, the case law has given rise to a number of rules that declare that a duty does or does not exist in specific factual settings.

Thus, for example, most courts hold that all individuals have a duty not to cause physical injury to those who foreseeably might be harmed by a failure to exercise reasonable care. At the same time, perhaps all courts hold

---

[9] See United States v. Carroll Towing Co., 159 F.2d 169 (2d Cir. 1947).

that a lawyer has no duty to exercise reasonable care to prevent even foreseeable economic loss to the opposing party in a litigation.

C. Strict Liability

The third category of tort duties is based on "strict liability" or "liability
without fault." Where strict liability is imposed, the defendant may have
acted without negligence or intent to injure and yet must compensate the
plaintiff for any resulting injury.

The classic modern example involves abnormally dangerous activity. The
rule creating liability for such conduct states that one is liable for compensation if one engages in abnormally dangerous activity that causes injury.

Strict liability is the least individualist of the three forms of tort liability.
The only exercise of individual will required is the act of engaging in the
activity.

The element of an abnormally dangerous activity is often defined by a
rule that lists a number of factors that may indicate that an activity is abnormally dangerous, although no one factor is dispositive. One factor exists, for example, where the activity poses a high risk of danger. Another exists where the danger cannot be prevented by the exercise of care. A third
factor exists where the value of the activity to the community is outweighed
by its dangerous attributes.

Courts have weighed the same utilitarian and rights-based theories of justice that they weighed in the case of negligence but have reached a different
result. Because abnormally dangerous activities are socially useful, they are
permitted. Justice for the individual victim, however, requires that the activities pay their way by compensating the injured.

The imposition of strict liability on abnormally dangerous activities illustrates the way in which a change in facts alters the relationship between
ends and means and thus produces a different result, even where the relative
weights of the policies remain the same.[10] Allowing abnormally dangerous
activities is potentially much more costly to the rights of victims and less
beneficial to society as a whole than allowing ordinary activities. Indeed,
one factor defining an abnormally dangerous activity is that the danger outweighs the benefit to the community. A negligence rule, which effectively encourages activity by insulating it from liability where reasonable precautions
have been taken, would be far more costly in terms of justice to the victim
and far less productive of social benefit in the case of abnormally dangerous
activities than in the case of ordinary activities. Indeed, because by definition abnormally dangerous activities are those that cannot be prevented by

---

[10] The shift to strict liability in any particular context, of course, could also be the result of
a shift toward rights-based theories of justice and away from utilitarianism.

reasonable care, a negligence rule would exonerate those who took preventative steps known in advance to be ineffective. The courts have thus decided that, in the case of abnormally dangerous activities, the greatest policy benefit will be derived from imposing a standard of strict liability rather than a standard of negligence. That is, in the case of abnormally dangerous activities, negligence is an inferior means, relative to strict liability, of furthering the policies sought by both rules.

Strict liability has also been imposed on manufacturers of defective consumer products. Under the doctrine of strict products liability, courts generally hold that one who sells a product that is in a "defective condition unreasonably dangerous" has a duty to compensate foreseeable users of the product who are injured by the defect, regardless of whether the defect was the result of negligence.

The strict products liability doctrine was originally modeled after breach of warranty in contract law. Courts noted that the law implied in contracts for the sale of goods a warranty that the goods were of merchantable quality. This warranty was breached when the goods were not of such quality.

Because warranties were implied in sales contracts regardless of whether the parties had included them in their promises, courts in the mid-twentieth century began to acknowledge that implied warranties created duties more akin to tort than contract. Accordingly, they imposed a tort duty not to sell a product in a defective condition unreasonably dangerous. Implied contractual warranties continued to exist but were subject to the technicalities of contract law. Thus, injured parties could often recover more easily under the tort doctrine of strict products liability than under the contract doctrine of implied warranty.

The policies underlying implied warranty and strict products liability included those of majoritarianism and a rights-based theory of justice. Under the policy of majoritarianism, parties were protected by the court against their failure to obtain express guarantees of safety. At the same time, courts thought it just to require the seller whose product had caused injury to compensate the injured. Some argued that strict products liability was also supported by a policy of efficiency because the doctrine forced manufacturers to internalize the cost of injuries caused by products and to build that cost into the price of the product. In that way, products that cause damage disproportionate to their social value (and thus are socially inefficient) will be priced at more than consumers are willing to pay and will thereby be forced from the market.

Strict products liability illustrates a situation in which policies that are inconsistent in theory are perceived to be consistent in their consequences. Majoritarianism and social efficiency are communitarian policies, whereas rights-based theories of justice are individualist. Yet, despite the fact that these policies in theory represent opposing poles in the tension between the community and the individual, all of them have been cited in support of imposing strict liability on manufacturers for defective products.

Strict products liability also illustrates the situation in which a policy conflict resolved at one level of generality reemerges at a lower level of generality. Because the conflict was resolved differently at alternate levels of generality, strict products liability also illustrates the situation in which a general rule is defined by more specific rules that are based on policies inconsistent with the policies underlying the general rule.

The general rule imposing strict liability on manufacturers of defective products is supported by a rights-based theory of justice. In adopting more specific rules to define the element of a defective product, however, the courts fashioned rules that resemble the definition of the breach of reasonable care in negligence theory. One definition of that element holds that a product is defective if the ordinary prudent manufacturer, aware of the risk, would not have put it into the stream of commerce, a standard suggestive of the reasonable person test.[11] Another definition states that a product is defective if it poses excessive preventable danger, which is determined by weighing the burden of preventing the danger against the degree of danger and the likelihood of its occurring,[12] a test reminiscent of the Hand Formula for negligence. As noted above, negligence theory rests on a utilitarian theory of justice rather than on a rights-based theory.

Thus, the policy conflict that appeared to have been resolved in adopting the strict products liability rule simply reemerged in the course of adopting more specific rules defining the general rule. Moreover, the courts resolved the policy conflicts differently in adopting the more specific rules than they did in adopting the general rule. For example, the rule imposing strict liability for the sale of defective products seemed initially to resolve the conflict between a rights-based theory of justice and utilitarianism in favor of the former. The conflict reemerged, however, in the course of formulating the more specific rule defining the term "defective." In defining "defective" in the ways that they did, courts seemed to embrace a utilitarian policy.

Unable to fully resolve the policy conflicts, the courts favor one policy in adopting a general rule and the opposing policy in defining the terms of the general rule. The policies underlying the definition ultimately serve to subvert the policies underlying the general rule.

The lawyer attempting to argue for a particular result in a case involving products liability doctrine can find policy support for any conceivable

---

[11] *See, e.g.,* Phillips v. Kimwood Machine Co., 269 Or. 485, 525 P.2d 1033 (1974).

[12] *See, e.g.,* Barker v. Lull Engineering, 20 Cal. 3d 413, 143 Cal. Rptr. 225, 573 P.2d 443 (1978).

outcome explicitly within the cases creating and defining the doctrine. The policies that supported initial creation of the doctrine support expanded liability for the manufacturer, whereas the policies that supported the definition of a defective product support a more limited potential liability for the manufacturer. Like negligence, strict products liability doctrine is supported by policies that simultaneously favor both expanded and contracted liability.

10

Constitutional Law

Constitutional law is the law defining those powers, rights, duties, privileges, and immunities created by a constitution. In other words, it is the law governing the application of the provisions of a constitution. As the term is commonly used by most American lawyers, it usually refers to the application of the provisions of the United States Constitution, and that is the primary sense in which the term is used here.

The Constitution is a charter that has four primary functions. First, it establishes a federal government and defines its powers. Second, it creates within the federal government three branches and allocates federal power among those branches. Third, it defines certain rights that individuals have against the government. Finally, it defines the powers and rights that exist among individual states.

I. CONSTITUTIONAL INTERPRETATION

The United States Constitution is a brief document that sets forth in very general terms the legal relationships that exist among the federal government, state governments, and private persons. Because constitutional provisions are so general, they are especially indeterminate. The result is that the language of the Constitution resolves relatively few disputes. The courts have addressed the problem of indeterminacy by adopting more specific rules of case law that define, apply, and limit the provisions of the Constitution.

The more specific case law rules add content to the Constitution's broad provisions and provide whatever predictability there is in constitutional law. For this reason, a constitutional scholar spends very little time studying the language of the Constitution. Rather, the study of constitutional law is almost entirely the study of cases.

Indeed, entire bodies of constitutional law have arisen that are not based on any specific provision. Such law may be based on the nature of the Constitution as a whole or on several provisions taken together. An example of the former is the doctrine of separation of powers. The Constitution does not anywhere use that term, and yet the Supreme Court has decided that certain limitations on the power of each branch of government are implicit in the Constitutional scheme. An example of a constitutional doctrine based on several provisions taken together is the right of privacy. The Constitution does not mention a right of privacy, but the Supreme Court has decided that it is created by "emanations" from several of the articles in the Bill of Rights.[1] In other words, like the separation of powers doctrine, the right of privacy is implied.

Constitutional interpretation is a weightier matter than statutory interpretation. One reason for this is that constitutional provisions, as the fundamental law of a nation-state, are intended to be more enduring than statutes and are generally difficult to amend. If a court misconstrues a statute, the legislature can amend the statute with relative ease to make clear the intended meaning. If the court errs in constitutional interpretation, however, the error cannot easily be corrected by an amendment.

Another reason that the ramifications of constitutional interpretation are usually much greater than the ramifications of statutory interpretation is that the Constitution is the supreme law of the land. An interpretation of the Constitution may invalidate laws ranging from federal statutes through local ordinances, whereas the effect of a statutory interpretation is usually far less sweeping.

The differences between constitutional and statutory interpretation have given rise to a rule of judicial restraint whereby the courts seek to decide cases without applying constitutional law, if possible. Assume, for example, that a criminal statute prohibits the sale of "pornography." A person charged with violation of the statute has at least two arguments: (1) the statute does not apply because what that person sold was not pornography as defined by the statute; and (2) even if it applies, the statute is invalid because it violates the Constitution's guarantee of free speech. If the court determines that the material is not pornographic, that decision requires that the charges be dismissed, regardless of whether the statute is constitutional or not. The court will usually consider the issue of statutory interpretation before reaching the issue of constitutional interpretation, because that approach may avoid the need to interpret the Constitution at all.

The tension between an interpretation based on text and one based on extrinsic evidence that pervades statutory interpretation[2] is reflected in constitutional interpretation as well. In interpreting the Constitution, courts vacillate between textualism, the theory that questions of constitutional law should be decided by reference to the language of the Constitution, and intentionalism, the theory that questions of constitutional law should be

---

[1] *See* Griswold v. Connecticut, 381 U.S. 479 (1965).
[2] *See* Chapters 2, 5, and 7.

decided by discerning the intent of the framers as expressed in sources outside the text. Textualism and intentionalism are sometimes referred to collectively as originalism because they ultimately look to the original understanding of the framers or as interpretivism because they seek to interpret either the language or the intent of the framers.

A third alternative, often called nonoriginalism or noninterpretivism, involves the attempt to interpret the Constitution according to some evolving set of community norms. This third approach is similar to intentionalism in that guidance is sought outside the text, but it differs from intentionalism in that the policies that it seeks to further are not those in the minds of the drafters but those of the contemporary community.

This nonoriginalist approach avoids the obvious limitations of the other approaches. It recognizes that the text of the Constitution is usually too vague to settle most disputes. At the same time, the attempt to discern the intent behind the language is doomed to failure since it is not possible to fathom the minds of men dead for nearly two hundred years and, in any event, the framers would have had no intent with respect to most issues that arise in the modern world. Indeed, all of the problems that characterize intentionalist theories of statutory interpretation apply with equal or greater force to intentionalist theories of constitutional interpretation. A nonoriginalist theory of interpretation permits a static document to evolve with the times, giving new meaning to terms in response to changing historical circumstances. Many argue that this flexible approach is especially appropriate for a Constitution, which is meant to endure over a period of centuries and thus must be adapted to new situations.

At the same time, nonoriginalism is subject to the criticism that it allows the court to rewrite the Constitution in accordance with its own views, under the pretext that these views represent community sentiment—a criticism that mirrors objections to nonoriginalist theories of statutory interpretation as well. Further, even if the court's interpretation of community sentiment is accurate, one purpose of the Constitution is to provide a stable set of legal principles that withstand shifts in political sentiment.

II. POWERS OF THE GOVERNMENT: FEDERALISM

A major purpose of the Constitution is to define the powers[3] of the federal government. A long series of clauses confers on the federal government the power to take various actions or enact certain types of laws.

---

[3] As noted in Chapter 1, a power—like a right or duty—is a type of legal relationship created by rules.

The distribution of powers between the federal and state governments reflects the theory of federalism. This section provides a basic description of that theory and illustrates how the Constitution empowers the federal government by discussing briefly one of those empowering clauses, the commerce clause.

The term "federalism" refers collectively to several rules and the underlying policies. One rule, codified in the Tenth Amendment to the Constitution, holds that the federal government has only those powers granted to it by the Constitution. Another rule, set forth in the Supremacy Clause, holds that where the federal government does have the power to enact a law, that law is the supreme law of the land and prevails over all inconsistent state and local laws in all American courts. The rules of federalism, in other words, limit the power of both the federal and the state governments.

Federalism represented a compromise between the opposing policies of protecting liberty and ensuring the efficaciousness of the government. A strong centralized government was thought more likely to destroy individual rights, but experience under the Articles of Confederation, the charter of the national government that preceded the Constitution, showed that if power was too decentralized, the national government would be unable to function. The compromise was to give the federal government only certain specified powers but to make it supreme within the ambit of those powers.

Federalism thus reflects the recurrent tension between the community and the individual. The welfare of the community demands an effective government, but protecting the rights of the individual requires limited and thus divided government.

Federalism also illustrates the phenomenon in which a policy stated at a moderately high level of generality is actually a means to an even more general policy. The framers did not consider the division of power between the federal and state governments to be an end in itself but merely a means to the end of preserving liberty.

One of the powers most often relied upon by the federal government in enacting legislation is the commerce clause. The commerce clause provides that Congress shall have the power to regulate commerce "among the several States." Thus, the constitutional rule creating this power has two elements. First, the statute must be a regulation of commerce. Second, the commerce must be among the several states.

Early in the nineteenth century in *Gibbons v. Ogden*,[4] the Supreme Court defined these elements. Commerce was defined as "intercourse," meaning more than mere trade and extending to navigation. Commerce among the states was defined as "that commerce which affects more states than one."

---

[4] 22 U.S. 1 (1824).

The rules defining these elements have changed over time, however, depending upon the political philosophy of the Supreme Court. In the late nineteenth century, for example, a Supreme Court hostile to federal economic regulation added rules limiting the scope of these elements. One such rule provided that the commerce power did not include the power to regulate manufacturing. That is, the term "commerce" was defined to exclude manufacturing.[5]

The Court's hostility to federal regulation of commerce ended in 1937 with *NLRB v. Jones & Laughlin Steel Corp.*,[6] in which the Court defined the commerce power to authorize regulation of any activity having a "close and substantial relation" to interstate commerce. Subsequent cases have refined this rule to require a substantial economic effect on interstate commerce. In *Wickard v. Filburn*,[7] the Court added a rule further defining the commerce power to include the power to regulate activity that, although trivial in itself, when aggregated with all other activity of the same class has a substantial economic effect on commerce.

Another line of cases has created a rule, sometimes called the protective principle, that is cumulative to the "effects" principle articulated by *Jones & Laughlin Steel*. The protective principle originated in 1903 with *Champion v. Ames*,[8] in which the Supreme Court held that Congress has the power to prohibit the interstate transportation of lottery tickets. The modern version of this rule provides that Congress has plenary power to exclude any article from commerce.[9] The effects principle and the protective principle are cumulative because if the facts satisfy the elements of *either* rule, then the federal power to regulate under the commerce clause exists.

The rules defining the commerce clause in modern times grant Congress far more power than it possessed prior to 1937. The shift in power from the states to the federal government reflected a change in the Supreme Court's judgment about the relationship between ends and means. The policy underlying federalism continued to be the protection of liberty. In the mid-1930s, however, the Supreme Court concluded that for many Americans the greatest threat to their freedom came from large corporations and other private entities that, by virtue of their national scope and their ability to relocate facilities, could not be effectively regulated by any one state. Thus, the Court decided that a stronger federal government capable of regulating these private entities anywhere in the nation would promote rather than impede individual liberty.

---

[5] *See* United States v. E.C. Knight Co., 156 U.S. 1 (1895).

[6] 310 U.S. 1 (1937).

[7] 317 U.S. 111 (1942).

[8] 188 U.S. 321 (1903).

[9] *See* United States v. Darby, 312 U.S. 100 (1941).

The rules defining the commerce power after 1937 also reflected a change in the relative weight accorded to policies, which was, more specifically, a shift from autonomy to paternalism. Prior to 1937, the Court was hostile to Congressional attempts to intervene in the private sphere to protect farmers, laborers, children, and other vulnerable groups. After 1937, no longer persuaded that many private transactions were truly free, the Court gave greater weight to the policy of paternalism, believing that the federal government has an extensive and constitutionally permissible role to play in regulating private transactions to protect the vulnerable.

One of the notable features of mid-twentieth-century commerce clause doctrine was that it seemed to confer very broad power on the federal government. Few areas of regulation seemed beyond the reach of Congress under the commerce clause. One explanation for this result is that the Court's conclusion that a stronger federal government was necessary to protect individual freedom seemed to suggest that, in this case, majoritarianism and individualism were consistent in their consequences. Protection of individual freedom was thought to be furthered by lodging greater power in the agent of the national community, the government. Thus, those who were normally sympathetic to majoritarian arguments were inclined to permit the expansion of federal power, whereas those who were normally sympathetic to individualist arguments were inclined to support the same result. Mainstream lawyers had reached a consensus that both poles of the tension between the community and the individual pushed in the same direction. The evolution of commerce clause doctrine in the twentieth century thus illustrates the point made in Chapter 7 that a particularly strong argument is one that seems to demonstrate that two policies that normally are perceived to be inconsistent in their consequences both support the result advocated by the lawyer.

Changes in the allocation of power between the federal and state governments in the twentieth century also illustrate the way in which policies stated at a high level of generality are indeterminate unless one makes additional assumptions about the relationship between ends and means in a particular factual context. Even assuming that one decides that individual liberty shall be protected against community power by the doctrine of federalism, resolving the tension between the community and the individual at that level of generality decides few questions. In the late nineteenth century, the protection of liberty was thought to be furthered by sharply limiting the power of the federal government, whereas in the mid-twentieth century it was thought to be furthered by a strong federal government. Stated at a high level of generality, the policy of individualism is largely indeterminate about the proper allocation of power between federal and state governments.

Only as courts make additional, more specific assumptions about the most effective means of protecting liberty does the policy of individualism become more determinate, and only then does it direct the lawyer to expand or contract federal power. These additional assumptions are drawn from the factual context in which the policy is to be applied. By ascertaining in a particular context the greatest threats to individual liberty and making judgments about how those threats are best counterbalanced, the lawyer is able to reach some conclusions about whether the individualist policy underlying federalism in that context calls for a stronger or weaker federal government.

III. INDIVIDUAL RIGHTS

The Constitution, particularly in the Bill of Rights, prescribes certain rights that individuals have. These provisions may be thought of as creating rules that limit the rules defining the power of the federal government. Moreover, because of the Supremacy Clause, to the extent that the rules codifying individual rights are interpreted as applicable to the states, they prevail over inconsistent state law. Thus, these rules also limit the power of state governments as defined in the state constitutions.

The framers of the Constitution conceived of natural law as creating certain rights that no government could lawfully impair. The Bill of Rights was considered a kind of codification of some of these rights, not an exclusive listing. Indeed, the Ninth Amendment expressly provides that "[t]he enumeration in the Constitution, of certain rights, shall not be construed to deny or disparage others retained by the people." That is, the framers believed that individuals have additional rights arising out of natural law that were not expressly included in the Bill of Rights.

In the years immediately following adoption of the Constitution, the Supreme Court sometimes claimed the power to invalidate legislation on the ground that it was inconsistent with natural law.[10] As belief in natural law diminished, however, that idea fell into disfavor. Today, the Supreme Court will not recognize a right as existing under the Constitution unless the right can be said to have been codified at least implicitly in one or more of the specific written provisions of the Constitution.

A. Free Speech

One of the most important rights enumerated in the Bill of Rights is that of free speech, which is set forth in the First Amendment. The text of the amendment provides that "Congress shall make no law . . . abridging the freedom of speech . . ."

---

[10] *See* Calder v. Bull, 3 U.S. 386 (1798).

Although this rule is phrased as a limitation on congressional power, it limits the power of the states as well.[11] It has three elements. If (1) an exercise of governmental power (2) abridges (3) freedom of speech, then the power to take the action is extinguished.

The Supreme Court has adopted case law rules defining each of these elements. The term "speech," for example, is defined as any activity that is intended to convey a message, where it is likely that an observer would understand the message. Thus, for example, wearing a black armband as a form of antiwar protest[12] or burning the American flag[13] have both been considered "speech," even if no words are spoken, because both actions communicate a message.

Defining speech to include expressive conduct as well as spoken utterances is based on certain policy considerations. One policy underlying the First Amendment is to permit the exchange of ideas necessary for a democracy to function. This may be thought of as a utilitarian theory of free expression, since it assumes that society as a whole enjoys greater happiness if expression is protected. Protecting all forms of expression, whether they involve words, conduct, or nonverbal symbols, furthers that policy.

Another policy underlying the First Amendment is to protect the rights of individuals, that is, to allow individuals to express themselves in ways that they find personally fulfilling. This may be thought of as a rights-based theory of free expression because it protects expression that is important to specific individuals, even if the expression does not necessarily contribute to the functioning of democracy or to improving the welfare of the society generally. This theory arguably supports a broader protection for free expression than the utilitarian theory because it calls for protecting speech of no value to anyone except the speaker.

One significant rule limiting the right of free speech is the obscenity doctrine. That doctrine states that the right of free speech does not protect obscene speech. That is, if speech is obscene, then the freedom of speech does not include the right to engage in it. Thus, the factual predicate has only one element: obscene speech.

The factual predicate of the obscenity doctrine has been defined by another rule, referred to as the *Miller*[14] test. Under that test, speech is obscene if (1) the average person, applying contemporary community standards, would find that the work, taken as a whole, appeals to the prurient in-

---

[11] The Supreme Court has held that the enactment of the Fourteenth Amendment resulted in the application of the First Amendment to the states as well as to the federal government. *See* Gitlow v. New York, 268 U.S. 652 (1925).

[12] *See* Tinker v. Des Moines Independent Community School Dist., 393 U.S. 503 (1969).

[13] *See* Texas v. Johnson, 491 U.S. 397 (1989).

[14] *See* Miller v. California, 413 U.S. 15 (1973).

terest; (2) the work depicts or describes, in a patently offensive way, sexual conduct specifically defined by the applicable state law; and (3) the work, taken as a whole, lacks serious literary, artistic, political, or scientific value.[15]

The rule that freedom of speech does not protect obscenity is based on a compromise between competing policy considerations. The policy of majoritarianism calls for deferring to the judgment of the legislature, in particular the judgment that obscenity must be suppressed for the good of the community. Balanced against this majoritarian policy is the policy of protecting individual expression, including that which may be objectionable to the majority.

Recall that balancing usually requires the lawyer to make two kinds of judgments. Specifically, the lawyer must make judgments about the relative importance of policies as well as about the relationship between ends and means.

In the case of obscenity, the courts have decided that obscenity does not contribute very much to the utilitarian values underlying free speech. Put another way, the propagation of obscenity is not a means that is closely related to promoting the functioning of a democracy, particularly given that obscenity, by definition, has no serious literary, artistic, political, or scientific value. The suppression of obscenity is thus thought not to impair significantly the utilitarian value of speech. Accordingly, the individual's right to self-expression in obscene ways is outweighed by the majority's desire to suppress obscenity.

As previously explained, utilitarianism is generally in conflict with rights-based theories because utilitarianism protects individual rights only to the extent that the society as a whole benefits from that protection. Thus, a utilitarian theory of free speech is inherently less protective than an individual rights theory. If one rests free speech on an individual rights theory, then obscenity has value if it furthers individual expression and fulfillment, even if it does not contribute anything to public debate. An individual rights theory of free speech would thus support a narrower definition of obscenity.

The rule defining obscenity illustrates the phenonemon by which rules are limited by more specific rules based on policies that subvert the policies underlying the general rule. Although the rule guaranteeing free speech is based on individualism, the rule is limited by the obscenity exception, which is based on a utilitarian conception of free speech. As previously noted, the policy of utilitarianism that underlies the obscenity doctrine is in conflict with the policy of individualism that underlies the more general rule of free speech.

---

[15] Miller v. California, 413 U.S. 15 (1973).

The rule defining obscenity also illustrates the indeterminacy of many legal rules. The definition of obscenity has frequently been criticized on the ground that reasonable people could differ concerning whether the definition applies to a particular instance of expression.[16] Indeed, the inherent difficulty of defining the term prompted Supreme Court Justice Potter Stewart to write in a much-quoted opinion that it would perhaps be impossible to define obscenity intelligibly, although, he said, "I know it when I see it."[17]

B. *Due Process*

The due process clause of the Constitution prohibits the federal or state governments from depriving any person of life, liberty, or property without due process of law.[18] This clause, like the First Amendment's guarantee of free expression, is phrased as a limitation on government power.

The due process clause actually imposes several different limitations on government power, each of which has been formulated as one or more rules. One such rule, sometimes called the doctrine of substantive due process, provides that the government may not deprive a person of liberty or property unless the deprivation is rationally related to a legitimate state interest—a rule sometimes referred to as the rational relationship test.

A second rule included in the doctrine of substantive due process provides that the government may not deprive a person of a *fundamental* right of liberty or property unless the deprivation is narrowly drawn to further a compelling state interest—a rule sometimes referred to as the strict scrutiny test.

The courts have not adopted any single definition of the term "fundamental right." Disagreements among the members of the Supreme Court concerning how to define a fundamental right illustrate the phenonemon in which a policy conflict that is resolved at one level of generality merely reemerges at a more specific level. The rule imposing strict scrutiny on infringements of fundamental rights seemed to resolve the conflict between majoritarianism and individualism in favor of individualism. The conflict reemerges, however, in the various attempts to formulate more specific rules defining fundamental rights. One suggested definition would require that

---

[16] For a discussion and criticism of the evolving standards, *see* the opinions in Miller v. California, 413 U.S. 15 (1973) and Paris Adult Theatre I v. Slaton, 413 U.S. 49 (1973).

[17] Jacobellis v. Ohio, 378 U.S. 184, 197 (1964).

[18] Technically, there are two due process clauses—one in the Fifth Amendment and one in the Fourteenth Amendment. The former applies to the federal government, whereas the latter applies to the states. The substance of the clauses is the same, and they are treated here as if they constitute a single clause.

such a right be "deeply rooted in this Nation's history and tradition,"[19] a definition that tends to limit the number of such rights and to base them on a national consensus. Another suggested definition would define a fundamental right as one that forms a "central . . . part of an individual's life,"[20] a definition that tends to expand the number of such rights and to identify them by their value to the individual rather than by their recognition by a national consensus. Thus, the first definition would move the law toward a policy of majoritarianism, whereas the second would move the law toward a policy of individualism.

A series of cases has illustrated the term "fundamental right." For example, one group of cases has held that the right of privacy is a fundamental right.

The right of privacy is not specifically mentioned in the Constitution and thus is a right that the Supreme Court has found implicit in several different provisions, including, among others, the First and the Ninth Amendments. The very existence of the right of privacy reflects a policy of nonoriginalist constitutional interpretation, in which the text is interpreted in light of community values rather than by reference to the language alone or the intent of the drafters.

The fundamental right of privacy has not been treated as a single, indivisible right. Rather, like many legal relationships,[21] the fundamental right of privacy actually refers to a collection of more specific rights, such as the right to use a contraceptive[22] and the right to an abortion.[23] At the same time, it does not include the right of homosexuals to engage in sodomy.[24]

The concept of a fundamental right illustrates the ways in which lawyers can manipulate the generality of rules in order to broaden or narrow their scope. In *Michael H. v. Gerald D.*,[25] members of the Court divided over whether the father of a child born to a woman married to another man had a fundamental right to establish his paternity. Justice Antonin Scalia's opinion announcing the judgment of the Court took the position that a fundamental right should be proven by reference to "the most specific level at which a relevant tradition protecting, or denying protection to, the asserted right can be identified."[26] Justice Scalia found that no prior case had

---

[19] *See* Moore v. East Cleveland, 431 U.S. 494, 503 (1977).

[20] Bowers v. Hardwick, 478 U.S. 186, 199 (1986) (Blackmun, J., dissenting).

[21] Recall the discussion from Chapter 2 of the fact that the term "right" or "duty" may refer collectively to several more specific rights or duties.

[22] Griswold v. Connecticut, 381 U.S. 479 (1965).

[23] Roe v. Wade, 410 U.S. 113 (1973).

[24] Bowers v. Hardwick, 478 U.S. 186 (1986)

[25] 491 U.S. 110 (1989).

[26] *Id.* at 127, note 6.

recognized as fundamental the right of a father to establish parental rights with respect to a child conceived within and born into a marriage other than his own. By reading the right recognized in each prior case at a very specific level, Justice Scalia effectively distinguished all prior cases and concluded that no case had recognized the right asserted by the father. Justice William Brennan's dissent, by contrast, read prior cases as protecting the parent-child relationship. By reading the right recognized in prior cases at a more general level, Justice Brennan found repeated protection of the parent-child relationship and concluded that the natural father's right to establish paternity was supported by precedent.

The two substantive due process rules described above (the rational relationship and strict scrutiny tests), to use the terminology of Chapter 3, are cumulative. That is, they are parallel to each other; either one alone may invalidate a state or federal law.

The form of these two rules is especially striking. Both rules make explicit that their application to a particular set of facts consists of a policy judgment. Specifically, both rules require the court to make a judgment about the relationship between ends and means and the relative importance of policies.

In the case of the first rule, the rational relationship test, in order to prevail the state must show that the law is reasonably related to a legitimate state policy. If it does, the law will not be void under the due process clause. Thus, the policy supporting the rule need not be particularly important, and the law may be a relatively attenuated means of advancing the policy.

In the case of the second rule, the strict scrutiny test, in order to prevail the state must make a much more difficult showing: It must demonstrate that the law is narrowly drawn to further a compelling policy of the state. The policy must be a more important one than under the rational relationship test, and the relationship between ends and means must be much more direct.

The factual predicate of the strict scrutiny rule thus has three elements. The law must be (1) narrowly drawn (2) to further (3) a compelling state interest. Let us consider each of these elements briefly.

First, the interest furthered by the law must be compelling. The courts have adopted no rule that determines which interests are compelling and which are not. Rather, the court simply makes a judgment about the weight of the policy underlying the challenged law. If the court believes that the policy is important enough, it will declare the government's interest in that law to be compelling. This element illustrates in the starkest possible terms the ad hoc nature of the policy judgments required by the process of applying law to fact.

Second, the law must further the policy of the state. That is, the law must make accomplishment of the policy more likely than if there were no law.

For example, in *Zablocki v. Redhail,*[27] the Supreme Court held unconstitutional a statute that denied a marriage license to noncustodial parents with unpaid child support obligations. The state's policy was to ensure that noncustodial parents support their children. The Court found, however, that the statute might simply cause such parents to cohabit with their lovers and produce children out of wedlock. The net result would be the birth of more children of unwed parents, which would not further any state policy. In other words, the law was not an effective means of furthering the state's ends.

Third, the law must be narrowly drawn. Courts have articulated various factors that they consider in determining whether a law is narrowly drawn. If the law is overinclusive or underinclusive, it may not be considered narrowly drawn. An overinclusive law regulates conduct that is not part of the mischief the legislature intended to remedy, whereas an underinclusive law addresses only part of the mischief that the legislature was attempting to remedy.

For example, in *Zablocki,* the Court held that the statute was not narrowly tailored enough to satisfy the requirements of the Constitution. The Court found the law underinclusive because it did not prevent the parent from assuming other costly obligations, such as the purchase of a house, that might equally prevent the parent from supporting his or her children. That is, the law addressed only a small part of the problem of parents who spend their money in ways other than to support their children.

The Court found the law overinclusive because marriage might make the parent more financially secure and thus better able to provide for his or her children. That is, the law applied to parents who were not part of the problem that the legislature was addressing. The fit between the legislative ends and the means chosen was too attenuated to justify the burden on the right to marry.

---

[27] 434 U.S. 374 (1978). The statute was challenged as a violation of both the due process and the equal protection clause. The equal protection clause imposes ends-means tests very similar to those imposed by the doctrine of substantive due process. Ultimately, the Supreme Court held that the law violated the equal protection clause. The case is discussed here, though, because its reasoning is equally applicable to a discussion of substantive due process.

11

Civil Procedure

Civil procedure is the law governing civil litigation in the courts. It prescribes the mechanisms by which parties obtain judicial determination of the rights and duties created by civil substantive law, such as contracts, torts, and constitutional law.

Civil procedure has largely been codified. Congress, in Title 28 of the United States Code, has enacted a number of statutes governing various aspects of federal court procedure. One such statute is the Rules Enabling Act of 1934,[1] which authorizes the Supreme Court to adopt rules of civil procedure, subject to congressional approval. Pursuant to this act, the Supreme Court has adopted the Federal Rules of Civil Procedure to govern procedure in the federal district courts, as well as several other sets of rules to govern procedure in the specialized trial courts and the appellate courts. A large number of states have adopted modified versions of the Federal Rules of Civil Procedure, and even those states that have not done so have adopted some of the innovations included in those rules.

Among the most important rules governing procedure are those that prescribe the jurisdiction of the courts, that is, the power[2] of the courts to decide cases. The power of a court over a case actually comprises two distinct powers, either of which may exist without the other: power over the defendant, and power with respect to the type of case. These powers are known, respectively, as personal jurisdiction and subject matter jurisdiction. The balance of this chapter is devoted to discussing some of the rules defining personal and subject matter jurisdiction.

I. PERSONAL JURISDICTION

A party can obtain judicial determination of a right only by filing suit in a court with power over the defendant, a power generally referred to as

---

[1] The current version is codified at 28 U.S.C. § 2072 (1988 and Supp. 1993).

[2] As explained in Chapter 2, a power, like a right or duty, is a type of legal relationship created by rules.

personal jurisdiction. For example, as will be seen shortly, a California court generally has no personal jurisdiction over a citizen of Kentucky who has never had any contact with California. Thus, the California court would have no power to adjudicate whether the Kentuckian owed a duty to someone.

Power over the defendant exists as a general matter where two elements are satisfied. First, the legislature by statute must have conferred power on the court. Second, the exercise of that power must be consistent with the due process clause of the Constitution.[3] Each of these elements is discussed in turn.

A. *Statutory Basis of Jurisdiction*

The first element of the rule defining the personal jurisdiction of the courts is the existence of a statute conferring on the courts power over the defendant. Some states, such as California, have authorized their state courts to exercise personal jurisdiction to the full extent permitted by the Constitution. Thus, any constitutional exercise of power is authorized by statute. In other states, however, the legislature has enacted narrower statutes that may provide the courts with less power than the Constitution would permit them to have.

In the case of the federal courts, Congress prescribed the limits of personal jurisdiction in Rule 4 of the Federal Rules of Civil Procedure. Thus, for a federal court to have power over the defendant, the defendant must be subject to service of process under Rule 4.

B. *Limitations Imposed by Due Process*

1. *Traditional Bases of Jurisdiction*

The second element, that personal jurisdiction be consistent with the due process clause, was imposed by the Supreme Court in the well-known case of *Pennoyer v. Neff.*[4] For the sake of simplicity, only the limitations that the due process clause imposes on personal jurisdiction exercised by *state* courts are discussed here.

Prior to the decision in *Pennoyer,* state courts generally exercised power over a defendant in only three situations: where the defendant was a citizen of the state in which the court was located; where the defendant was served

---

[3] As noted in Chapter 10, the Constitution has two due process clauses, one in the Fifth Amendment and the other in the Fourteenth Amendment. The former applies to the federal government, whereas the latter applies to the state governments. They are treated here as a single clause.

[4] 95 U.S. 714 (1877).

with legal process while present in the state's territory; or where the defendant had consented to the court's jurisdiction. These traditional limitations were based in part on a concern that a defendant who did not fall into one of those categories as a practical matter might be able to ignore the court's order, to the great embarrassment of the court.

Pennoyer stated, however, that these limitations were not merely voluntary limitations based on policy but were imposed by the due process clause. That is, under *Pennoyer*, a court's exercise of jurisdiction would violate the Constitution unless one of the three traditional bases of power just described was present.

The traditional bases of power proved increasingly inadequate under modern circumstances. For example, a nonresident motorist who caused a collision and then left the state seemed beyond the power of the courts as defined in *Pennoyer*. States responded by enacting statutes that deemed certain conduct, such as driving within the state, to be implied consent to jurisdiction, an approach held to be consistent with the due process clause in *Hess v. Pawlowski*.[5] By adopting the legal fiction of implied consent, states were able to expand the power of the courts while staying within the literal terms of the rule in *Pennoyer*.

Another problem was posed by the existence of corporations engaged in interstate transactions. Assume, for example, that a Massachusetts corporation breached a contract that its sales agent had negotiated with a California supplier. Although the Massachusetts corporation may have property and employees in California, the corporation itself is an abstract legal concept and is not physically present in California or anywhere else. Thus, the only possible basis the California courts would have for exercising jurisdiction over the Massachusetts corporation would be consent, which might not be forthcoming. To solve this problem, courts again resorted to various fictions, finding that an out-of-state corporation's conduct of business in state constituted "presence" in the state, or an implied consent to suit.

2. Minimum Contacts

As a result of the growing dissatisfaction with the restrictiveness of the traditional bases of jurisdiction, the Supreme Court created a new basis in *International Shoe Co. v. State of Washington*.[6] In that case, the Court adopted a rule that a state has power over individuals who have "minimum contacts" with the territory such that the exercise of jurisdiction over them would not offend traditional notions of fair play and substantial justice. The minimum contacts rule permitted courts to exercise jurisdiction over

---

[5] 274 U.S. 352 (1927).
[6] 326 U.S. 310 (1945).

out-of-state motorists and corporations without having to resort to the legal fiction of implied consent or presence. Those legal fictions had allowed the courts to assert jurisdiction in cases where jurisdiction seemed unwarranted under the traditional bases of jurisdiction. The adoption of the minimum contacts rule represented an abandonment of the pretense and a concession that the law had in fact changed.

In a series of subsequent decisions, the Supreme Court has defined two different types of power that the court may have over the defendant under *International Shoe*. One type of power, called general jurisdiction, permits the court to assert power over the defendant with respect to any claim the plaintiff may allege. The other type of power, called specific jurisdiction, permits the court to assert power over the defendant only with respect to a claim related to the contacts that form the basis for the power. Each of these two types of power is created by a separate rule.

a. General Jurisdiction

General jurisdiction exists if the defendant's contacts with the state are systematic and continuous.[7] Thus, the factual predicate necessary to establish general jurisdiction has only one element: systematic and continuous contacts.

b. Specific Jurisdiction

Specific jurisdiction exists if (1) the defendant has purposefully availed himself or herself of the benefits and protections of the laws of the state and (2) the exercise of jurisdiction would be reasonable under the circumstances. The factual predicate necessary to establish specific jurisdiction thus has two elements. Additional rules have further defined and limited each of these two elements.

(1) Purposeful Availment

The first element is purposeful availment of the benefits and protections of the laws of the forum state. In *World-Wide Volkswagen Corp. v. Woodson*,[8] the Supreme Court cited the rule that the unilateral act of someone unaffiliated with the defendant does not constitute purposeful availment. More specifically, the Court held that the decision of the plaintiff to drive to Oklahoma a car sold to him by a New York car dealer did not constitute purposeful availment of the benefits and protections of Oklahoma law by the New York dealer.

---

[7] *See, e.g.,* Perkins v. Benguet Consolidated Mining Co., 342 U.S. 437 (1952).
[8] 444 U.S. 286 (1980).

An exception to this rule exists, however, where the defendant places a product in a stream of commerce that foreseeably will carry the product to the forum state.[9] Even though the product may be carried to the forum state by individuals with no affiliation with the defendant, the defendant's act of placing the product in the stream of commerce is considered a form of purposeful availment.

There are currently two versions of the stream of commerce rule, neither of which has yet obtained the support of a majority of the members of the Supreme Court. In *Asahi Metal Industry Co., Ltd. v. Superior Court*,[10] Justice Brennan wrote an opinion supported by four of the nine justices of the Court endorsing a rule that purposeful availment exists where the defendant places the product in the stream of commerce with *knowledge* that it will reach the forum state. Justice Sandra Day O'Connor wrote an opinion, also supported by four of the nine justices, stating that purposeful availment exists where the defendant places the product in the stream of commerce with some indication of a *purpose* that the product reach the forum state. Justice O'Connor's opinion suggested, by way of illustration, that one such indication of purpose would be designing a product for sale in the forum state. Which version of the rule is correct will remain unclear until the Supreme Court clarifies that question in a future case.

(2) Reasonableness

The second element of specific jurisdiction, that the exercise of power be reasonable, was also further defined in *World-Wide Volkswagen*. The Supreme Court adopted the rule that the reasonableness of jurisdiction is determined by balancing five elements: the burden on the defendant, the convenience to the plaintiff, the interest of the forum state, judicial efficiency, and any substantive policies affected by the choice of forum.

The definition of this second element is an example of the use of a standard in place of a formal rule. The law does not state that if certain facts are present, jurisdiction will be reasonable. It merely states the policies to be achieved—such as minimizing burden on the defendant, providing a convenient forum for the plaintiff, and promoting efficient adjudication—and then leaves to future courts the task of applying these policies to particular factual situations. Like any standard, the reasonableness test permits the court to arrive at the fairest result in any particular case, though at some cost to predictability and uniformity in the law.

The reasonableness test, again like standards generally, permits a court to reach virtually any result it believes just. Although cases arise in which a

---

[9] The "forum" state is the state in which the court adjudicating the case is located.
[10] 480 U.S. 102 (1987).

particular result would further all of the policies, often a given result promotes some policies while impeding others. Because the test does not indicate how much weight each policy is to be given, the court can assign the greatest weight to the policies that would be furthered by what it believes to be the best outcome.

In the case of the reasonableness test, once more as in the case of standards generally, precedent is less likely to seem controlling than in cases where the law prescribes a rigid rule. Whereas a rigid rule specifies the facts that must be present for a particular legal consequence to occur, the reasonableness standard allows any set of facts to give rise to the legal consequence of power over the defendant, as long as those facts seem to further at least some of the policies underlying the standard. With so many facts potentially relevant, the likelihood is low that the relevant facts of one case will be similar enough to the relevant facts of a later case to require the conclusion that the earlier case controls the later case.

c. Jurisdictional Rules as a Compromise

The due process clause's limitation on court power seems to represent a compromise between the policies of individualism and majoritarianism.[11] An individualist policy suggests that the state should have minimal power over individuals, whereas a majoritarian policy is consistent with the government's having power to enforce its laws against wrongdoers. Were individualism to prevail all the time, a court's power over persons might be limited to cases in which the defendant consented to jurisdiction. Were majoritarianism to prevail all the time, a court's power might extend to all persons wherever located.

The Supreme Court has reached a compromise in which a defendant's claim to freedom from the minimal exercise of state power represented by specific jurisdiction ends once the defendant has reached out to the forum state in a purposeful way and jurisdiction is reasonable. Because general jurisdiction is a more substantial exercise of state power, the defendant's claim to freedom from general jurisdiction is lost only where the defendant has engaged in systematic and continuous contacts with the forum state or meets one of the traditional bases of jurisdiction. That is, a greater act of will by the defendant in relation to the forum state must exist before the state can exercise the more sweeping form of power represented by general jurisdiction.

The rules defining minimum contacts illustrate the phenonemon in which a general rule is defined by a more specific rule that is supported by policies

---

[11] For a fuller discussion, see Vandevelde, *Ideology, Due Process and Civil Procedure,* 67 St. John's L. Rev. 265 (1993).

that are inconsistent with the policies underlying the general rule. The minimum contacts rule was based on a majoritarian policy that justified the state's projection of power over defendants. The first cases applying the minimum contacts rule seemed to embrace that same policy choice in that they continued the expansion of jurisdiction begun by *International Shoe*.[12] In 1958, however, the U.S. Supreme Court in *Hanson v. Denckla*,[13] held for the first time that minimum contacts existed only where the defendant had "purposefully avail[ed]" himself or herself of the benefits and protections of the laws of the forum state. In adopting the purposeful availment test, the Court embraced a policy of individualism: Jurisdiction would exist only where the defendant had exercised his or her will. That is, although the minimum contacts rule was based on a majoritarian policy, in defining minimum contacts to require purposeful availment the Court adopted a definition based on the opposing policy of individualism. The policy underlying the definitional rule thus subverts the policy underlying the rule that it defines.

The history of the minimum contacts rule also illustrates the way in which policy conflicts that appear to be resolved at one level of generality simply reemerge at a lower level of generality. In adopting the minimum contacts rule, the Court seemed to resolve the conflict between majoritarianism and individualism in favor of majoritarianism. The conflict reemerged, however, in the course of adopting a more specific rule defining minimum contacts. In adopting the purposeful availment requirement, the Court seemed to resolve the dispute at that level of generality in favor of individualism. The conflict nevertheless reemerged yet again in the course of defining purposeful availment in the stream of commerce cases. Four Justices, led by Justice O'Connor, sought to resolve the conflict in favor of the policy of individualism by requiring that the defendant acted purposefully, while four other Justices, led by Justice Brennan, sought to resolve the conflict in the direction of majoritarianism by requiring only knowledge. As of 1995, the Court had not resolved the conflict at that very specific level.

The adoption of the minimum contacts standard also illustrates the way in which policies that are inconsistent in theory may be consistent in their consequences. In adopting the minimum contacts standard, courts moved from a formalist, rule-based system of defining personal jurisdiction to a more instrumentalist, standard-based system. The rigid *Pennoyer* triad of consent, citizenship, and presence was supplanted by the flexible standard of minimum contacts.

---

[12] *See* Travelers Health Ass'n v. Virginia, 339 U.S. 643 (1950); Mullane v. Central Hanover Bank & Trust Co., 339 U.S. 306 (1950); McGee v. International Life Insurance, 355 U.S. 220 (1957).

[13] 357 U.S. 235 (1958).

Thus, the shift from an individualist theory of jurisdiction to a more majoritarian one was accompanied by a shift from a formalist concept to a more instrumental one. As has been shown, formalism at a very high level of generality is inconsistent with individualism. The inconsistency was noted, for example, in the use of the objective standard in contract and tort law, where the formalism of the objective standard subverted the individualism underlying the doctrine of offer and acceptance in contract law and the negligence and consent doctrines in tort law.[14] In the case of personal jurisdiction, however, a formalist approach was perceived as more protective of individual will, whereas the flexible minimum contacts standard seemed to provide the state a broader opportunity to impose its will.

II. SUBJECT MATTER JURISDICTION

A court can enforce a right only if it has power with respect to the type of claim being brought, a form of power generally known as subject matter jurisdiction. The extent of a court's subject matter jurisdiction is defined by statute.

State judicial systems typically have one group of courts of general jurisdiction, that is, courts that have the power to adjudicate disputes involving all areas of the law.[15] State judicial systems also have a number of courts of limited jurisdiction, such as probate court, family court, or small claims court. These courts have power to adjudicate certain types of disputes, such as those involving a will, a divorce, or a claim for less than a prescribed amount of money.

All federal courts are courts of limited subject matter jurisdiction. This fact reflects the doctrine of federalism, which holds that the federal government possesses only the limited powers delegated to it by the Constitution.[16] Given the limited nature of federal power, the framers of the Constitution thought it inappropriate to create federal courts of general jurisdiction.

Accordingly, the Constitution authorizes Congress to confer on the federal courts the power to hear only certain categories of cases. Congress, however, has chosen not to confer on the federal courts all of the subject matter jurisdiction authorized by the Constitution. In this section, two of the most important forms of jurisdiction conferred by Congress on the federal courts are examined: federal question jurisdiction and diversity jurisdiction.

---

[14] *See* Chapters 8 and 9.

[15] The term "general jurisdiction," when used in the context of subject matter jurisdiction, has a different meaning than when used in the context of personal jurisdiction.

[16] Federalism is discussed in greater detail in Chapter 10.

A. Federal Question Jurisdiction

A first statute confers on the federal district courts power over cases "arising under" federal law,[17] a form of jurisdiction generally referred to as federal question jurisdiction. Federal question jurisdiction exists so that federal courts can hear cases in which federal law will in some sense be controlling. In this way, the federal government can ensure that the policies underlying federal law are advanced by the courts applying that law.

The courts have adopted several cumulative rules defining the phrase "arising under" as used in the statute. These rules are cumulative in that, if any one of them is satisfied, the case "arises under" federal law.

One rule provides that a case arises under federal law if the cause of action was created by federal law.[18] For example, claims alleging a violation of a federal civil rights statute arise under federal law because the civil rights statute creates the cause of action.

Another rule provides that a case arises under federal law if the cause of action was created by state law, but the success of the plaintiff's claim depends upon an interpretation or application of federal law.[19] For example, a negligence claim alleging that a corporation was negligent because it violated a federal safety regulation could be held to arise under federal law. Although the cause of action for negligence is created by state law, in order to prevail the defendant must prove that the federal safety regulation was violated. Thus, the success of the claim depends upon an application of federal law.

The statute granting federal question jurisdiction to the district courts has been limited by a judicially enacted rule known as the "well-pleaded complaint" rule.[20] Under this rule, the federal question must be a necessary part of the plaintiff's complaint. That is, a federal question raised by a defense does not bring the case within federal subject matter jurisdiction.

For example, assume that a retail store sues a manufacturer for breach of contract because the manufacturer failed to ship some toys that the retail store had ordered. The manufacturer raises as its sole defense the fact that after the order was placed, the federal government issued regulations banning this type of toy. Although the result in the case may well depend on an interpretation or application of the federal toy regulation, that federal law was raised as part of a defense and not as a necessary part of the plaintiff's claim. The plaintiff's claim was for breach of contract and could be set forth in its entirety without ever mentioning the toy regulation. Thus, under the

---

[17] 28 U.S.C. § 1331 (1988).

[18] *See* American Well Works Co. v. Layne & Bowler Co., 241 U.S. 257 (1916).

[19] *See* Smith v. Kansas City Title & Trust Co., 255 U.S. 180 (1921).

[20] *See* Louisville & Nashville Railroad Company v. Mottley, 211 U.S. 149 (1908).

well-pleaded complaint rule, the court probably would not have federal question jurisdiction over the retailer's claim.

The well-pleaded complaint rule is based on a policy determination by the federal courts that in order to promote the efficient functioning of the court system, a federal court must be able to ascertain at the commencement of a lawsuit whether it has jurisdiction, rather than having to wait until all the pleadings have been filed to see if any party raised a federal question. Of course, the fact that a federal law is applicable to a crucial defense, as opposed to the plaintiff's claim, does not in any way lessen the federal government's interest in furthering the policies underlying that law. Yet, under this rule, where the federal question arises in connection with a defense rather than the plaintiff's complaint, federal question jurisdiction does not exist. Thus, the courts have determined, in effect, that the policy of efficiency underlying the well-pleaded complaint rule outweighs the policy of empowering the federal courts to decide issues of federal law.

As has been discussed, federalism reflects the tension between the community and the individual and was originally conceived as essentially an individualist doctrine.[21] That is, although the efficient functioning of government for the good of the community might have suggested that the federal government should have plenary power, the power of the federal government was limited in order to prevent it from becoming oppressive. In the 1930s, courts reconceived the source of the primary threats to freedom, moving from an approach consistent with the policy of autonomy to one consistent with the policy of paternalism. Whereas in the nineteenth century the courts had seen the government as the primary threat to freedom, in the mid-twentieth century they saw private economic power as a greater threat and thus authorized an expansion of federal power to control that threat. That is, federalism continued to be based on an individualist policy, but individualism was now seen as consistent in consequence with a stronger federal government.

The well-pleaded complaint rule, however, reintroduces a new limitation on federal power in the name of efficiency. Thus, the tension between the community and the individual that was initially resolved by adopting the doctrine of federalism and creating courts with limited power reemerged at the level of the various subrules defining the precise terms of that federal judicial power. The well-pleaded complaint rule represents a victory for the communitarian policy of efficiency over the more individualist policies that, in the twentieth century, have underlain expanded federal power. The well-pleaded complaint rule thus illustrates the situation in which a specific rule qualifying a more general rule is based on policies inconsistent with the policies underlying the more general rule.

---

[21] *See* Chapter 10.

B. *Diversity Jurisdiction*

A second statute confers on the federal district court power over cases between citizens of different states,[22] a form of power known as diversity jurisdiction. The rule created by this statute has been defined by the courts to require "complete diversity," meaning that no plaintiff may be a citizen of the same state as any defendant.[23] As a rule of judicial interpretation, the complete diversity requirement illustrates the situation in which a case law rule ostensibly interpreting a statutory rule may give the statutory rule a different scope than its language might have seemed to warrant.

The term "citizen" has been defined to include one who is a United States citizen and who is domiciled in a state. The term domicile, in turn, has been defined as the place where one resides with the intent to remain indefinitely.

The apparent policy behind diversity jurisdiction was to allow out-of-state litigants to adjudicate their claims in federal courts, which might be less prejudiced against an out-of-state party than a state court, an assumption that has by no means been proven. Assuming that this is correct, however, the rule creating diversity jurisdiction is far broader than this policy would require. Put another way, it is overinclusive. For example, a federal district court in Kentucky has subject matter jurisdiction over a claim filed by a citizen of Massachusetts against a citizen of California in Kentucky, despite the fact that both litigants are from out of state and thus there is no reason to believe that the court would favor either party over the other. Similarly, a Kentuckian suing a Californian in Kentucky may file the complaint in federal court, even though the Kentuckian has no reason to fear the prejudice of the local state courts.

The rule is underinclusive as well. For example, if twenty-five Kentuckians sued twenty-five Californians and one Kentuckian in Kentucky, the fact that there was at least one Kentuckian on each side would preclude the exercise of diversity jurisdiction, even though the presence of so many Californians among the defendants seems to invite uneven justice.

In the case of diversity jurisdiction, then, the precise line drawn by the statutory rule seems difficult to explain on policy grounds. The diversity rule illustrates the problem discussed in Chapter 2 of identifying a legislative policy that adequately explains a statute, particularly where the statute is based on a series of crude compromises. It also illustrates the tendency of rigid rules to be overinclusive and as well as underinclusive.

---

[22] 28 U.S.C. § 1332 (1988).

[23] *See* Strawbridge v. Curtiss, 7 U.S. (3 Cranch) 267 (1806). The Constitution would have permitted Congress to confer on the federal district courts power over claims in which diversity was not complete, but Congress elected not to do so. *See* State Farm Fire & Cas. Co. v. Tashire, 386 U.S. 523 (1967).

Conclusion

These preceding chapters have had a single goal—to teach the techniques of thinking like a lawyer. By now it should be clear, however, that legal reasoning is not a mechanical process, but rather one involving the exercise of judgment.

Thus, the result that the lawyer reaches through the legal reasoning process can depend to a very great degree on the policies or values that the lawyer believes a court would prefer.[1] Where the lawyer is counseling a client, the lawyer can make clear that more than one outcome is possible and explain the considerations that would militate in favor of each. The lawyer's knowledge of the prevailing policy preferences of the local courts may assist the lawyer in estimating the probability that a court would reach any given result. Where the lawyer is an advocate, the lawyer is expected by the norms of the profession to urge the court to prefer those policies that will lead to the result most favorable to the client, regardless of the lawyer's personal preferences.

The legal reasoning process thus deals with advocacy and prediction, not with fixed truth. The lawyer is not engaged in mechanically explicating what the law is, but rather in formulating a series of arguments about what the law ought to be as applied to a particular situation. In that process, political and moral values play as large a role as neutral logic or reason.

Faced with the intrinsically political nature of law, lawyers adopt a variety of poses. Some believe that they have no obligation other than that imposed by the professional code of ethics and that they may use their skills

---

[1] There is an old joke that reflects this unalterable truth. A mathematician, an economist, and a lawyer are asked this question: "How much is two and two?" The mathematician pulls out a paper and pencil, scribbles for a moment, and announces, "Four." The economist consults a series of charts, puzzles over them, and finally says, "Well, if all current trends continue, I project that the answer will be four." The lawyer stands up, shuts the door, lowers the shades, leans close to the questioner, and asks in a conspiratorial whisper, "How much do you *want* it to be?"

for all who would employ them. Others see every case as political advocacy and find it difficult to represent anyone whose views are not their own. Many lawyers find themselves somewhere between these poles—perhaps being generally willing to represent nearly anyone who retains them, except for certain specific types of clients or cases.

In writing this book, I have avoided passing judgment on the question of the purposes for which a lawyer should or may provide legal representation. I have tried, insofar as I can, simply to teach the tricks of the trade.

This book, in other words, has been a kind of "how-to" book. The author of a how-to book in some sense empowers other people, without having any control over the way in which the power is used. The automotive repair manual can as easily be used to fix the getaway car as to repair the church bus.

A how-to book can equally distract attention from the fact that obtaining a replacement would be better than making repairs. The automotive repair manual makes it possible to keep the lemon running a little longer, when what the owner really should do is haul it to the junkyard and buy a new car.

Although I have avoided expressing my judgment on questions of political policy and moral value, I hope that I have not distracted the reader from recognizing that such questions are inherent in every act of legal reasoning. It is my hope, as well, that in learning how to think like men and women of the law, we do not forget how to judge like people of conscience.

Selected Bibliography

BOOKS

B. ACKERMAN, RECONSTRUCTING AMERICAN LAW (1984).
A. ALTMAN, CRITICAL LEGAL STUDIES: A LIBERAL CRITIQUE (1990).
P. ATIYAH & R. SUMMERS, FORM AND SUBSTANCE IN ANGLO-AMERICAN LAW (1987).
M. BRINT & W. WEAVER, EDS. PRAGMATISM IN LAW & SOCIETY (1991).
S. BURTON, AN INTRODUCTION TO LAW AND LEGAL REASONING (1985).
R. DWORKIN, TAKING RIGHTS SERIOUSLY (1977).
R. DWORKIN, A MATTER OF PRINCIPLE (1985).
R. DWORKIN, LAW'S EMPIRE (1986).
G. GILMORE, THE AGES OF AMERICAN LAW (1977).
H. HART & A. SACKS, THE LEGAL PROCESS (1994).
J. HERGET, AMERICAN JURISPRUDENCE, 1870–1970: A HISTORY (1990).
M. HORWITZ, THE TRANSFORMATION OF AMERICAN LAW, 1780–1860 (1977).
M. HORWITZ, THE TRANSFORMATION OF AMERICAN LAW, 1870–1960 (1992).
D. KAIRYS, ED. THE POLITICS OF LAW: A PROGRESSIVE CRITIQUE (1990).
M. KELMAN, A GUIDE TO CRITICAL LEGAL STUDIES (1987).
E. LEVI, AN INTRODUCTION TO LEGAL REASONING (1949).
K. LLEWELLYN, THE BRAMBLE BUSH (1930).
D. LUBAN, LEGAL MODERNISM (1994).
R. MALLOY, LAW AND ECONOMICS: A COMPARATIVE APPROACH TO THEORY AND PRACTICE (1990).
A. POLINSKY, AN INTRODUCTION TO LAW AND ECONOMICS (2d ed. 1989).
R. POSNER, ECONOMIC ANALYSIS OF LAW (4th ed. 1992).
E. PURCELL, THE CRISIS OF DEMOCRATIC THEORY (1973).
M. RADIN, REINTERPRETING PROPERTY (1993).
R. UNGER, KNOWLEDGE AND POLITICS (1975).
R. UNGER, THE CRITICAL LEGAL STUDIES MOVEMENT (1986).
G. WHITE, PATTERNS OF AMERICAN LEGAL THOUGHT (1978).

ARTICLES

Ackerman, *Law, Economics, and the Problem of Legal Culture,* 1986 DUKE L.J. 929 (1989).
Balkin, *The Crystalline Structure of Legal Thought,* 39 RUTGERS L. REV. 1 (1986).
Blatt, *The History of Statutory Interpretation,* 6 CARDOZO L. REV. 799 (1985).
Boyle, *The Anatomy of a Torts Class,* 34 AM. U. L. REV. 1003 (1985).
Boyle, *The Politics of Reason,* 133 U. PA. L. REV. 685 (1985).
Brest, *Interpretation and Interest,* 34 STAN. L. REV. 765 (1982).

Carrington, *Of Law and the River*, 34 J. LEGAL EDUC. 222 (1984).

Chow, *Trashing Nihilism*, 65 TUL. L. REV. 221 (1990).

Coleman, *The Normative Basis of Economic Analysis: A Critical Review of Richard Posner's* The Economics of Justice, 34 STAN. L. REV. 1105 (1982).

Cornell, *Toward a Modern/Postmodern Reconstruction of Ethics*, 133 U. PA. L. REV. 291 (1985).

Dalton, *An Essay in the Deconstruction of Contract Doctrine*, 94 YALE L.J. 997 (1985).

Ernst, *The Critical Tradition in the Writing of American Legal History*, 102 YALE L.J. 1019 (1993).

Eskridge & Frickey, *Statutory Interpretation as Practical Reasoning*, 42 STAN. L. REV. 321 (1984).

Farber, *Legal Pragmatism and the Constitution*, 72 MINN. L. REV. 1331 (1988).

Farber & Frickey, *Practical Reasoning and the First Amendment*, 34 U.C.L.A. L. REV. 1615 (1987).

Fiss, *Objectivity and Interpretation*, 34 STAN. L. REV. 739 (1982).

Golding, *Jurisprudence and Legal Philosophy in Twentieth Century America— Major Themes and Developments*, 36 J. LEGAL EDUC. 441 (1986).

Gordley, *Legal Reasoning: An Introduction*, 72 CAL. L. REV. 138 (1984).

Gordon, *Historicism in Legal Scholarship*, 90 YALE L.J. 1017 (1981).

Gordon, *Critical Legal Histories*, 36 STAN. L. REV. 57 (1984).

Graff, *"Keep Off the Grass," "Drop Dead," and Other Indeterminacies: A Response to Sanford Levinson*, 60 TEX. L. REV. 405 (1982).

Grey, *Langdell's Orthodoxy*, 45 U. PITT. L. REV. 1 (1983).

Grey, *Holmes and Legal Pragmatism*, 41 STAN. L. REV. 787 (1989).

Hantzis, *Legal Innovation Within the Wider Intellectual Tradition: The Pragmatism of Oliver Wendell Holmes, Jr.*, 82 Nw. U. L. REV. 541 (1988).

Hoeflich, *Law and Geometry: Legal Science from Leibnitz to Langdell*, 30 AM. J. LEGAL HIST. 95 (1986).

Johnson, *Do You Sincerely Want to Be Radical?* 36 STAN. L. REV. 247 (1984).

Kelman, *Trashing*, 36 STAN. L. REV. 293 (1984).

Kennedy, *Legal Formality*, 2 J. LEG. STUD. 351 (1973).

Kennedy, *Form and Substance in Private Law Adjudication*, 89 HARV. L. REV. 1685 (1976).

Kennedy, *The Structure of Blackstone's Commentaries*, 28 BUFF. L. REV. 205 (1979).

Kennedy, *Cost-Benefit Analysis of Entitlement Problems: A Critique*, 33 STAN. L. REV. 387 (1981).

Kennedy, *Distributive and Paternalistic Motives in Contract and Tort Law, with Special Reference to Compulsory Terms and Unequal Bargaining Power*, 41 MD. L. REV. 563 (1982).

Kennedy, *A Semiotics of Legal Argument*, 42 SYRACUSE L. REV. 75 (1991).

Kennedy & Klare, *A Bibliography of Critical Legal Studies*, 94 YALE L.J. 461 (1984).

Kennedy & Michelman, *Are Property and Contract Efficient?* 8 HOFSTRA L. REV. 711 (1980).

Leff, *Economic Analysis of Law: Some Realism About Nominalism,* 60 VA. L. REV. 451 (1974).

Llewellyn, *Some Realism About Realism—Responding to Dean Pound,* 44 HARV. L. REV. 1222 (1931).

Lyons, *Legal Formalism and Instrumentalism—A Pathological Study,* 66 CORNELL L. REV. 949 (1981).

Markovitz, *Duncan's Do Nots: Cost-Benefit Analysis and the Determination of Legal Entitlements,* 36 STAN. L. REV. 1169 (1984).

Michelman, *Norms and Normativity in the Economic Theory of Law,* 62 MINN. L. REV. 1015 (1978).

Minda, *The Jurisprudential Movements of the 1980s,* 50 OHIO ST. L.J. 599 (1989).

Minda, *Jurisprudence at Century's End,* 43 J. LEGAL EDUC. 27 (1993).

Moore, *The Interpretive Turn in Modern Legal Theory: A Turn for the Worse?* 41 STAN. L. REV. 871 (1989).

Note, *'Round and 'Round the Bramble Bush: From Legal Realism to Critical Legal Scholarship,* 95 HARV. L. REV. 1669 (1982).

Peller, *The Metaphysics of American Law,* 73 CAL. L. REV. 1152 (1985).

Posner, *The Decline of the Law as an Autonomous Discipline 1962–1987,* 100 HARV. L. REV. 761 (1987).

Pound, *Mechanical Jurisprudence,* 8 COLUM. L. REV. 605 (1908).

Pound, *Law in Books and Law in Action,* 44 AM. L. REV. 12 (1910).

Pound, *The Scope and Purpose of Sociological Jurisprudence,* 25 HARV. L. REV. 489 (1912).

Radin, *Reconsidering the Rule of Law,* 69 B. U. L. REV. 69 (1989).

Radin & Michelman, *Pragmatist and Poststructuralist Critical Legal Practice,* 139 U. PA. L. REV. 1019 (1991).

Schanck, *Understanding Postmodern Thought and Its Implications for Statutory Interpretation,* 65 S. CAL. L. REV. 2505 (1992).

Schauer, *Easy Cases,* 58 S. CAL. L. REV. 399 (1985).

Schauer, *Slippery Slopes,* 99 HARV. L. REV. 361 (1985).

Schauer, *Precedent,* 39 STAN. L. REV. 571 (1987).

Schauer, *Formalism,* 97 YALE L.J. 509 (1988).

Schlag, *Rules and Standards,* 33 U.C.L.A. L. REV. 379 (1985).

Schlag, *The Problem of the Subject,* 69 TEX. L. REV. 1627 (1991).

Schlegel, *American Legal Realism and Empirical Social Science: From the Yale Experience,* 28 BUFF. L. REV. 459 (1979).

Schlegel, *American Legal Realism and Empirical Social Science: The Singular Case of Underhill Moore,* 29 BUFF. L. REV. 195 (1980).

Schlegel, *Notes Toward an Intimate, Opinionated, and Affectionate History of the Conference on Critical Legal Studies,* 36 STAN. L. REV. 391 (1984).

Shiffron, *Liberalism, Radicalism and Legal Scholarship,* 30 U.C.L.A. L. REV. 1103 (1983).

Singer, *The Legal Rights Debate in Analytical Jurisprudence from Bentham to Hohfeld,* 1982 WISC. L. REV. 975 (1982).

Singer, *The Player and the Cards: Nihilism and Legal Theory,* 94 YALE L.J. 1 (1984).

Smith, *The Pursuit of Pragmatism,* 100 YALE L.J. 409 (1990).

Solum, *On the Indeterminacy Crisis: Critiquing Critical Dogma,* 54 U. CHI. L. REV. 462 (1987).

Stick, *Can Nihilism Be Pragmatic?* 100 HARV. L. REV. 332 (1986).

Summers, *Pragmatic Instrumentalism in Twentieth Century American Legal Thought: A Synthesis and Critique of Our Dominant General Theory About Law and Its Use,* 66 CORNELL L. REV. 861 (1981).

Symposium, *Symposium on Critical Legal Studies,* 36 STAN. L. REV. 1 (1984).

Symposium, *Interpetation Symposium,* 58 S. CAL. L. REV. 1 (1985).

Symposium, *Symposium on Post-Chicago Law and Economics,* 65 CHI.-KENT L. REV. 1 (1989).

Symposium, *Symposium on the Renaissance of Pragmatism in American Legal Thought,* 63 S. CAL. L. REV. 1569 (1990).

Symposium, *Symposium on the Future of Law and Economics,* 20 HOFSTRA L. REV. 757 (1992).

Turley, *The Hitchhiker's Guide to CLS, Unger and Deep Thought,* 81 NW. U. L. REV. 593 (1987).

Tushnet, *Critical Legal Studies and Constitutional Law: An Essay in Deconstruction,* 36 STAN. L. REV. 623 (1984).

Tushnet, *Following the Rules Laid Down: A Critique of Interpretation and Neutral Principles,* 96 HARV. L. REV. 781 (1985).

Tushnet, *Critical Legal Studies: An Introduction to Its Origins and Underpinnings,* 36 J. LEGAL EDUC. 505 (1986).

Tushnet, *Critical Legal Studies: A Political History,* 100 YALE L.J. 1515 (1991).

Vetter, *Postwar Legal Scholarship on Judicial Decisionmaking,* 33 J. LEGAL EDUC. 412 (1983).

Wellman, *Practical Reasoning and Judicial Justification: Toward an Adequate Theory,* 57 U. COLO. L. REV. 45 (1985).

Wellman, *Dworkin and the Legal Process Tradition: The Legacy of Hart and Sacks,* 29 ARIZ. L. REV. 413 (1987).

White, *From Sociological Jurisprudence to Realism: Jurisprudence and Social Change in Early Twentieth Century America,* 58 VA. L. REV. 999 (1972).

White, *The Inevitability of Critical Legal Studies,* 36 STAN. L. REV. 649 (1984).

White, *From Realism to Critical Legal Studies: A Truncated Intellectual History,* 40 SW. L.J. 819 (1986).

White, *Law as Language: Reading Law and Reading Literature,* 60 TEX. L. REV. 415 (1982).

Williams, *Critical Legal Studies: The Death of Transcendence and the Rise of the New Langdells,* 62 N.Y.U. L. REV. 429 (1987).

Winter, *Foreword: On Building Houses,* 69 TEX. L. REV. 1595 (1991).

Woodard, *The Limits of Legal Realism: An Historical Perspective,* 54 VA. L. REV. 689 (1968).

About the Book and Author

Students of the law are often told that they must learn to "think like a lawyer," but they are given surprisingly little help in understanding just what this amounts to. Generally, they are expected to pick up this ability by example and perhaps by osmosis. But it remains the case that very few lawyers—even very good ones—are consciously aware of what it means to think like a lawyer.

In this insightful and highly revealing book, Kenneth J. Vandevelde identifies, explains, and interprets the goals and methods of the well-trained lawyer. This is not a book about the content of the law; it is about a well-developed and valuable way of thinking that can be applied to many fields.

Both practical and sophisticated, *Thinking Like a Lawyer* avoids the pitfalls common to most books on legal reasoning: It neither assumes too much legal knowledge nor condescends to its readers. Invaluable for law students and practicing lawyers, the book will also effectively interpret legal thinking for lay readers seeking a better understanding of the often mysterious ways of the legal profession.

Kenneth J. Vandevelde is dean and professor of law at Thomas Jefferson School of Law in San Diego. He is author of *United States Investment Treaties: Policy and Practice* and many papers, primarily on international law and American legal history.

Index